PERSEPOLIS

PERSEPOLIS

MARJANE SATRAPI

PANTHEON

Translation copyright © 2003 by L'Association, Paris, France

All rights reserved under International and Pan-American Copyright Conventions. Published in the United States by Pantheon Books, a division of Random House, Inc., New York, and simultaneously in Canada by Random House of Canada, Limited, Toronto. Originally published in France in two volumes as *Persepolis 1* and *Persepolis 2* by L'Association, 16 rue de la Pierre Levée, 75011 Paris, in 2000 and 2001, respectively. This translation originally published in hardcover by Pantheon Books, a division of Random House, Inc., New York, in 2003.

L'Association

Pantheon Books and colophon are registered trademarks of Random House, Inc.

A portion previously appeared in *Ms.* magazine

Library of Congress Cataloging-in-Publication Data
Satrapi, Marjane, 1969-
[Persepolis. English]
Persepolis / Marjane Satrapi.
   p. cm.
ISBN 0-375-71457-X
1. Satrapi, Marjane, 1969–Comic books, strips, etc. I. Title.
PN6747.S245 P4713 2003   741.5'944–dc21   2002190806

www.pantheonbooks.com
Printed in India
First American Paperback Edition

51st Printing

INTRODUCTION

In the second millennium B.C., while the Elam nation was developing a civilization alongside Babylon, Indo-European invaders gave their name to the immense Iranian plateau where they settled. The word "Iran" was derived from "Ayryana Vaejo," which means "the origin of the Aryans." These people were semi-nomads whose descendants were the Medes and the Persians. The Medes founded the first Iranian nation in the seventh century B.C.; it was later destroyed by Cyrus the Great. He established what became one of the largest empires of the ancient world, the Persian Empire, in the sixth century B.C. Iran was referred to as Persia – its Greek name – until 1935 when Reza Shah, the father of the last Shah of Iran, asked everyone to call the country Iran.

Iran was rich. Because of its wealth and its geographic location, it invited attacks: From Alexander the Great, from its Arab neighbors to the west, from Turkish and Mongolian conquerors, Iran was often subject to foreign domination. Yet the Persian language and culture withstood these invasions. The invaders assimilated into this strong culture, and in some ways they became Iranians themselves.

In the twentieth century, Iran entered a new phase. Reza Shah decided to modernize and westernize the country, but meanwhile a fresh source of wealth was discovered: oil. And with the oil came another invasion. The West, particularly Great Britain, wielded a strong influence on the Iranian economy. During the Second World War, the British, Soviets, and Americans asked Reza Shah to ally himself with them against Germany. But Reza Shah, who sympathized with the Germans, declared Iran a neutral zone. So the Allies invaded and occupied Iran. Reza Shah was sent into exile and was succeeded by his son, Mohammad Reza Pahlavi, who was known simply as the Shah.

In 1951, Mohammed Mossadeq, then prime minister of Iran, nationalized the oil industry. In retaliation, Great Britain organized an embargo on all exports of oil from Iran. In 1953, the CIA, with the help of British intelligence, organized a coup against him. Mossadeq was overthrown and the Shah, who had earlier escaped from the country, returned to power. The Shah stayed on the throne until 1979, when he fled Iran to escape the Islamic revolution.

Since then, this old and great civilization has been discussed mostly in connection with fundamentalism, fanaticism, and terrorism. As an Iranian who has lived more than half of my life in Iran, I know that this image is far from the truth. This is why writing *Persepolis* was so important to me. I believe that an entire nation should not be judged by the wrongdoings of a few extremists. I also don't want those Iranians who lost their lives in prisons defending freedom, who died in the war against Iraq, who suffered under various repressive regimes, or who were forced to leave their families and flee their homeland to be forgotten.

One can forgive but one should never forget.

Marjane Satrapi
Paris, September 2002

PERSEPOLIS

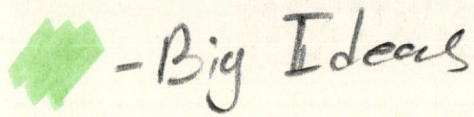 - Big Ideas

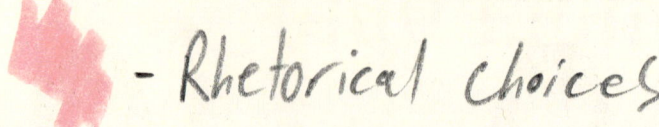 - Rhetorical choices

 - Appeals

THE VEIL

THIS IS ME WHEN I WAS 10 YEARS OLD. THIS WAS IN 1980.
AND THIS IS A CLASS PHOTO. I'M SITTING ON THE FAR LEFT SO YOU DON'T SEE ME. FROM LEFT TO RIGHT: GOLNAZ, MAHSHID, NARINE, MINNA.
IN 1979 A REVOLUTION TOOK PLACE. IT WAS LATER CALLED "THE ISLAMIC REVOLUTION".
THEN CAME 1980: THE YEAR IT BECAME OBLIGATORY TO WEAR THE VEIL AT SCHOOL.
WEAR THIS!
WE DIDN'T REALLY LIKE TO WEAR THE VEIL, ESPECIALLY SINCE WE DIDN'T UNDERSTAND WHY WE HAD TO.
IT'S TOO HOT OUT!
EXECUTION IN THE NAME OF FREEDOM.
GIVE ME MY VEIL BACK!
YOU'LL HAVE TO LICK MY FEET!
GIDDYAP!
OOH! I'M THE MONSTER OF DARKNESS.

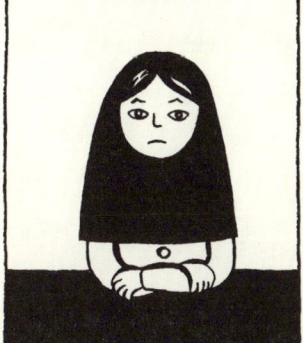

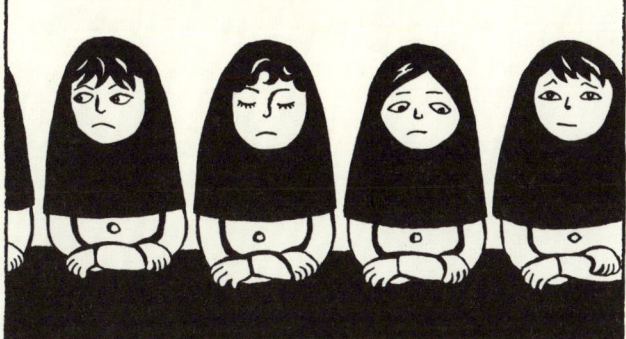

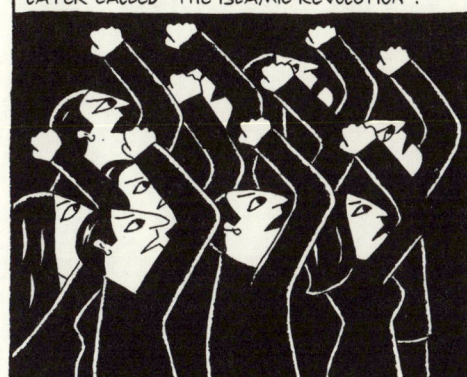

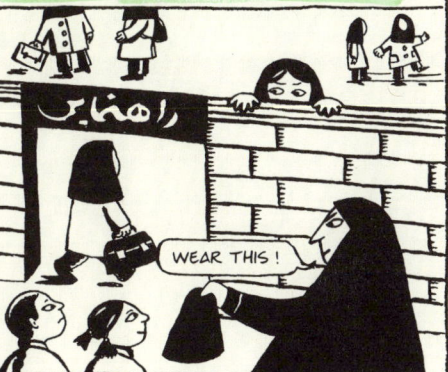

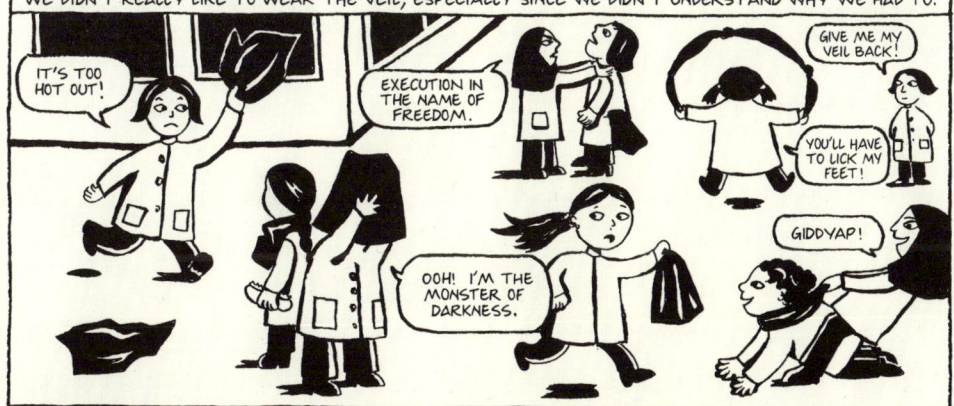

Religious Control

Making his face close up and not giving him a mouth to make him scarier

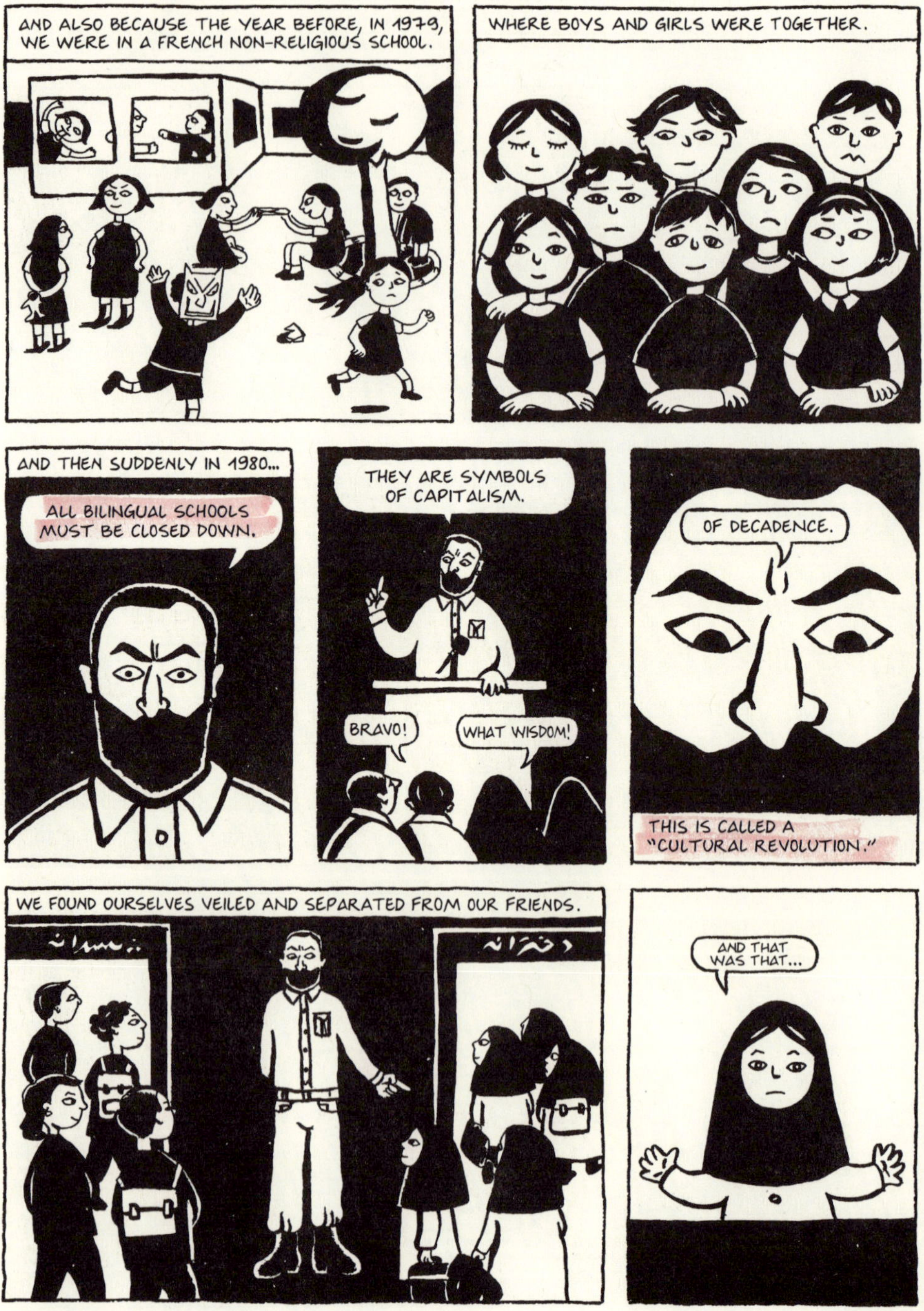

AND ALSO BECAUSE THE YEAR BEFORE, IN 1979, WE WERE IN A FRENCH NON-RELIGIOUS SCHOOL.
WHERE BOYS AND GIRLS WERE TOGETHER.
AND THEN SUDDENLY IN 1980...
ALL BILINGUAL SCHOOLS MUST BE CLOSED DOWN.
THEY ARE SYMBOLS OF CAPITALISM.
BRAVO!
WHAT WISDOM!
OF DECADENCE.
THIS IS CALLED A "CULTURAL REVOLUTION."
WE FOUND OURSELVES VEILED AND SEPARATED FROM OUR FRIENDS.
AND THAT WAS THAT...

Loss of identity

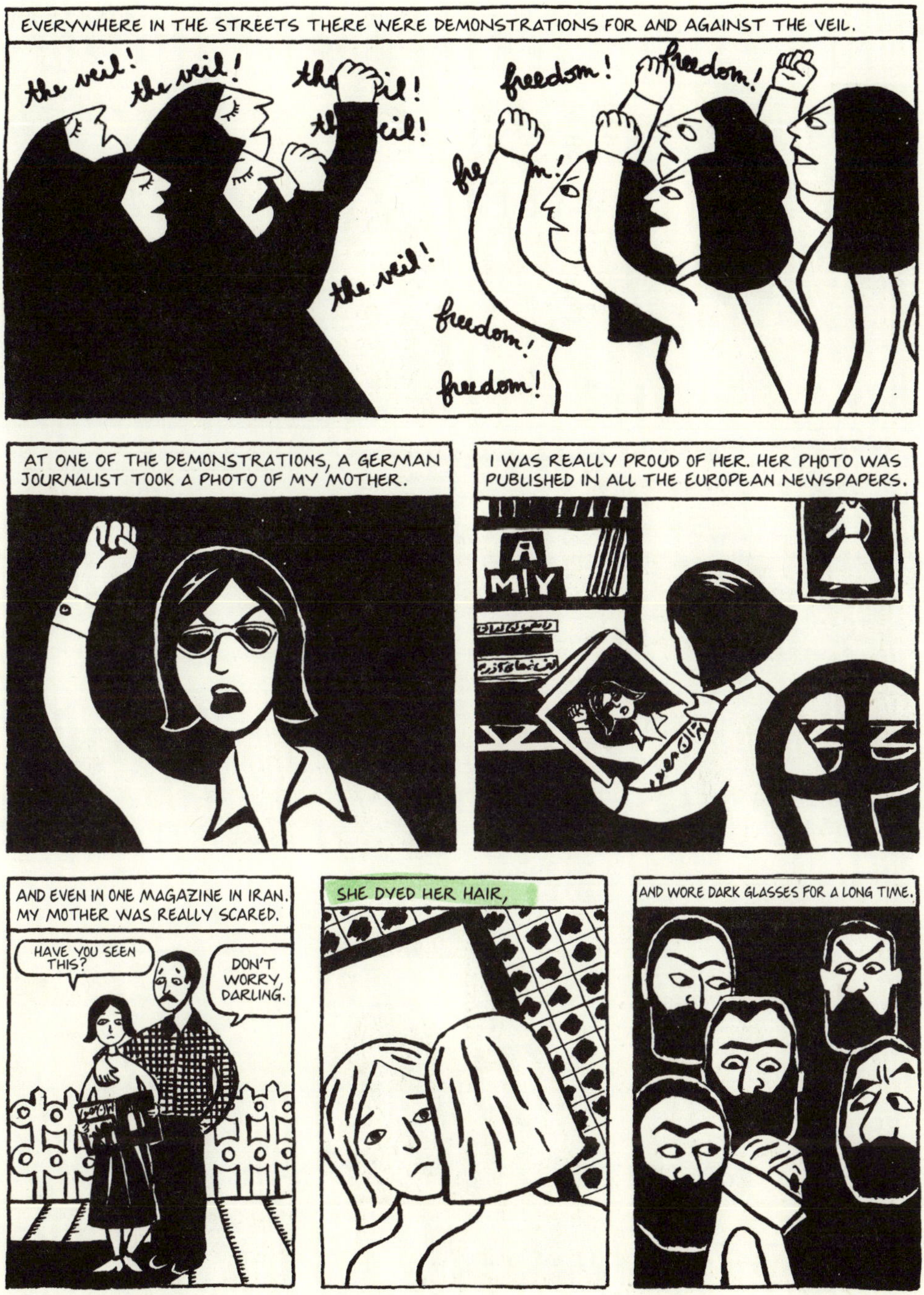
EVERYWHERE IN THE STREETS THERE WERE DEMONSTRATIONS FOR AND AGAINST THE VEIL.
the veil!
the veil!
the veil!
the veil!
the veil!
freedom!
freedom!
freedom!
freedom!
AT ONE OF THE DEMONSTRATIONS, A GERMAN JOURNALIST TOOK A PHOTO OF MY MOTHER.
I WAS REALLY PROUD OF HER. HER PHOTO WAS PUBLISHED IN ALL THE EUROPEAN NEWSPAPERS.
AND EVEN IN ONE MAGAZINE IN IRAN. MY MOTHER WAS REALLY SCARED.
HAVE YOU SEEN THIS?
DON'T WORRY, DARLING.
SHE DYED HER HAIR,
AND WORE DARK GLASSES FOR A LONG TIME.

Shows her face as the sun to appeal to our sense of wonder

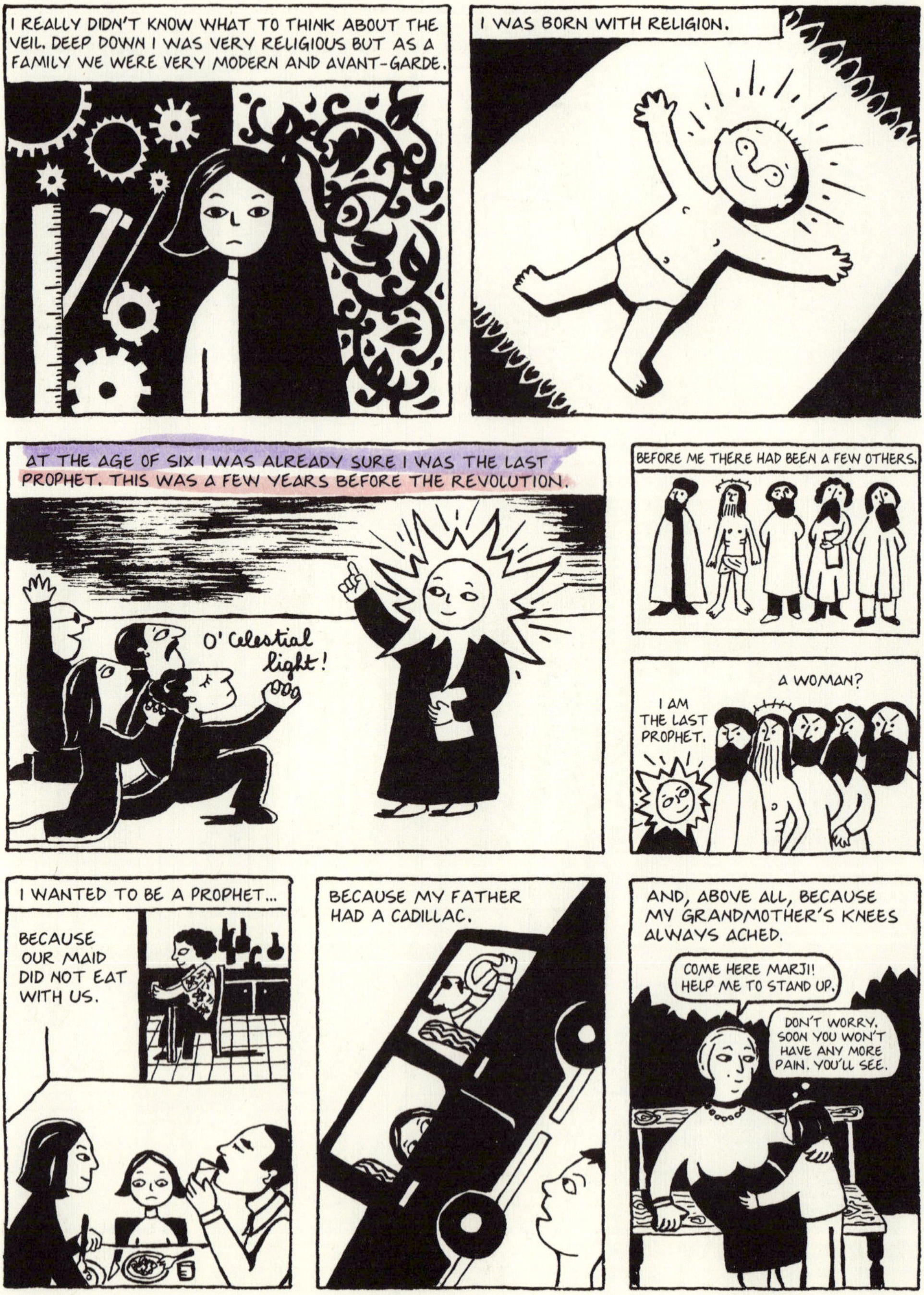
I REALLY DIDN'T KNOW WHAT TO THINK ABOUT THE VEIL. DEEP DOWN I WAS VERY RELIGIOUS BUT AS A FAMILY WE WERE VERY MODERN AND AVANT-GARDE.
I WAS BORN WITH RELIGION.
AT THE AGE OF SIX I WAS ALREADY SURE I WAS THE LAST PROPHET. THIS WAS A FEW YEARS BEFORE THE REVOLUTION.
O' Celestial light!
BEFORE ME THERE HAD BEEN A FEW OTHERS.
I AM THE LAST PROPHET.
A WOMAN?
I WANTED TO BE A PROPHET...
BECAUSE OUR MAID DID NOT EAT WITH US.
BECAUSE MY FATHER HAD A CADILLAC.
AND, ABOVE ALL, BECAUSE MY GRANDMOTHER'S KNEES ALWAYS ACHED.
COME HERE MARJI! HELP ME TO STAND UP.
DON'T WORRY. SOON YOU WON'T HAVE ANY MORE PAIN. YOU'LL SEE.

Allusion to history

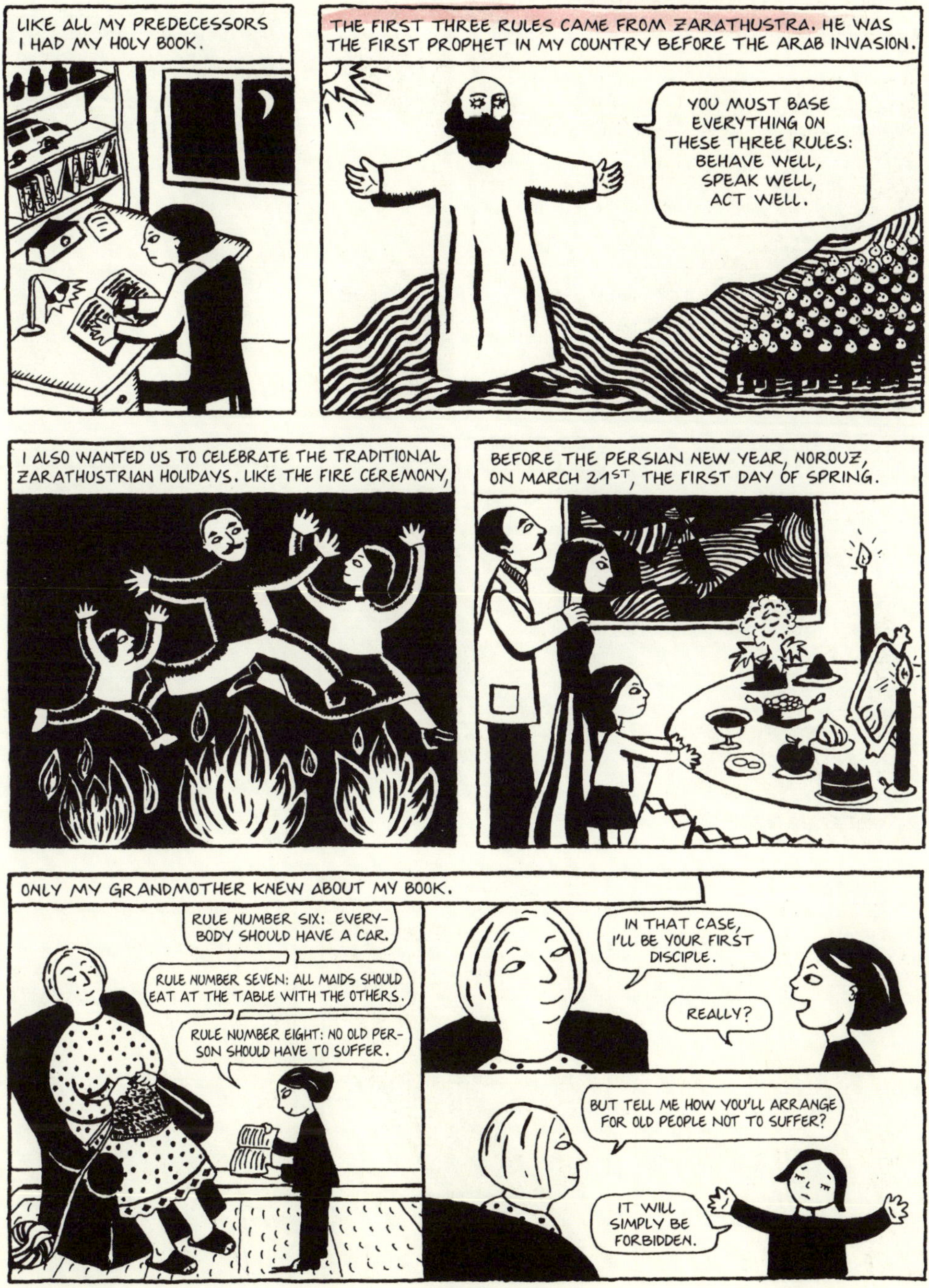
LIKE ALL MY PREDECESSORS I HAD MY HOLY BOOK.
THE FIRST THREE RULES CAME FROM ZARATHUSTRA. HE WAS THE FIRST PROPHET IN MY COUNTRY BEFORE THE ARAB INVASION.
YOU MUST BASE EVERYTHING ON THESE THREE RULES: BEHAVE WELL, SPEAK WELL, ACT WELL.
I ALSO WANTED US TO CELEBRATE THE TRADITIONAL ZARATHUSTRIAN HOLIDAYS. LIKE THE FIRE CEREMONY,
BEFORE THE PERSIAN NEW YEAR, NOROUZ, ON MARCH 21ST, THE FIRST DAY OF SPRING.
ONLY MY GRANDMOTHER KNEW ABOUT MY BOOK.
RULE NUMBER SIX: EVERYBODY SHOULD HAVE A CAR.
RULE NUMBER SEVEN: ALL MAIDS SHOULD EAT AT THE TABLE WITH THE OTHERS.
RULE NUMBER EIGHT: NO OLD PERSON SHOULD HAVE TO SUFFER.
IN THAT CASE, I'LL BE YOUR FIRST DISCIPLE.
REALLY?
BUT TELL ME HOW YOU'LL ARRANGE FOR OLD PEOPLE NOT TO SUFFER?
IT WILL SIMPLY BE FORBIDDEN.

Shows God as old with a beard to make him appear wise

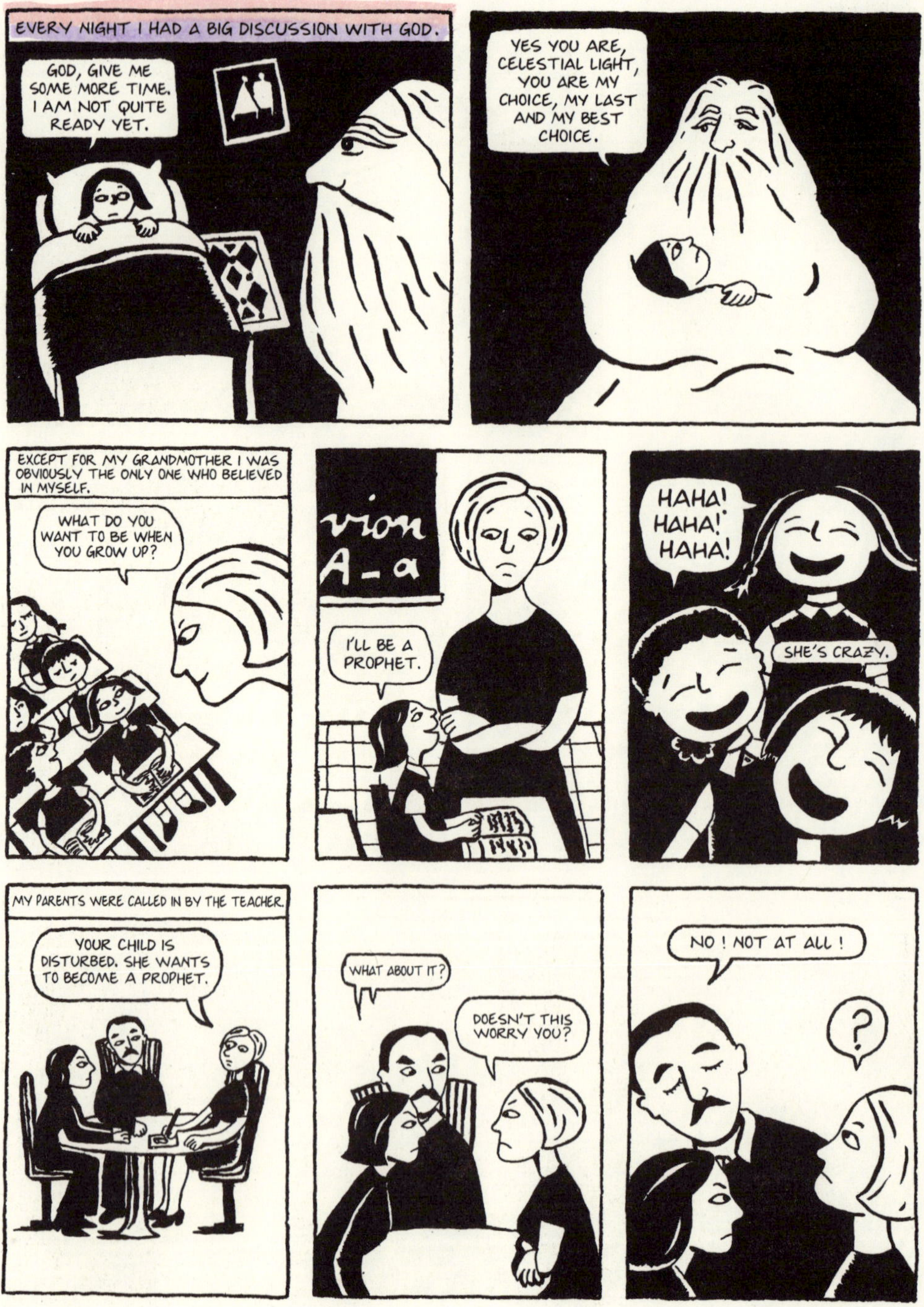

EVERY NIGHT I HAD A BIG DISCUSSION WITH GOD.
GOD, GIVE ME SOME MORE TIME. I AM NOT QUITE READY YET.
YES YOU ARE, CELESTIAL LIGHT, YOU ARE MY CHOICE, MY LAST AND MY BEST CHOICE.
EXCEPT FOR MY GRANDMOTHER I WAS OBVIOUSLY THE ONLY ONE WHO BELIEVED IN MYSELF.
WHAT DO YOU WANT TO BE WHEN YOU GROW UP?
vion
A – a
I'LL BE A PROPHET.
HAHA! HAHA! HAHA!
SHE'S CRAZY.
MY PARENTS WERE CALLED IN BY THE TEACHER.
YOUR CHILD IS DISTURBED. SHE WANTS TO BECOME A PROPHET.
WHAT ABOUT IT?
DOESN'T THIS WORRY YOU?
NO ! NOT AT ALL !
?

Hiding one's identity

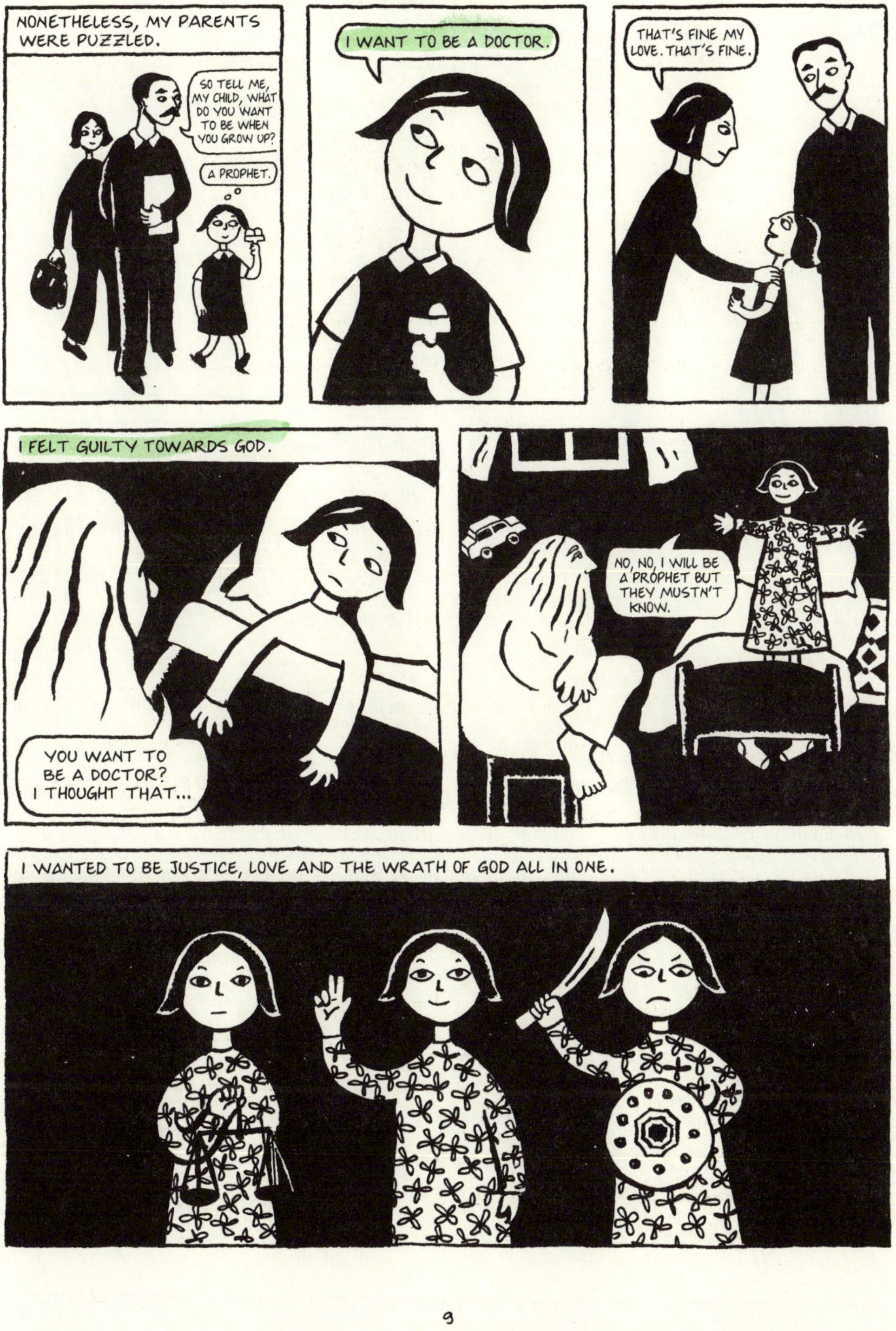
NONETHELESS, MY PARENTS WERE PUZZLED.
SO TELL ME, MY CHILD, WHAT DO YOU WANT TO BE WHEN YOU GROW UP?
A PROPHET.
I WANT TO BE A DOCTOR.
THAT'S FINE MY LOVE. THAT'S FINE.
I FELT GUILTY TOWARDS GOD.
YOU WANT TO BE A DOCTOR? I THOUGHT THAT...
NO, NO, I WILL BE A PROPHET BUT THEY MUSTN'T KNOW.
I WANTED TO BE JUSTICE, LOVE AND THE WRATH OF GOD ALL IN ONE.

Appeals to pathos by showing kids as soldiers

THE BICYCLE

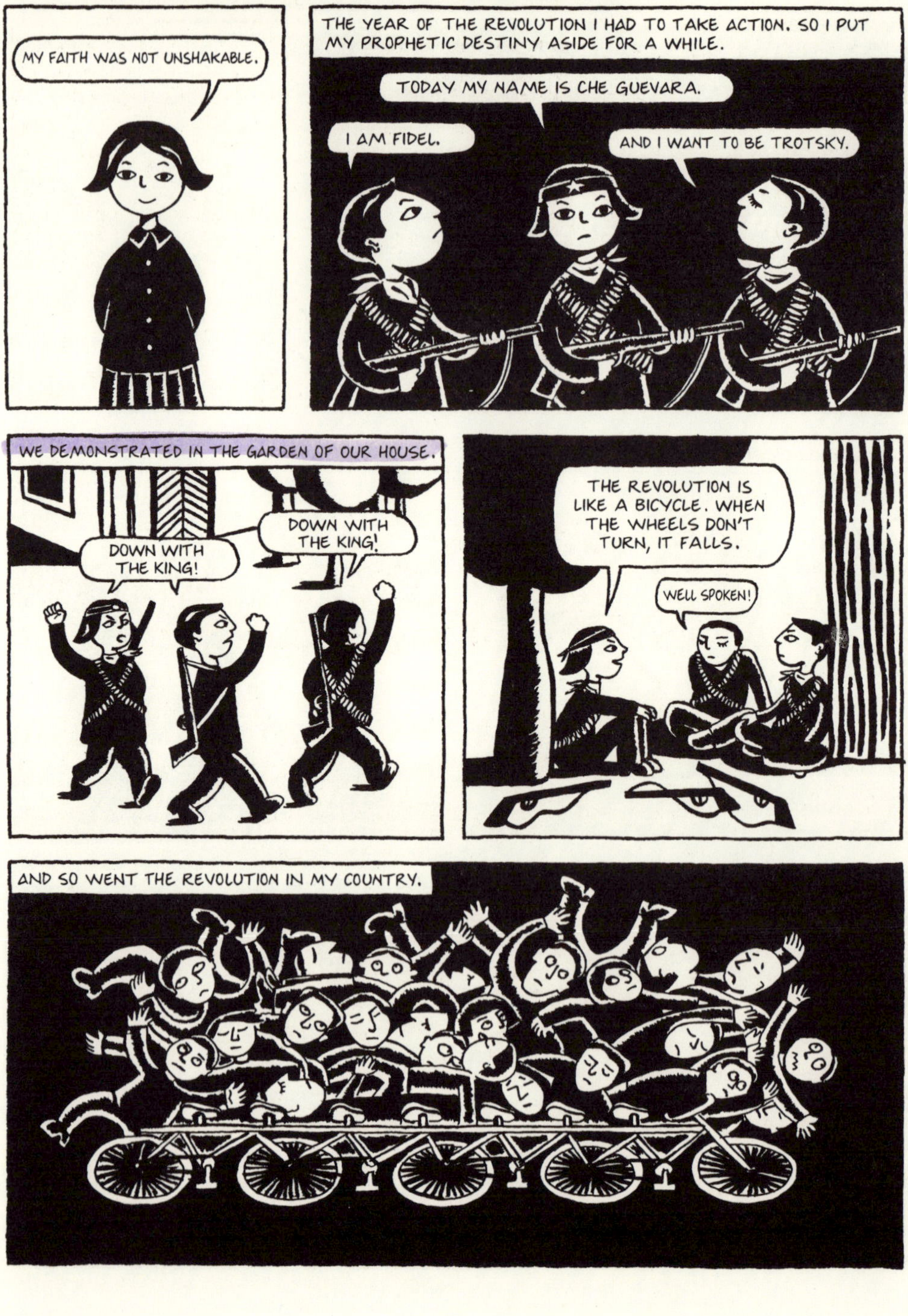
MY FAITH WAS NOT UNSHAKABLE.
THE YEAR OF THE REVOLUTION I HAD TO TAKE ACTION. SO I PUT MY PROPHETIC DESTINY ASIDE FOR A WHILE.
TODAY MY NAME IS CHE GUEVARA.
I AM FIDEL.
AND I WANT TO BE TROTSKY.
WE DEMONSTRATED IN THE GARDEN OF OUR HOUSE.
DOWN WITH THE KING!
DOWN WITH THE KING!
THE REVOLUTION IS LIKE A BICYCLE. WHEN THE WHEELS DON'T TURN, IT FALLS.
WELL SPOKEN!
AND SO WENT THE REVOLUTION IN MY COUNTRY.

Shows ppl asleep to demonstrate the awakening literally

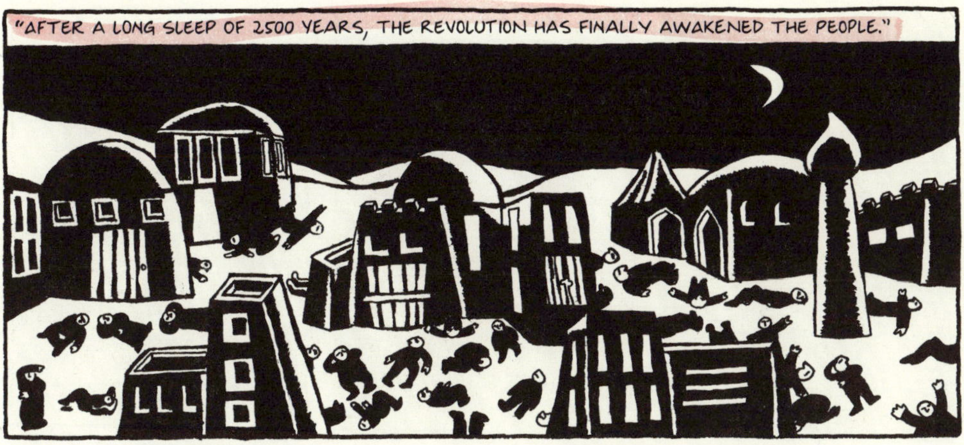
"AFTER A LONG SLEEP OF 2500 YEARS, THE REVOLUTION HAS FINALLY AWAKENED THE PEOPLE."

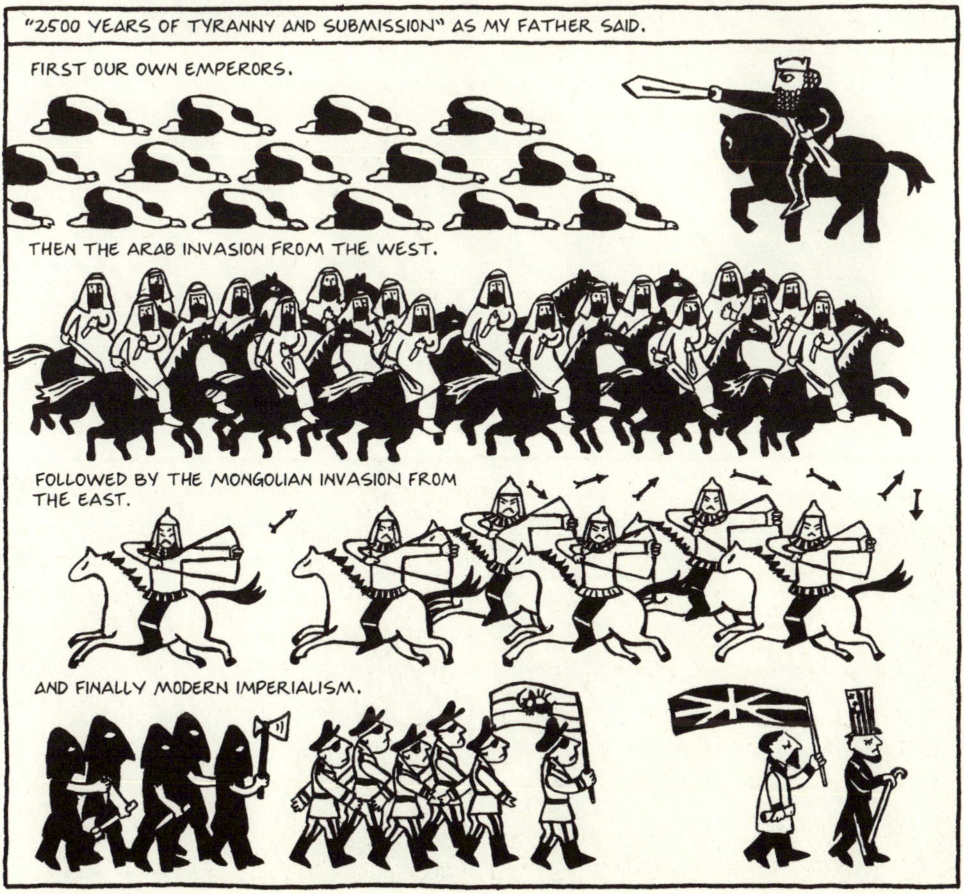
"2500 YEARS OF TYRANNY AND SUBMISSION" AS MY FATHER SAID.
FIRST OUR OWN EMPERORS.
THEN THE ARAB INVASION FROM THE WEST.
FOLLOWED BY THE MONGOLIAN INVASION FROM THE EAST.
AND FINALLY MODERN IMPERIALISM.

shows lots of books

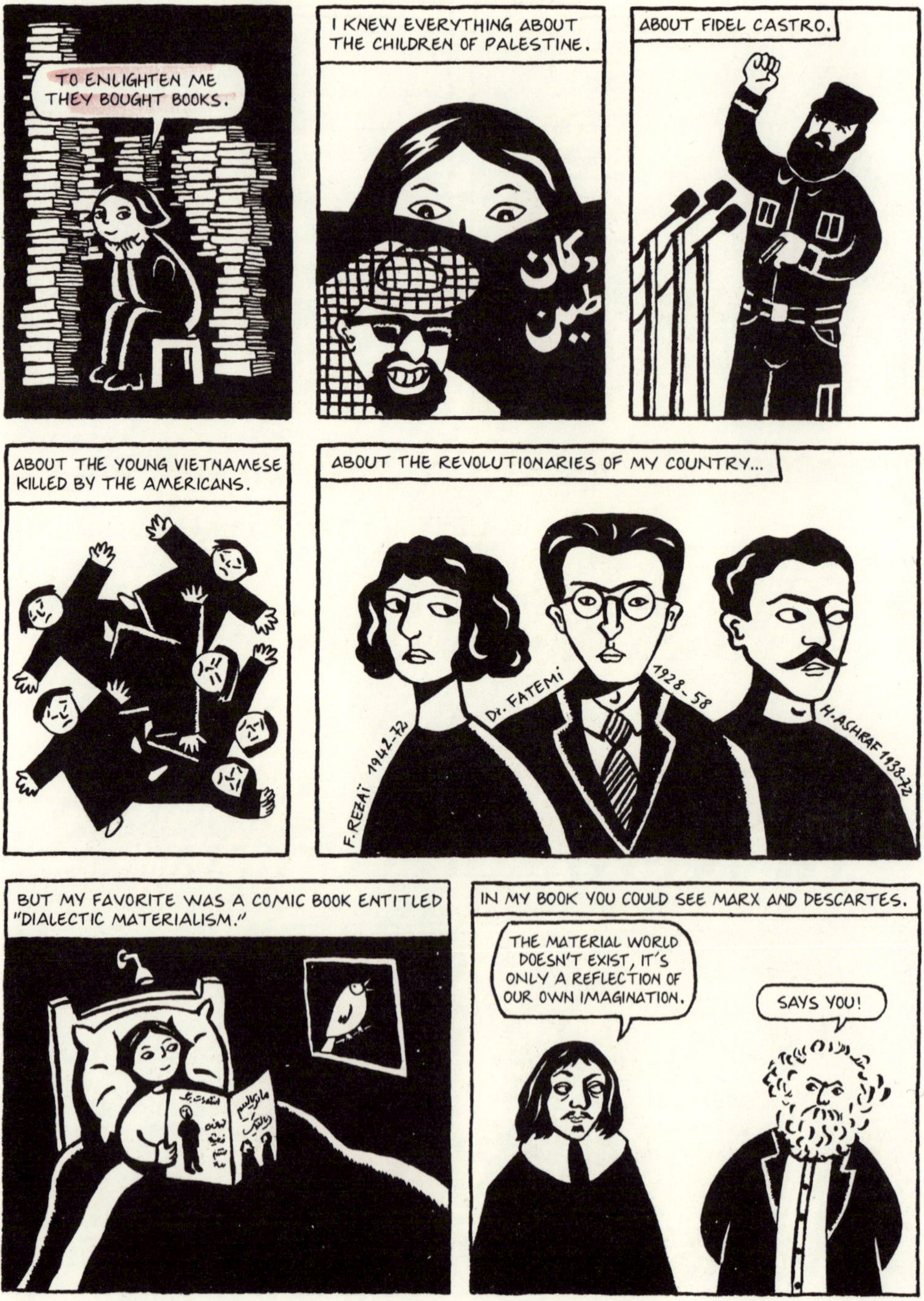

TO ENLIGHTEN ME THEY BOUGHT BOOKS.
I KNEW EVERYTHING ABOUT THE CHILDREN OF PALESTINE.
ABOUT FIDEL CASTRO.
ABOUT THE YOUNG VIETNAMESE KILLED BY THE AMERICANS.
ABOUT THE REVOLUTIONARIES OF MY COUNTRY...
F. REZAÏ 1942-72
Dr. FATEMI 1928-58
H. ASHRAF 1938-72
BUT MY FAVORITE WAS A COMIC BOOK ENTITLED "DIALECTIC MATERIALISM."
IN MY BOOK YOU COULD SEE MARX AND DESCARTES.
THE MATERIAL WORLD DOESN'T EXIST, IT'S ONLY A REFLECTION OF OUR OWN IMAGINATION.
SAYS YOU!

Shows Marx and God as the same to show her worldview

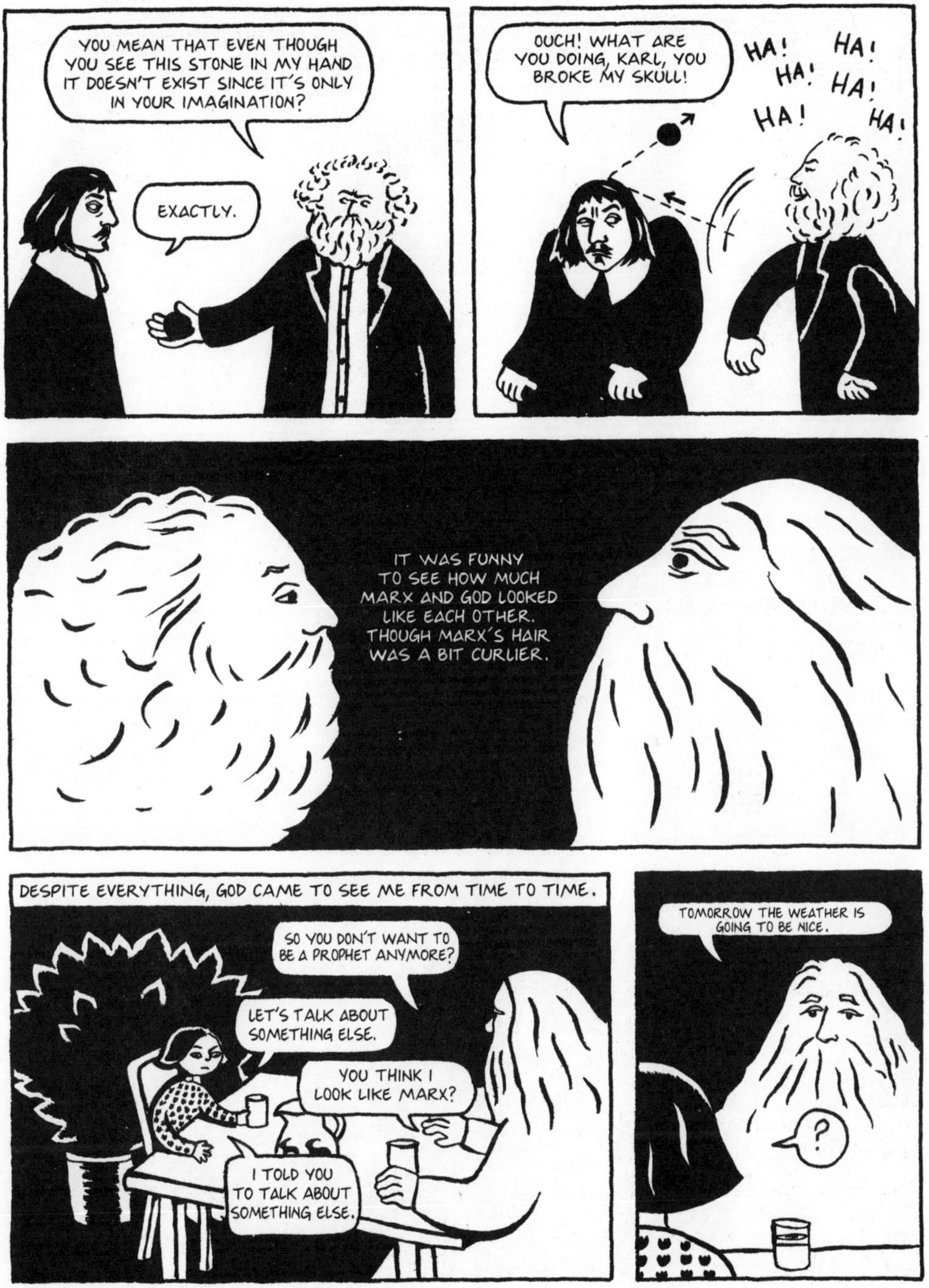
YOU MEAN THAT EVEN THOUGH YOU SEE THIS STONE IN MY HAND IT DOESN'T EXIST SINCE IT'S ONLY IN YOUR IMAGINATION?
EXACTLY.
OUCH! WHAT ARE YOU DOING, KARL, YOU BROKE MY SKULL!
HA! HA! HA! HA! HA! HA!
IT WAS FUNNY TO SEE HOW MUCH MARX AND GOD LOOKED LIKE EACH OTHER. THOUGH MARX'S HAIR WAS A BIT CURLIER.
DESPITE EVERYTHING, GOD CAME TO SEE ME FROM TIME TO TIME.
SO YOU DON'T WANT TO BE A PROPHET ANYMORE?
LET'S TALK ABOUT SOMETHING ELSE.
YOU THINK I LOOK LIKE MARX?
I TOLD YOU TO TALK ABOUT SOMETHING ELSE.
TOMORROW THE WEATHER IS GOING TO BE NICE.
?

Depicts the men as big to show control

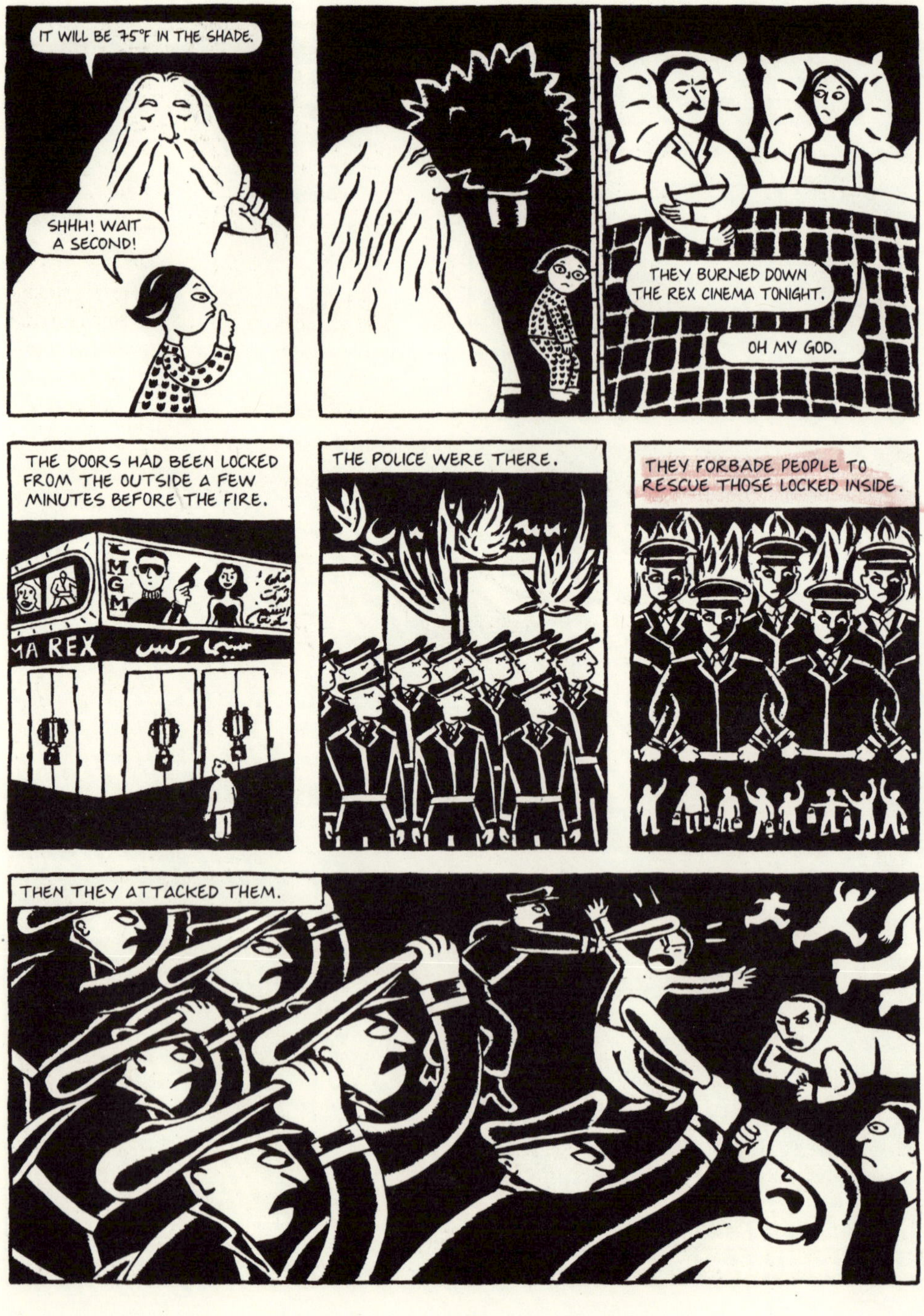

IT WILL BE 75°F IN THE SHADE.
SHHH! WAIT A SECOND!
THEY BURNED DOWN THE REX CINEMA TONIGHT.
OH MY GOD.
THE DOORS HAD BEEN LOCKED FROM THE OUTSIDE A FEW MINUTES BEFORE THE FIRE.
MGM
MA REX
THE POLICE WERE THERE.
THEY FORBADE PEOPLE TO RESCUE THOSE LOCKED INSIDE.
THEN THEY ATTACKED THEM.

Burning bodies to appeal to pathos

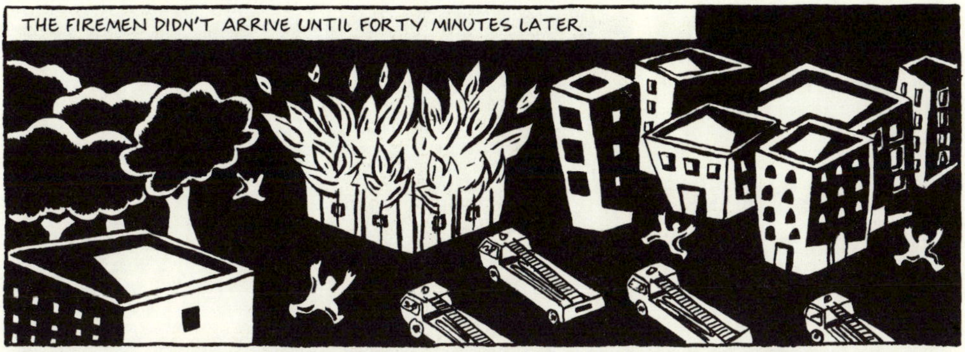
THE FIREMEN DIDN'T ARRIVE UNTIL FORTY MINUTES LATER.

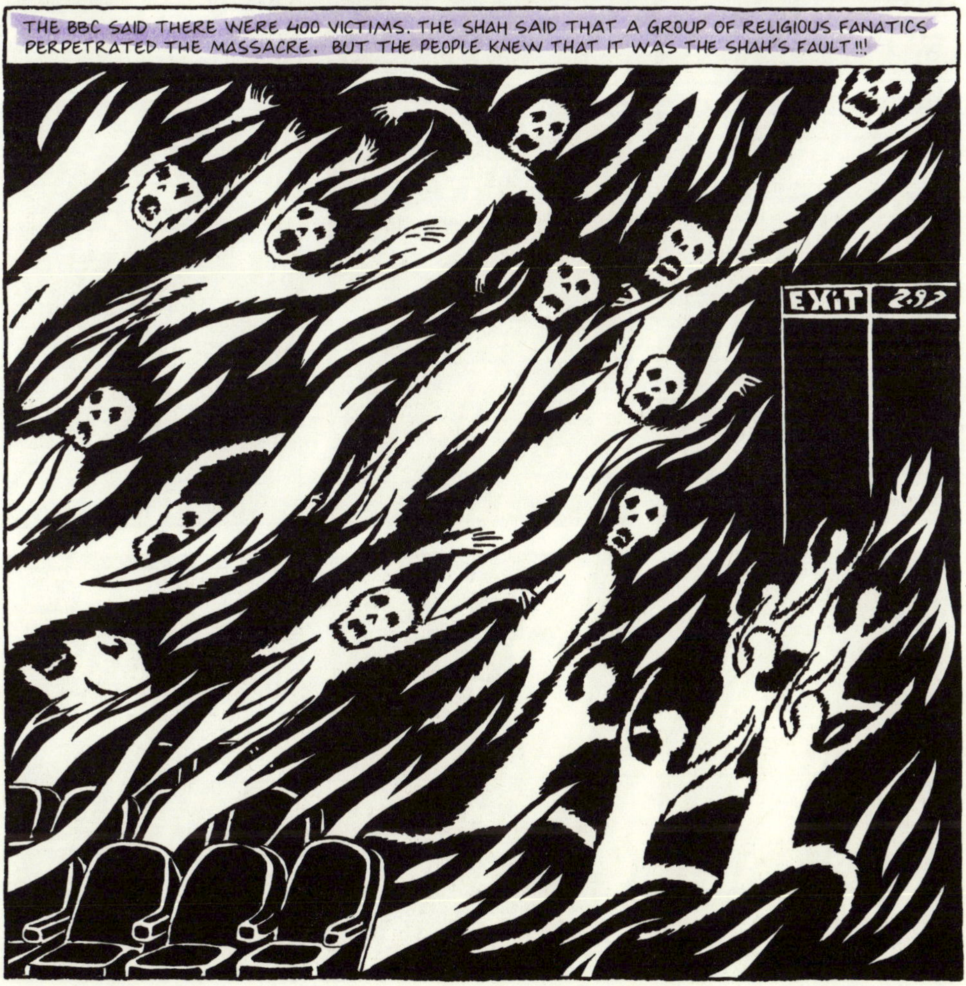
THE BBC SAID THERE WERE 400 VICTIMS. THE SHAH SAID THAT A GROUP OF RELIGIOUS FANATICS PERPETRATED THE MASSACRE. BUT THE PEOPLE KNEW THAT IT WAS THE SHAH'S FAULT!!!
EXIT

Hat to depict her aspirations to be a hero

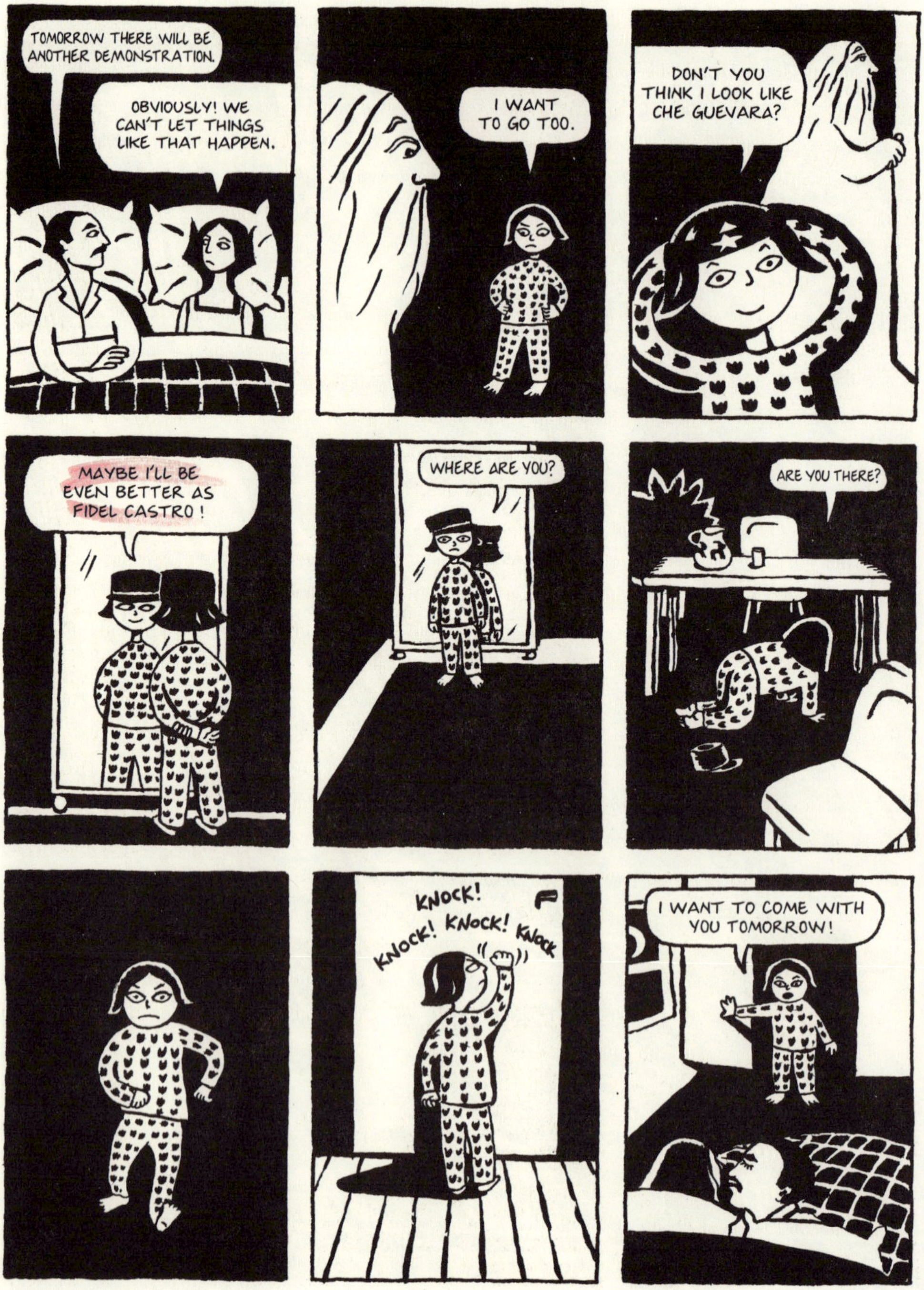

TOMORROW THERE WILL BE ANOTHER DEMONSTRATION.
OBVIOUSLY! WE CAN'T LET THINGS LIKE THAT HAPPEN.
I WANT TO GO TOO.
DON'T YOU THINK I LOOK LIKE CHE GUEVARA?
MAYBE I'LL BE EVEN BETTER AS FIDEL CASTRO!
WHERE ARE YOU?
ARE YOU THERE?
KNOCK! KNOCK! KNOCK! KNOCK
I WANT TO COME WITH YOU TOMORROW!

Changing worldview

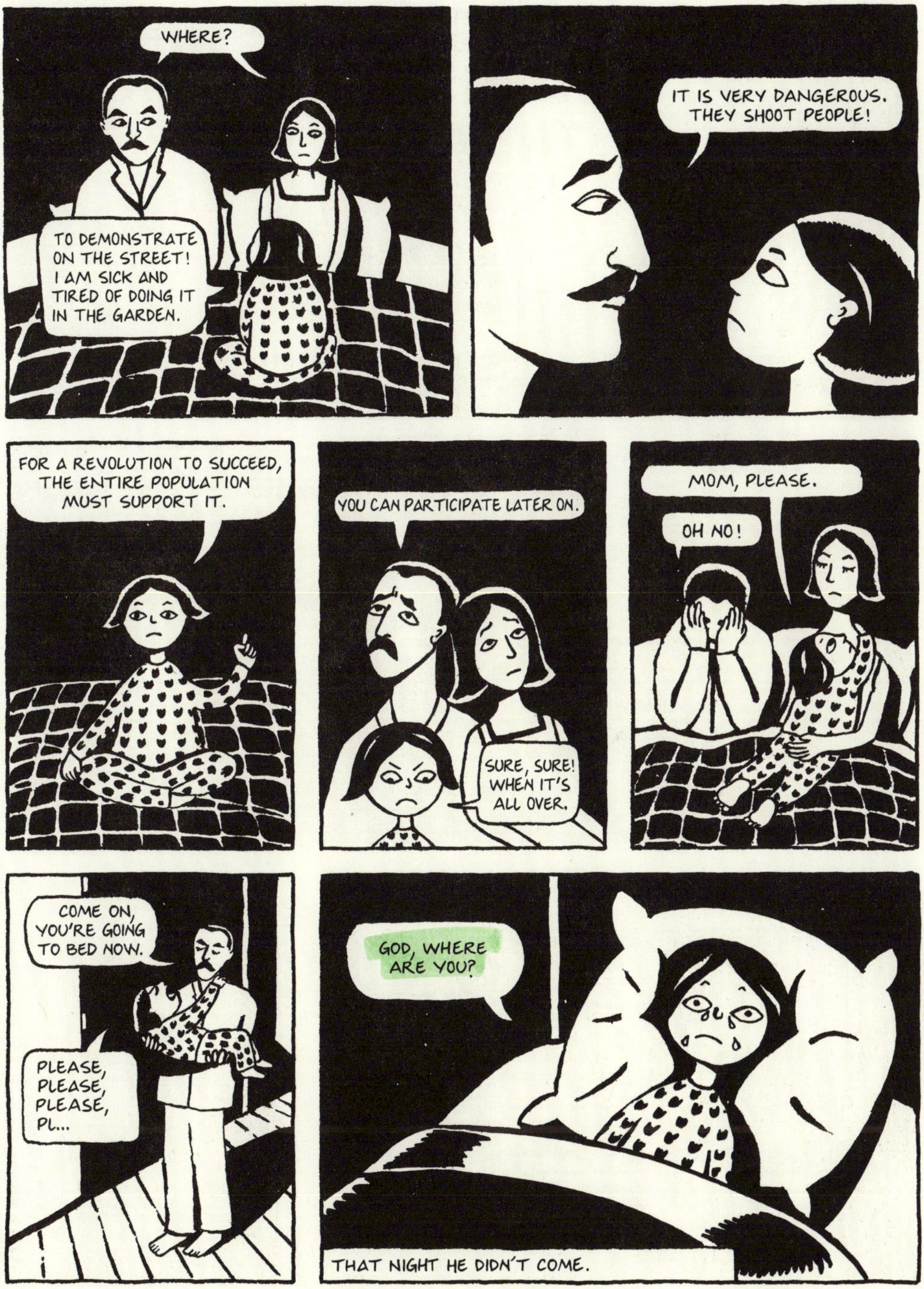
WHERE?
TO DEMONSTRATE ON THE STREET! I AM SICK AND TIRED OF DOING IT IN THE GARDEN.
IT IS VERY DANGEROUS. THEY SHOOT PEOPLE!
FOR A REVOLUTION TO SUCCEED, THE ENTIRE POPULATION MUST SUPPORT IT.
YOU CAN PARTICIPATE LATER ON.
SURE, SURE! WHEN IT'S ALL OVER.
MOM, PLEASE.
OH NO!
COME ON, YOU'RE GOING TO BED NOW.
PLEASE, PLEASE, PLEASE, PL...
GOD, WHERE ARE YOU?
THAT NIGHT HE DIDN'T COME.

Twisting their words to show her perception

THE WATER CELL

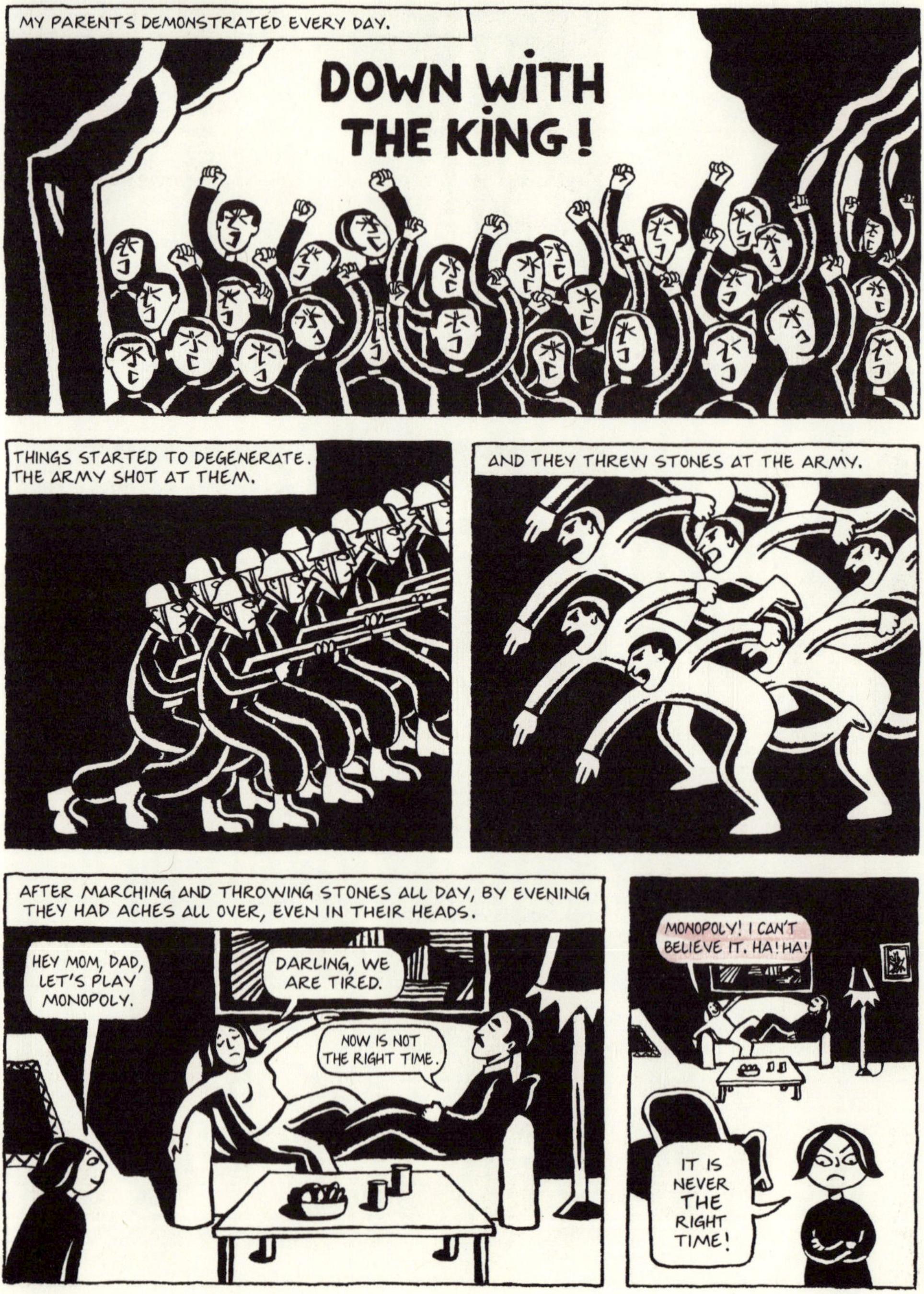
MY PARENTS DEMONSTRATED EVERY DAY.
DOWN WITH THE KING!
THINGS STARTED TO DEGENERATE. THE ARMY SHOT AT THEM.
AND THEY THREW STONES AT THE ARMY.
AFTER MARCHING AND THROWING STONES ALL DAY, BY EVENING THEY HAD ACHES ALL OVER, EVEN IN THEIR HEADS.
HEY MOM, DAD, LET'S PLAY MONOPOLY.
DARLING, WE ARE TIRED.
NOW IS NOT THE RIGHT TIME.
MONOPOLY! I CAN'T BELIEVE IT. HA! HA!
IT IS NEVER THE RIGHT TIME!

Educational indoctrination

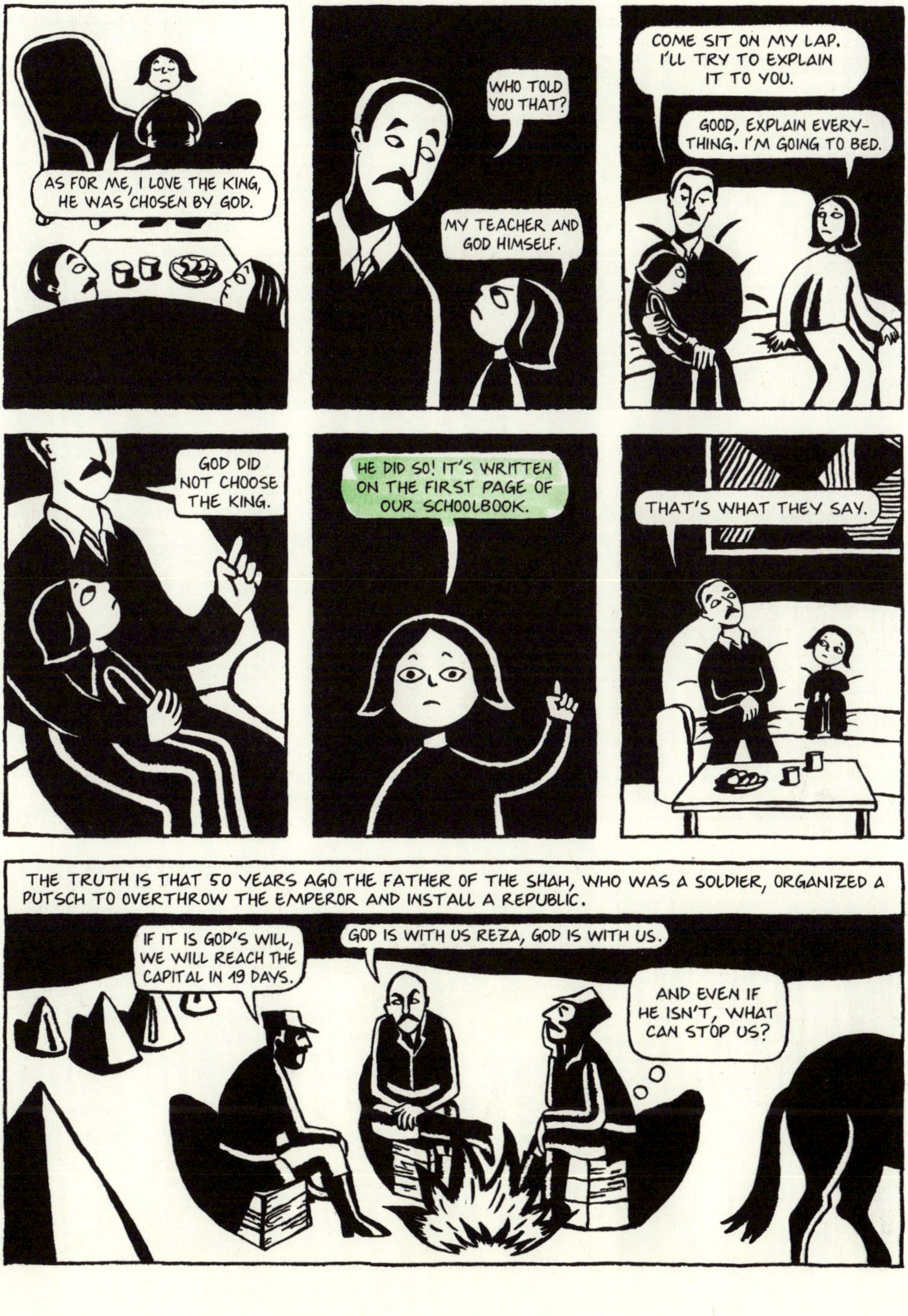
AS FOR ME, I LOVE THE KING, HE WAS CHOSEN BY GOD.
WHO TOLD YOU THAT?
MY TEACHER AND GOD HIMSELF.
COME SIT ON MY LAP. I'LL TRY TO EXPLAIN IT TO YOU.
GOOD, EXPLAIN EVERYTHING. I'M GOING TO BED.
GOD DID NOT CHOOSE THE KING.
HE DID SO! IT'S WRITTEN ON THE FIRST PAGE OF OUR SCHOOLBOOK.
THAT'S WHAT THEY SAY.
THE TRUTH IS THAT 50 YEARS AGO THE FATHER OF THE SHAH, WHO WAS A SOLDIER, ORGANIZED A PUTSCH TO OVERTHROW THE EMPEROR AND INSTALL A REPUBLIC.
IF IT IS GOD'S WILL, WE WILL REACH THE CAPITAL IN 19 DAYS.
GOD IS WITH US REZA, GOD IS WITH US.
AND EVEN IF HE ISN'T, WHAT CAN STOP US?

Clocked

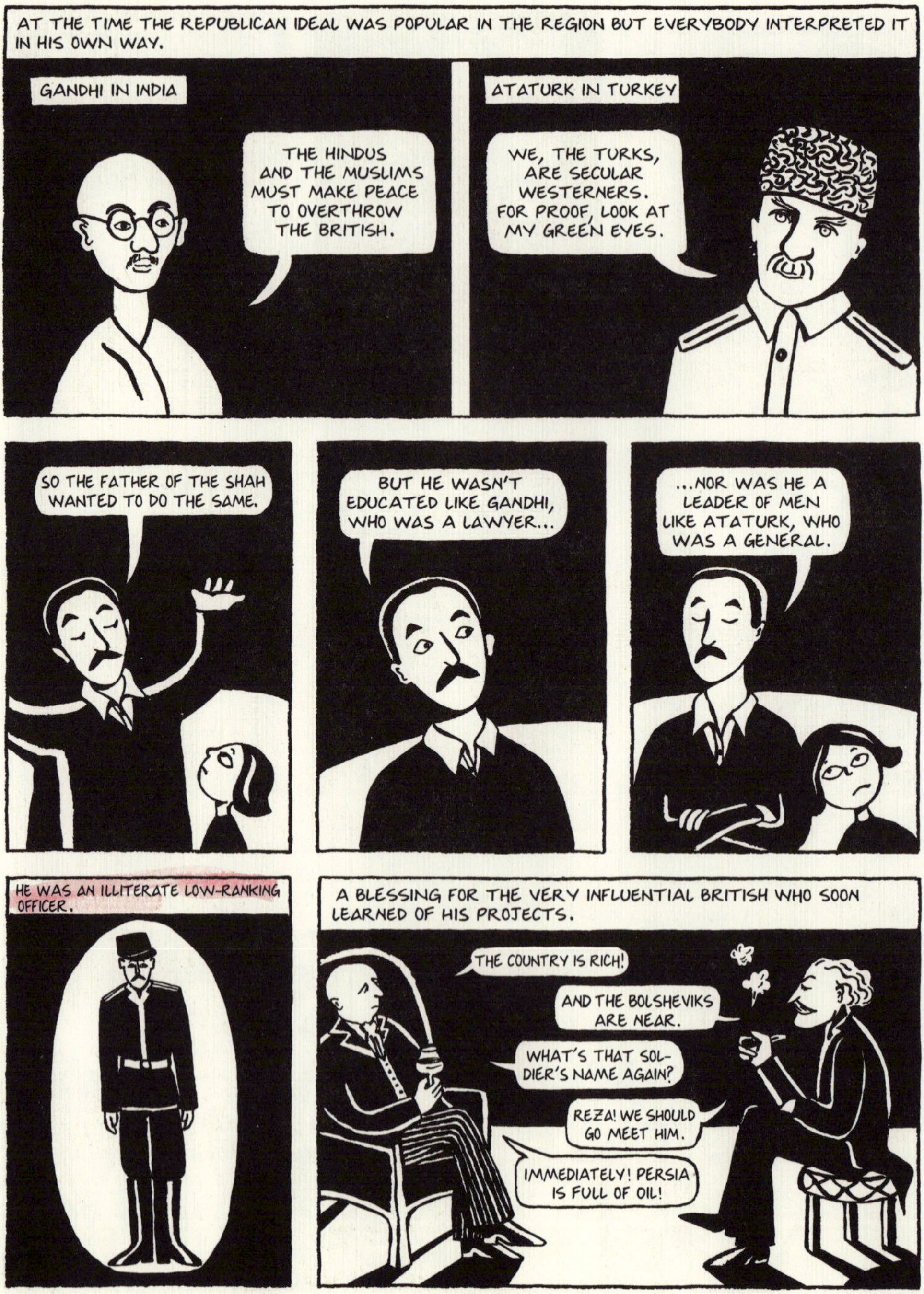
AT THE TIME THE REPUBLICAN IDEAL WAS POPULAR IN THE REGION BUT EVERYBODY INTERPRETED IT IN HIS OWN WAY.
GANDHI IN INDIA
THE HINDUS AND THE MUSLIMS MUST MAKE PEACE TO OVERTHROW THE BRITISH.
ATATURK IN TURKEY
WE, THE TURKS, ARE SECULAR WESTERNERS. FOR PROOF, LOOK AT MY GREEN EYES.
SO THE FATHER OF THE SHAH WANTED TO DO THE SAME.
BUT HE WASN'T EDUCATED LIKE GANDHI, WHO WAS A LAWYER...
...NOR WAS HE A LEADER OF MEN LIKE ATATURK, WHO WAS A GENERAL.
HE WAS AN ILLITERATE LOW-RANKING OFFICER.
A BLESSING FOR THE VERY INFLUENTIAL BRITISH WHO SOON LEARNED OF HIS PROJECTS.
THE COUNTRY IS RICH!
AND THE BOLSHEVIKS ARE NEAR.
WHAT'S THAT SOLDIER'S NAME AGAIN?
REZA! WE SHOULD GO MEET HIM.
IMMEDIATELY! PERSIA IS FULL OF OIL!

Holt shifted face to appeal to a sense of unease

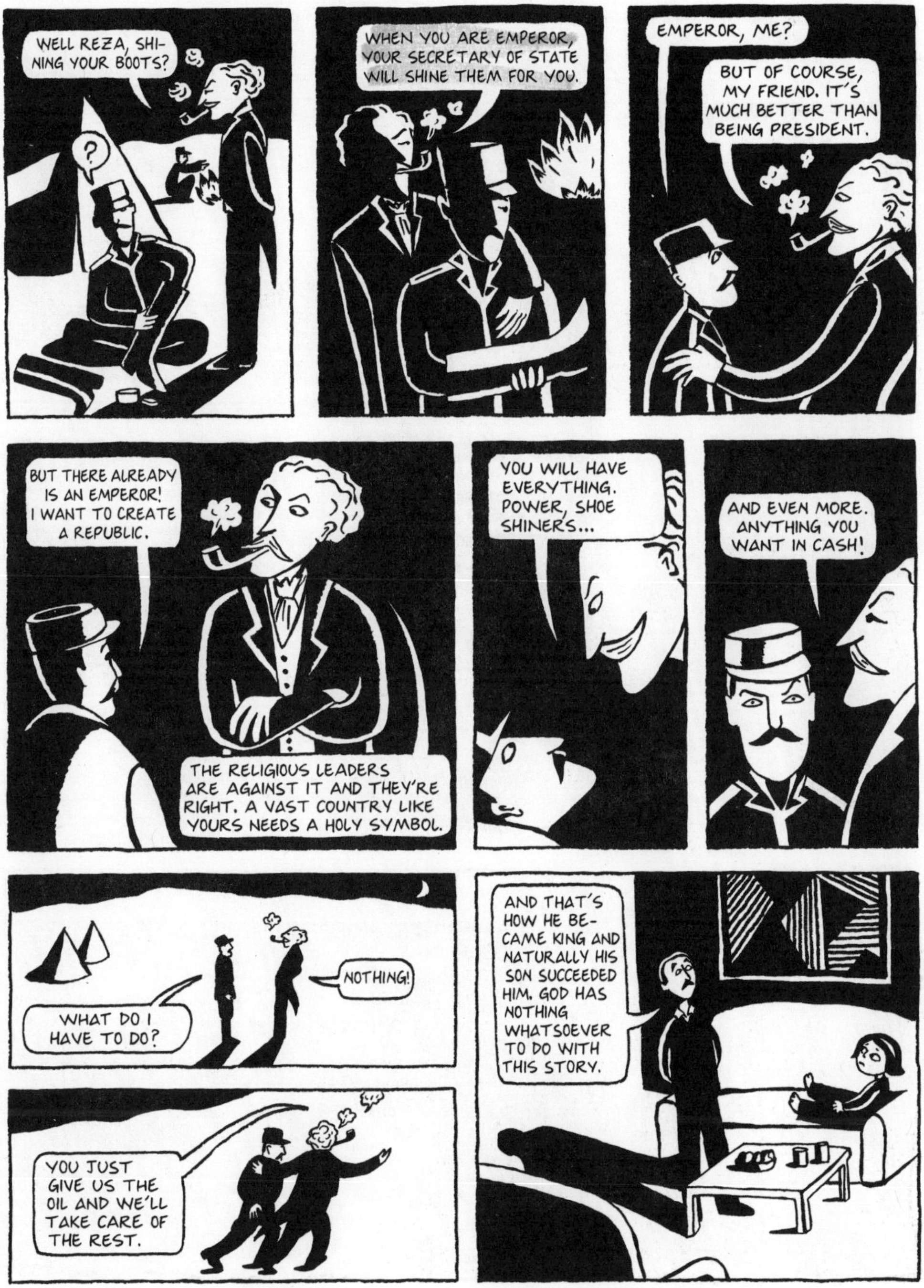

WELL REZA, SHINING YOUR BOOTS?
?
WHEN YOU ARE EMPEROR, YOUR SECRETARY OF STATE WILL SHINE THEM FOR YOU.
EMPEROR, ME?
BUT OF COURSE, MY FRIEND. IT'S MUCH BETTER THAN BEING PRESIDENT.
BUT THERE ALREADY IS AN EMPEROR! I WANT TO CREATE A REPUBLIC.
THE RELIGIOUS LEADERS ARE AGAINST IT AND THEY'RE RIGHT. A VAST COUNTRY LIKE YOURS NEEDS A HOLY SYMBOL.
YOU WILL HAVE EVERYTHING. POWER, SHOE SHINERS...
AND EVEN MORE. ANYTHING YOU WANT IN CASH!
WHAT DO I HAVE TO DO?
NOTHING!
YOU JUST GIVE US THE OIL AND WE'LL TAKE CARE OF THE REST.
AND THAT'S HOW HE BECAME KING AND NATURALLY HIS SON SUCCEEDED HIM. GOD HAS NOTHING WHATSOEVER TO DO WITH THIS STORY.

Child like wonder

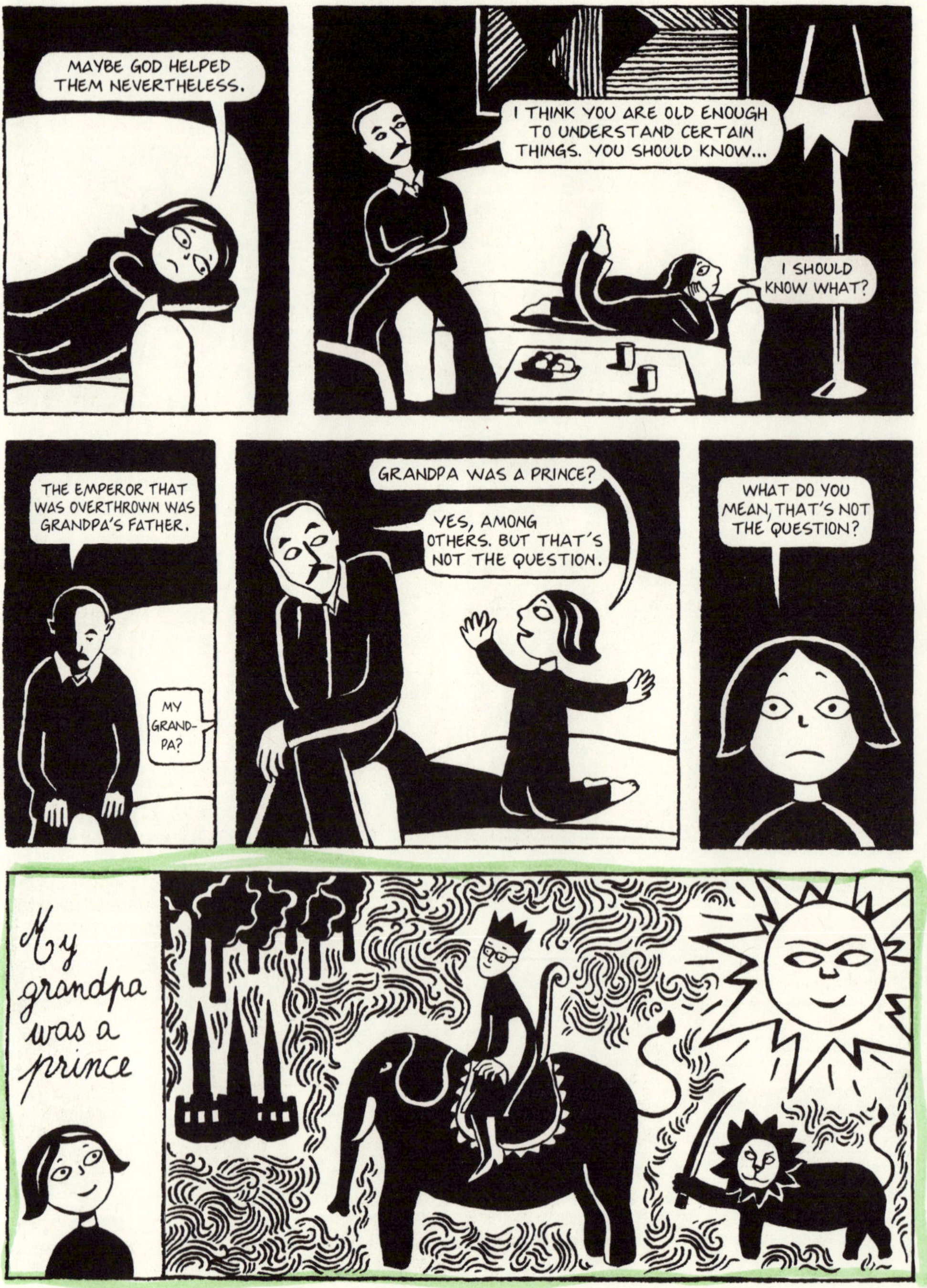
MAYBE GOD HELPED THEM NEVERTHELESS.
I THINK YOU ARE OLD ENOUGH TO UNDERSTAND CERTAIN THINGS. YOU SHOULD KNOW...
I SHOULD KNOW WHAT?
THE EMPEROR THAT WAS OVERTHROWN WAS GRANDPA'S FATHER.
MY GRANDPA?
GRANDPA WAS A PRINCE?
YES, AMONG OTHERS. BUT THAT'S NOT THE QUESTION.
WHAT DO YOU MEAN, THAT'S NOT THE QUESTION?
My grandpa was a prince

Appeals to sense of resolve

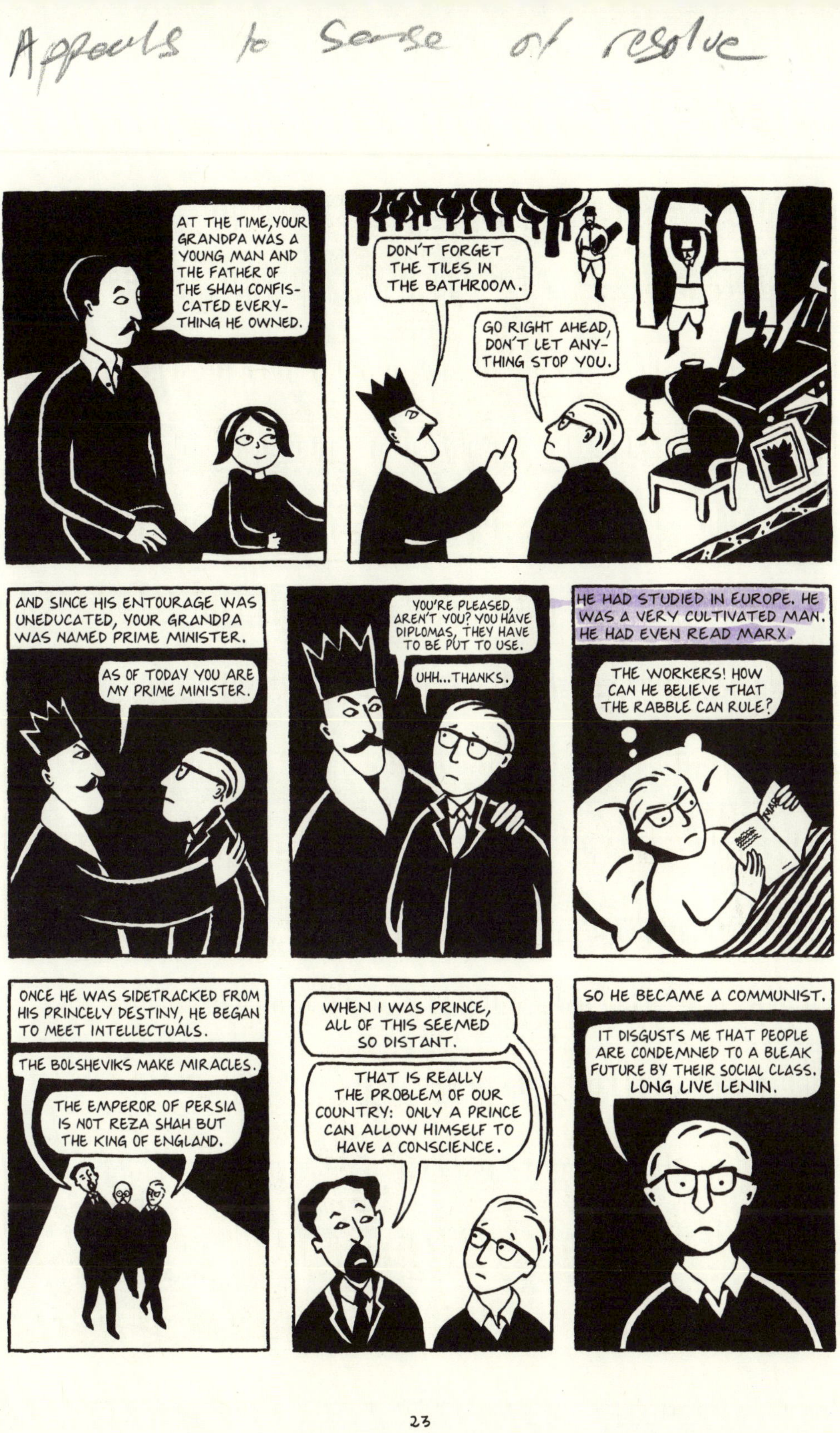
AT THE TIME, YOUR GRANDPA WAS A YOUNG MAN AND THE FATHER OF THE SHAH CONFISCATED EVERYTHING HE OWNED.
DON'T FORGET THE TILES IN THE BATHROOM.
GO RIGHT AHEAD, DON'T LET ANYTHING STOP YOU.
AND SINCE HIS ENTOURAGE WAS UNEDUCATED, YOUR GRANDPA WAS NAMED PRIME MINISTER.
AS OF TODAY YOU ARE MY PRIME MINISTER.
YOU'RE PLEASED, AREN'T YOU? YOU HAVE DIPLOMAS, THEY HAVE TO BE PUT TO USE.
UHH...THANKS.
HE HAD STUDIED IN EUROPE. HE WAS A VERY CULTIVATED MAN. HE HAD EVEN READ MARX.
THE WORKERS! HOW CAN HE BELIEVE THAT THE RABBLE CAN RULE?
ONCE HE WAS SIDETRACKED FROM HIS PRINCELY DESTINY, HE BEGAN TO MEET INTELLECTUALS.
THE BOLSHEVIKS MAKE MIRACLES.
THE EMPEROR OF PERSIA IS NOT REZA SHAH BUT THE KING OF ENGLAND.
WHEN I WAS PRINCE, ALL OF THIS SEEMED SO DISTANT.
THAT IS REALLY THE PROBLEM OF OUR COUNTRY: ONLY A PRINCE CAN ALLOW HIMSELF TO HAVE A CONSCIENCE.
SO HE BECAME A COMMUNIST.
IT DISGUSTS ME THAT PEOPLE ARE CONDEMNED TO A BLEAK FUTURE BY THEIR SOCIAL CLASS. LONG LIVE LENIN.

Loss of innocence / Axicty

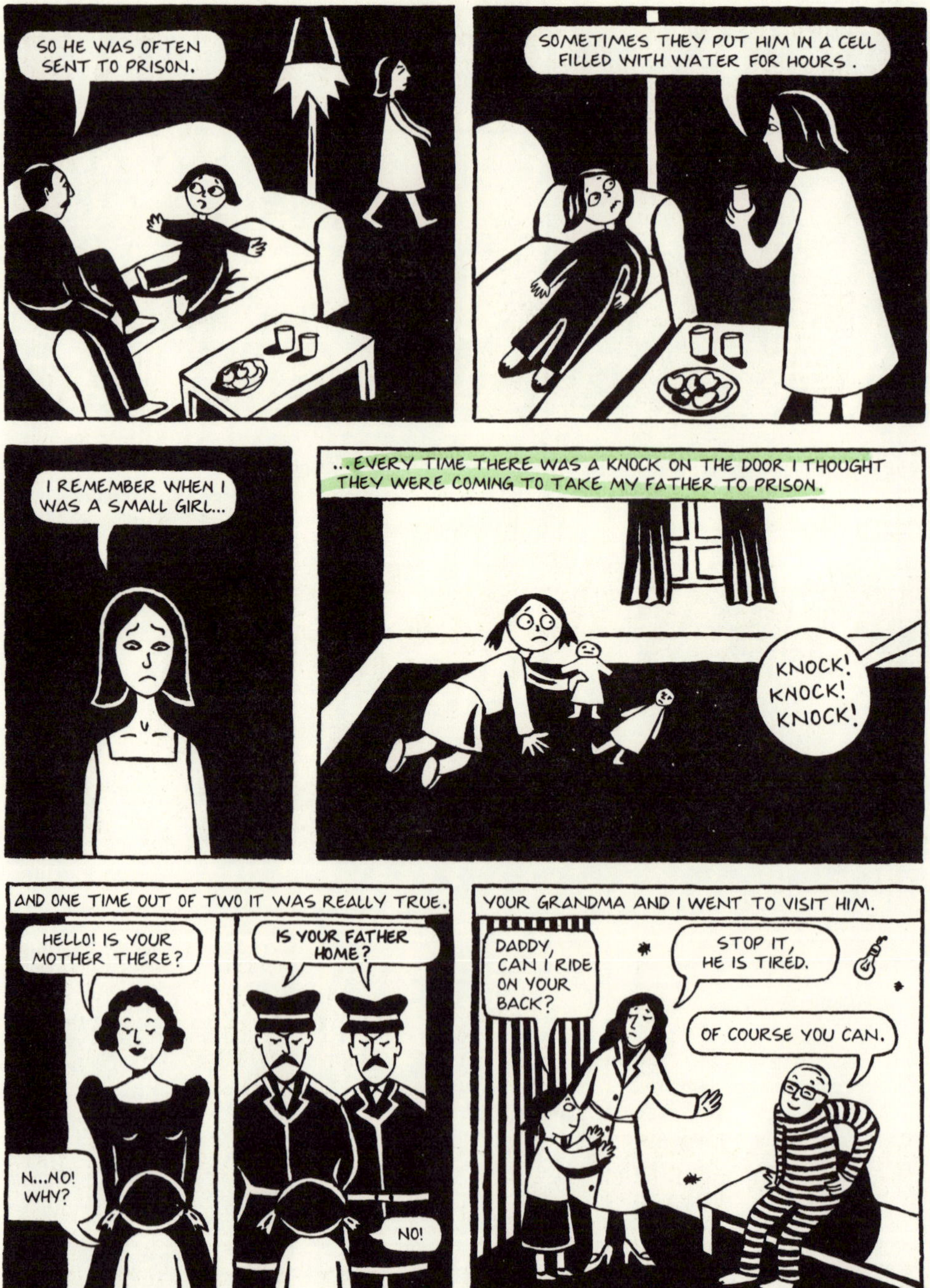
SO HE WAS OFTEN SENT TO PRISON.
SOMETIMES THEY PUT HIM IN A CELL FILLED WITH WATER FOR HOURS.
I REMEMBER WHEN I WAS A SMALL GIRL...
...EVERY TIME THERE WAS A KNOCK ON THE DOOR I THOUGHT THEY WERE COMING TO TAKE MY FATHER TO PRISON.
KNOCK! KNOCK! KNOCK!
AND ONE TIME OUT OF TWO IT WAS REALLY TRUE.
HELLO! IS YOUR MOTHER THERE?
N...NO! WHY?
IS YOUR FATHER HOME?
NO!
YOUR GRANDMA AND I WENT TO VISIT HIM.
DADDY, CAN I RIDE ON YOUR BACK?
STOP IT, HE IS TIRED.
OF COURSE YOU CAN.

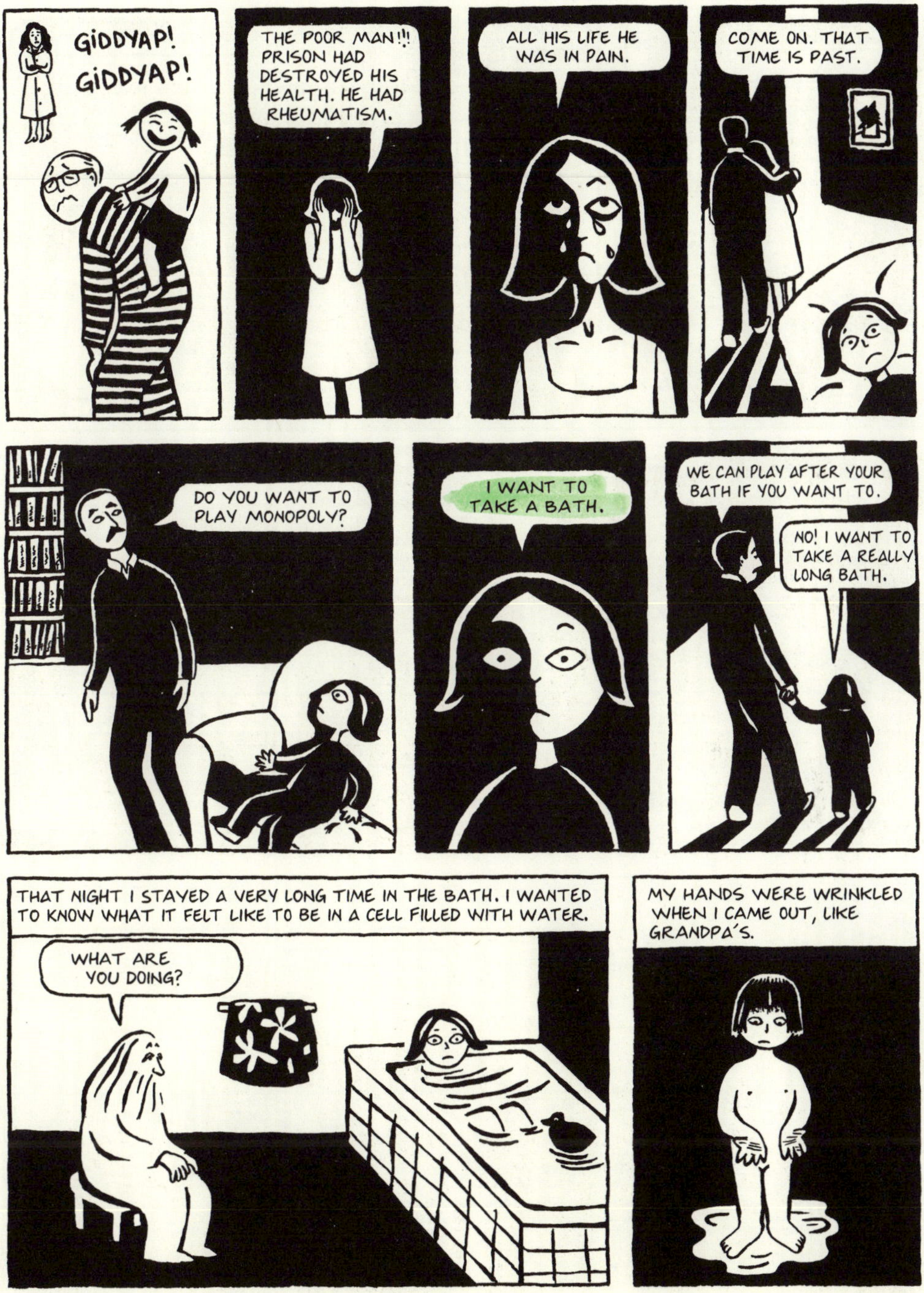
GIDDYAP! GIDDYAP!
THE POOR MAN!!! PRISON HAD DESTROYED HIS HEALTH. HE HAD RHEUMATISM.
ALL HIS LIFE HE WAS IN PAIN.
COME ON. THAT TIME IS PAST.
DO YOU WANT TO PLAY MONOPOLY?
I WANT TO TAKE A BATH.
WE CAN PLAY AFTER YOUR BATH IF YOU WANT TO.
NO! I WANT TO TAKE A REALLY LONG BATH.
THAT NIGHT I STAYED A VERY LONG TIME IN THE BATH. I WANTED TO KNOW WHAT IT FELT LIKE TO BE IN A CELL FILLED WITH WATER.
WHAT ARE YOU DOING?
MY HANDS WERE WRINKLED WHEN I CAME OUT, LIKE GRANDPA'S.

Face hidden to show authority

PERSEPOLIS

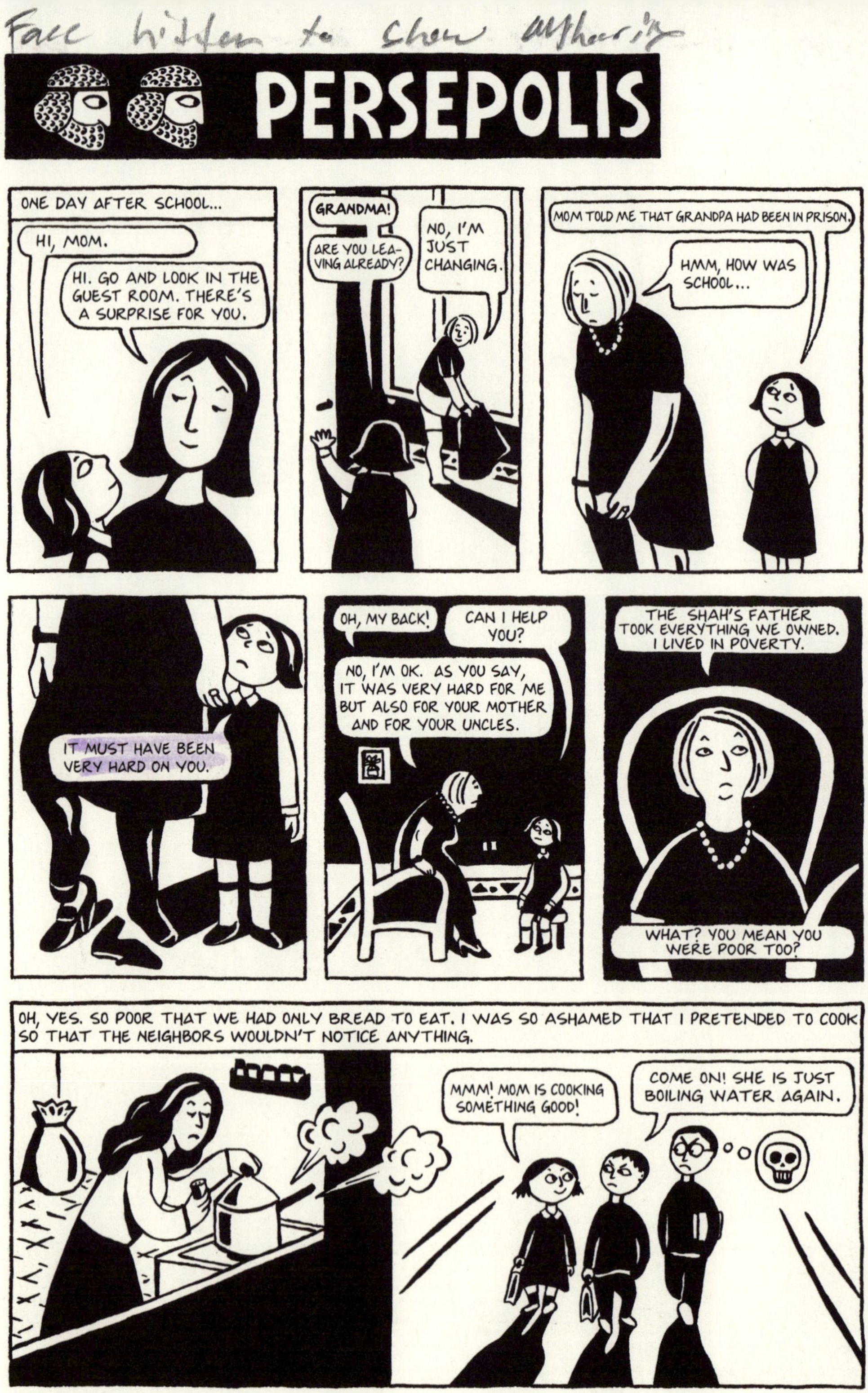

ONE DAY AFTER SCHOOL...
HI, MOM.
HI. GO AND LOOK IN THE GUEST ROOM. THERE'S A SURPRISE FOR YOU.
GRANDMA!
ARE YOU LEAVING ALREADY?
NO, I'M JUST CHANGING.
MOM TOLD ME THAT GRANDPA HAD BEEN IN PRISON.
HMM, HOW WAS SCHOOL...
IT MUST HAVE BEEN VERY HARD ON YOU.
OH, MY BACK!
CAN I HELP YOU?
NO, I'M OK. AS YOU SAY, IT WAS VERY HARD FOR ME BUT ALSO FOR YOUR MOTHER AND FOR YOUR UNCLES.
THE SHAH'S FATHER TOOK EVERYTHING WE OWNED. I LIVED IN POVERTY.
WHAT? YOU MEAN YOU WERE POOR TOO?
OH, YES. SO POOR THAT WE HAD ONLY BREAD TO EAT. I WAS SO ASHAMED THAT I PRETENDED TO COOK SO THAT THE NEIGHBORS WOULDN'T NOTICE ANYTHING.
MMM! MOM IS COOKING SOMETHING GOOD!
COME ON! SHE IS JUST BOILING WATER AGAIN.

In the moon to shed lights on history

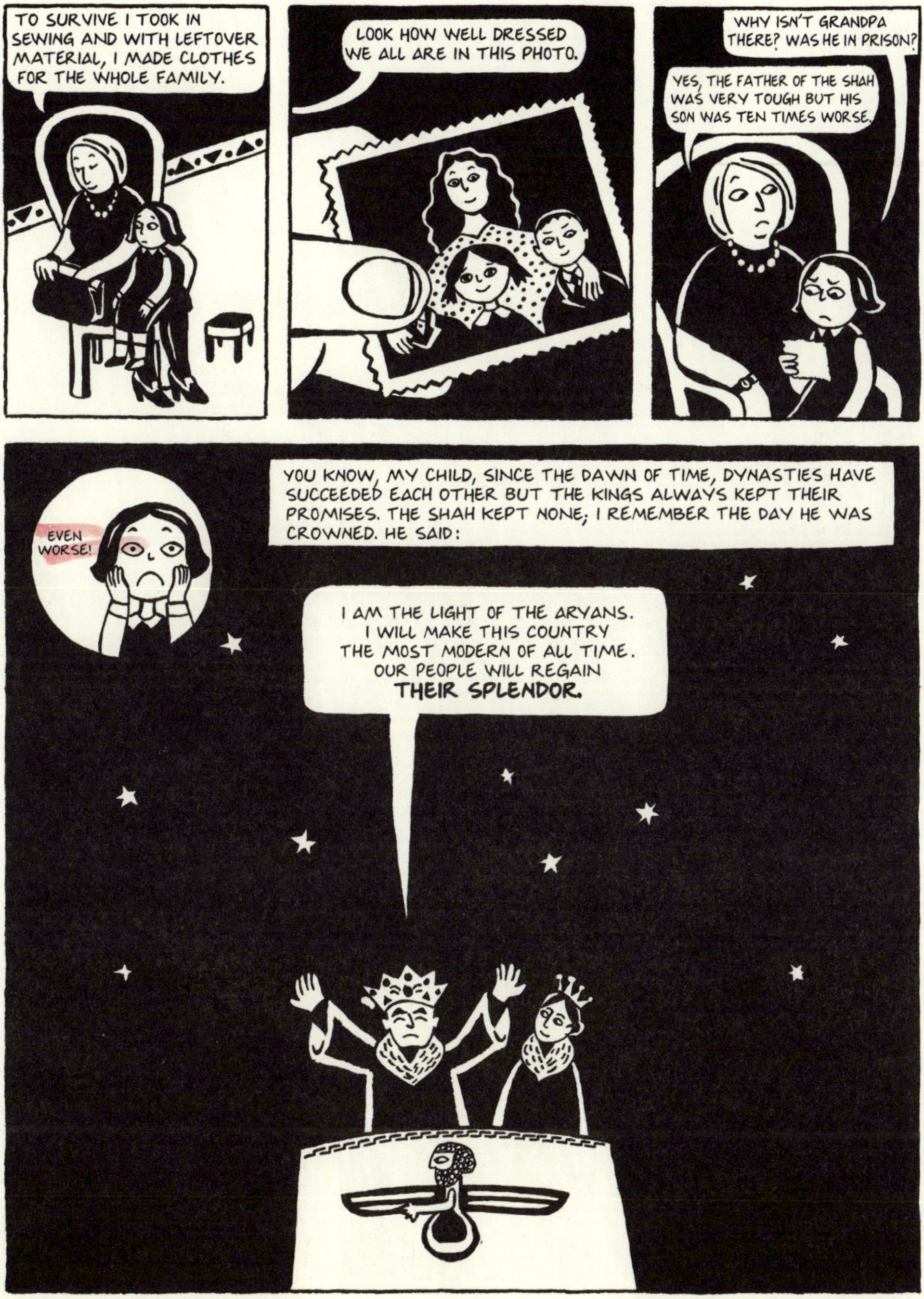
TO SURVIVE I TOOK IN SEWING AND WITH LEFTOVER MATERIAL, I MADE CLOTHES FOR THE WHOLE FAMILY.
LOOK HOW WELL DRESSED WE ALL ARE IN THIS PHOTO.
WHY ISN'T GRANDPA THERE? WAS HE IN PRISON?
YES, THE FATHER OF THE SHAH WAS VERY TOUGH BUT HIS SON WAS TEN TIMES WORSE.
EVEN WORSE!
YOU KNOW, MY CHILD, SINCE THE DAWN OF TIME, DYNASTIES HAVE SUCCEEDED EACH OTHER BUT THE KINGS ALWAYS KEPT THEIR PROMISES. THE SHAH KEPT NONE; I REMEMBER THE DAY HE WAS CROWNED. HE SAID:
I AM THE LIGHT OF THE ARYANS. I WILL MAKE THIS COUNTRY THE MOST MODERN OF ALL TIME. OUR PEOPLE WILL REGAIN **THEIR SPLENDOR.**

Hes big to show his power

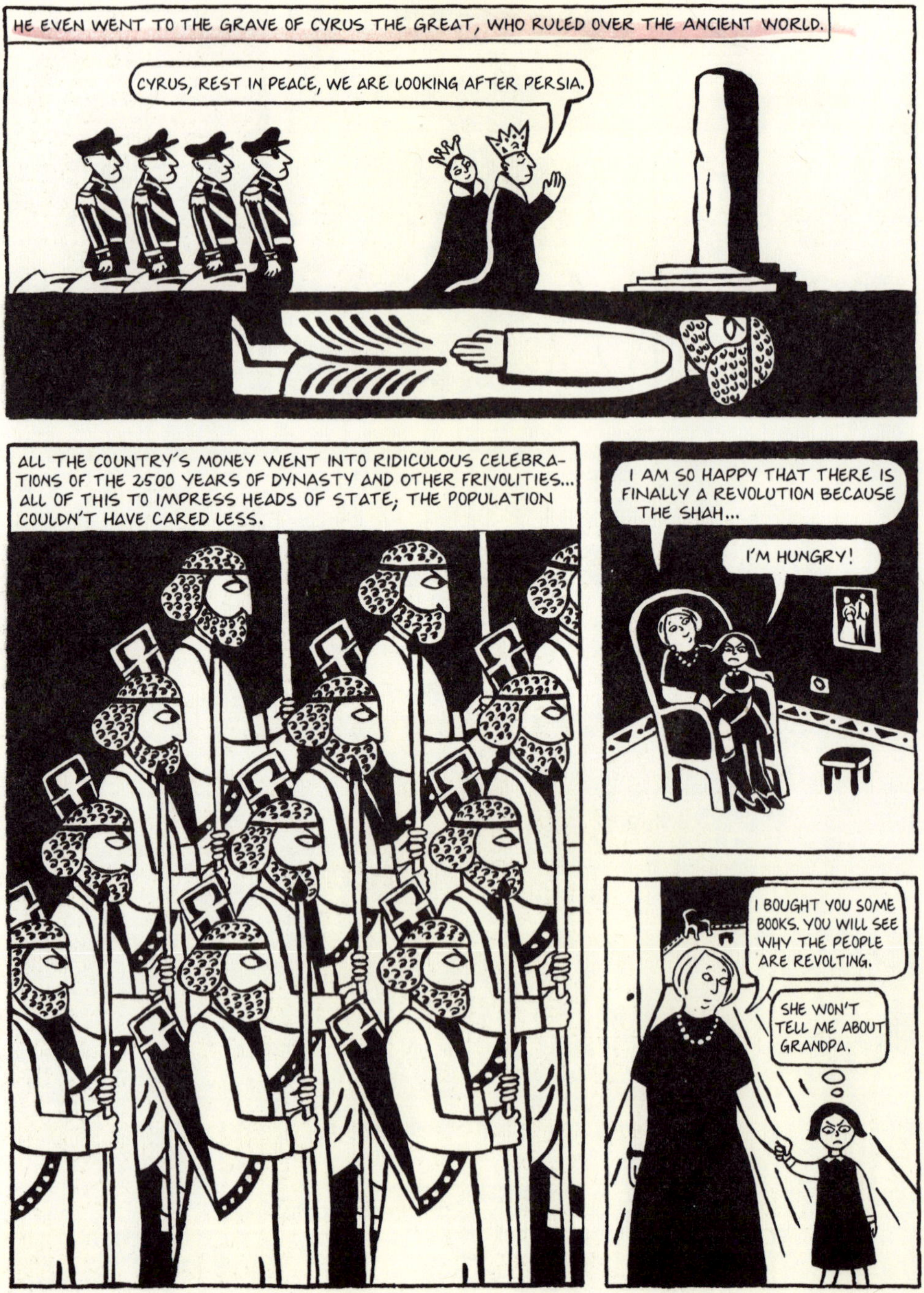
HE EVEN WENT TO THE GRAVE OF CYRUS THE GREAT, WHO RULED OVER THE ANCIENT WORLD.
CYRUS, REST IN PEACE, WE ARE LOOKING AFTER PERSIA.
ALL THE COUNTRY'S MONEY WENT INTO RIDICULOUS CELEBRATIONS OF THE 2500 YEARS OF DYNASTY AND OTHER FRIVOLITIES... ALL OF THIS TO IMPRESS HEADS OF STATE; THE POPULATION COULDN'T HAVE CARED LESS.
I AM SO HAPPY THAT THERE IS FINALLY A REVOLUTION BECAUSE THE SHAH...
I'M HUNGRY!
I BOUGHT YOU SOME BOOKS. YOU WILL SEE WHY THE PEOPLE ARE REVOLTING.
SHE WON'T TELL ME ABOUT GRANDPA.

Loss of language

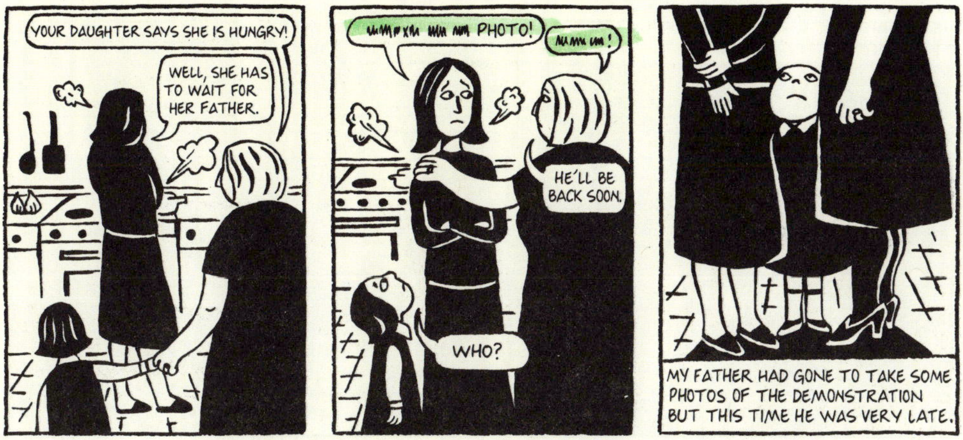

YOUR DAUGHTER SAYS SHE IS HUNGRY!
WELL, SHE HAS TO WAIT FOR HER FATHER.
PHOTO!
HE'LL BE BACK SOON.
WHO?
MY FATHER HAD GONE TO TAKE SOME PHOTOS OF THE DEMONSTRATION BUT THIS TIME HE WAS VERY LATE.

HE TOOK PHOTOS EVERY DAY. IT WAS STRICTLY FORBIDDEN. HE HAD EVEN BEEN ARRESTED ONCE BUT ESCAPED AT THE LAST MINUTE.

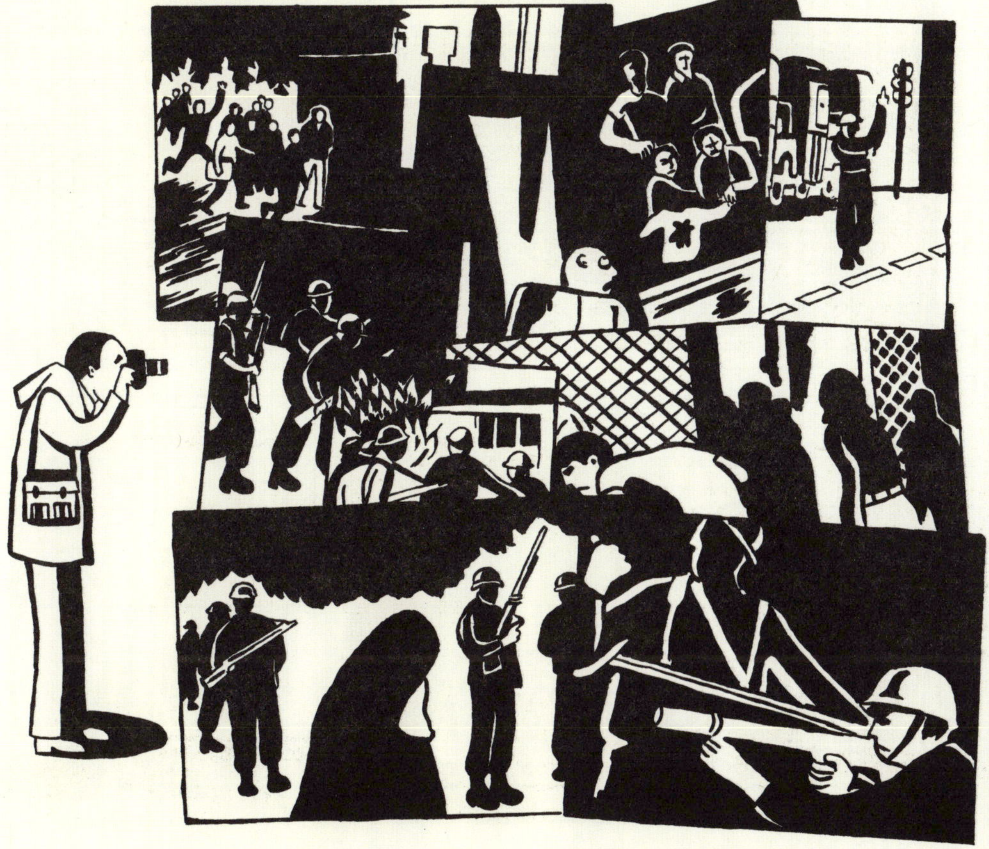

void to show is absence

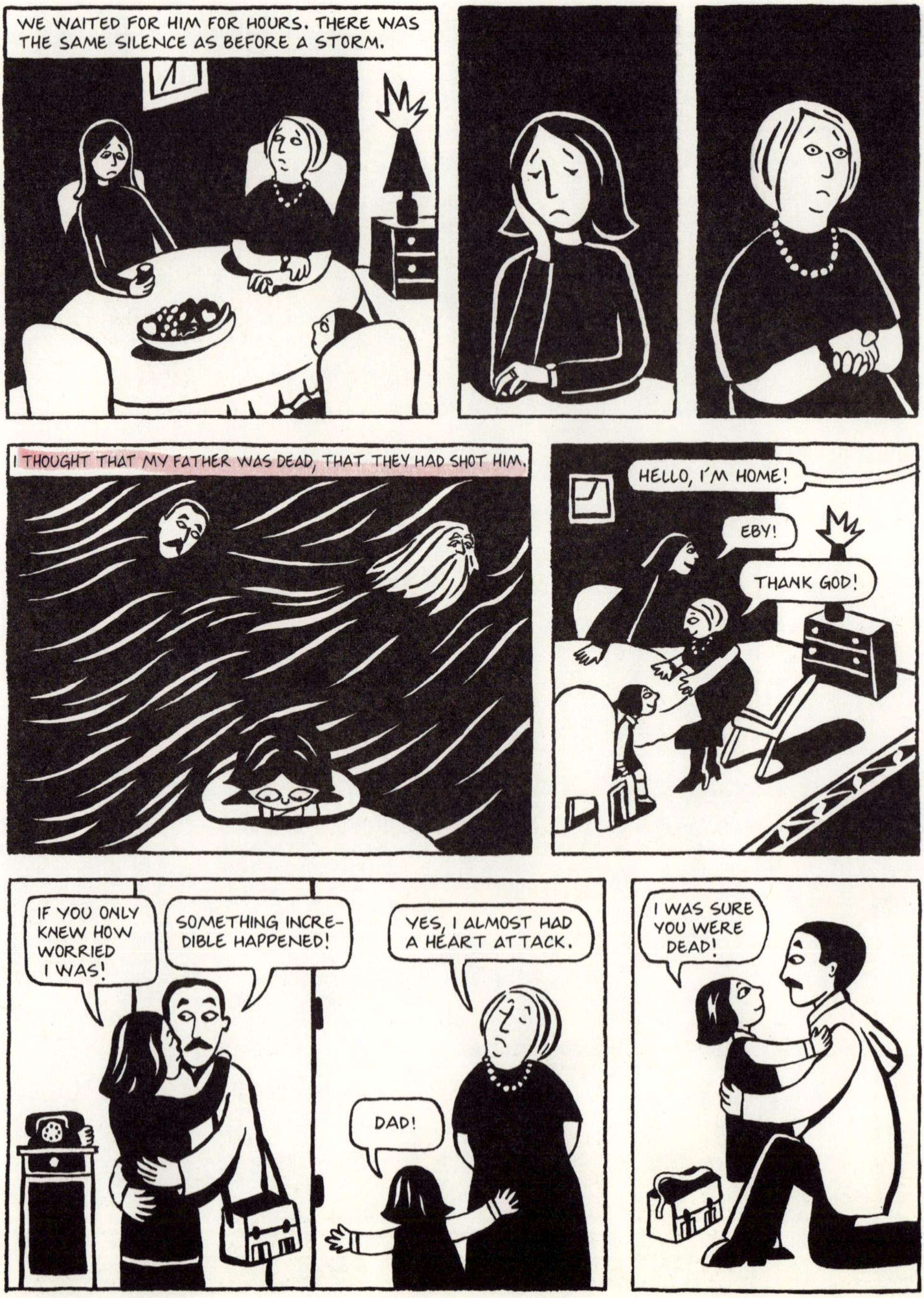

WE WAITED FOR HIM FOR HOURS. THERE WAS THE SAME SILENCE AS BEFORE A STORM.
I THOUGHT THAT MY FATHER WAS DEAD, THAT THEY HAD SHOT HIM.
HELLO, I'M HOME!
EBY!
THANK GOD!
IF YOU ONLY KNEW HOW WORRIED I WAS!
SOMETHING INCREDIBLE HAPPENED!
YES, I ALMOST HAD A HEART ATTACK.
DAD!
I WAS SURE YOU WERE DEAD!

Appeals to pathos with hollowed eyes

(Panel 1) TODAY I WENT TO REY HOSPITAL WITH MY CAMERA.

(Panel 2) PEOPLE CAME OUT CARRYING THE BODY OF A YOUNG MAN KILLED BY THE ARMY. HE WAS HONORED LIKE A MARTYR. A CROWD GATHERED TO TAKE HIM TO THE BAHESHTE ZAHRA CEMETERY.

(Panel 3) THEN THERE WAS ANOTHER CADAVER, AN OLD MAN CARRIED OUT ON A STRETCHER. THOSE WHO DIDN'T FOLLOW THE FIRST ONE WENT OVER TO THE OLD MAN, SHOUTING REVOLUTIONARY SLOGANS AND CALLING HIM A HERO.

HERE IS ANOTHER MARTYR.

(Panel 4) WELL, I WAS TAKING MY PHOTOS WHEN I NOTICED AN OLD WOMAN NEXT TO ME. I UNDERSTOOD THAT SHE WAS THE WIDOW OF THE VICTIM. I HAD SEEN HER LEAVE THE HOSPITAL WITH THE BODY.

PLEASE! STOP IT! STOP IT!

(Panel 5) WHAT? WHAT IS IT?
STOP IT!
WHO ARE YOU?
HIS WIDOW!

(Panel 6) ARE YOU A ROYALIST?
NO, BUT MY HUSBAND DIED OF CANCER...

Shows happy memories to appear to pathos

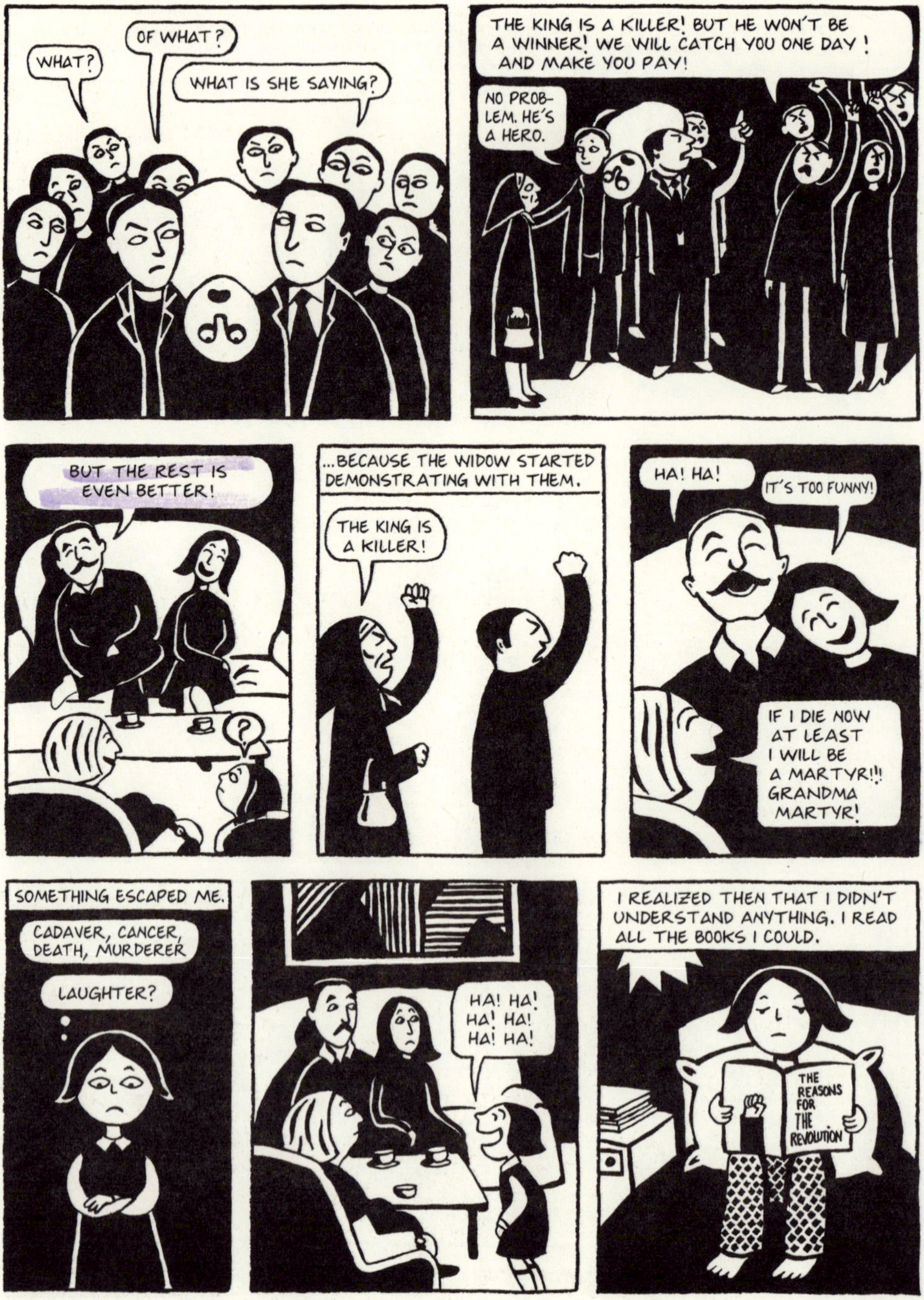

Childlike innocence

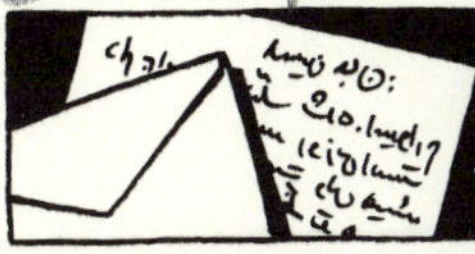

THE LETTER

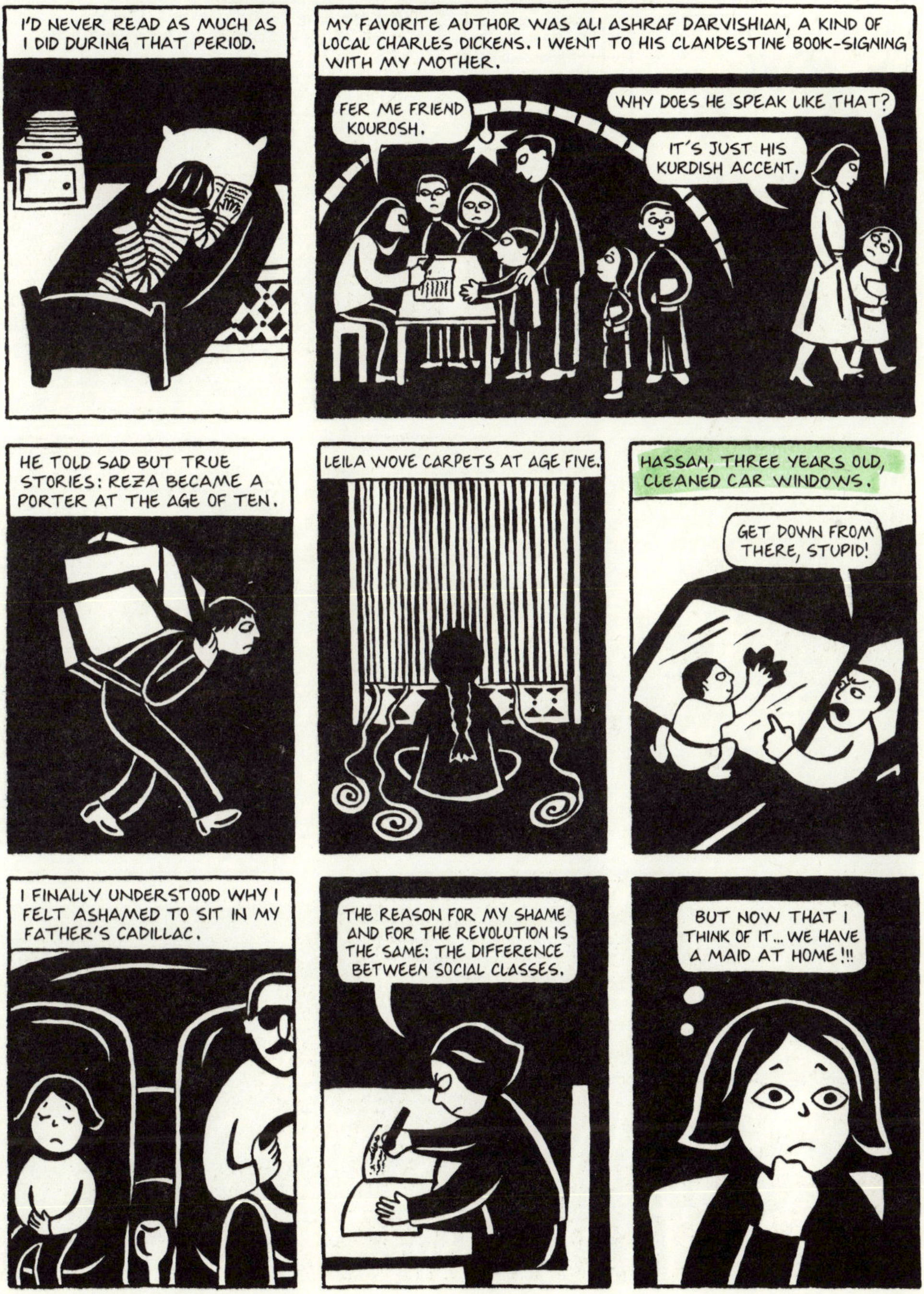

I'D NEVER READ AS MUCH AS I DID DURING THAT PERIOD.
MY FAVORITE AUTHOR WAS ALI ASHRAF DARVISHIAN, A KIND OF LOCAL CHARLES DICKENS. I WENT TO HIS CLANDESTINE BOOK-SIGNING WITH MY MOTHER.
FER ME FRIEND KOUROSH.
WHY DOES HE SPEAK LIKE THAT?
IT'S JUST HIS KURDISH ACCENT.
HE TOLD SAD BUT TRUE STORIES: REZA BECAME A PORTER AT THE AGE OF TEN.
LEILA WOVE CARPETS AT AGE FIVE.
HASSAN, THREE YEARS OLD, CLEANED CAR WINDOWS.
GET DOWN FROM THERE, STUPID!
I FINALLY UNDERSTOOD WHY I FELT ASHAMED TO SIT IN MY FATHER'S CADILLAC.
THE REASON FOR MY SHAME AND FOR THE REVOLUTION IS THE SAME: THE DIFFERENCE BETWEEN SOCIAL CLASSES.
BUT NOW THAT I THINK OF IT... WE HAVE A MAID AT HOME!!!

shows her feelings literally

HER → THIS IS MEHRI.

SHE WAS EIGHT YEARS OLD WHEN SHE HAD TO LEAVE HER PARENTS' HOME TO COME TO WORK FOR US. JUST LIKE REZA, LEILA AND HASSAN.

"WE HAVE TOO MANY CHILDREN, 14 OR 15 INCLUDING HER."

"SHE WILL EAT WELL AT YOUR HOUSE."

"WE WILL TAKE CARE OF HER."

SHE WAS JUST TEN YEARS OLD WHEN I WAS BORN... SHE TOOK CARE OF ME.

SHE PLAYED WITH ME.

AND SHE ALWAYS FINISHED MY FOOD.

SHE ALSO TOLD ME STORIES ABOUT JACKALS THAT SCARED ME.

"AND IT CAME CLOSER! AND IT CAME CLOSER!"

IN OTHER WORDS, WE GOT ALONG WELL.

Childhood bonding

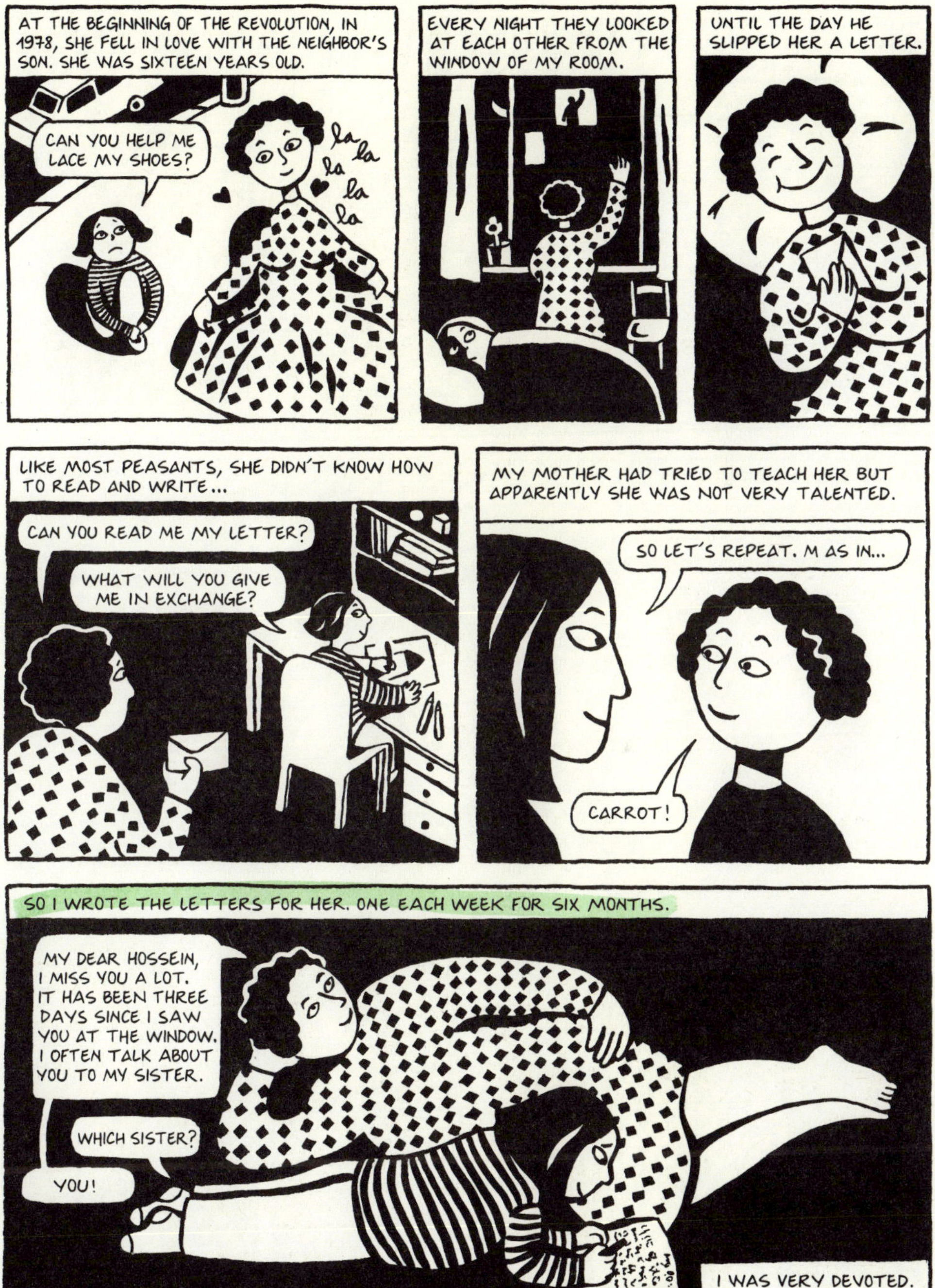

Shows the manipulation of the truth

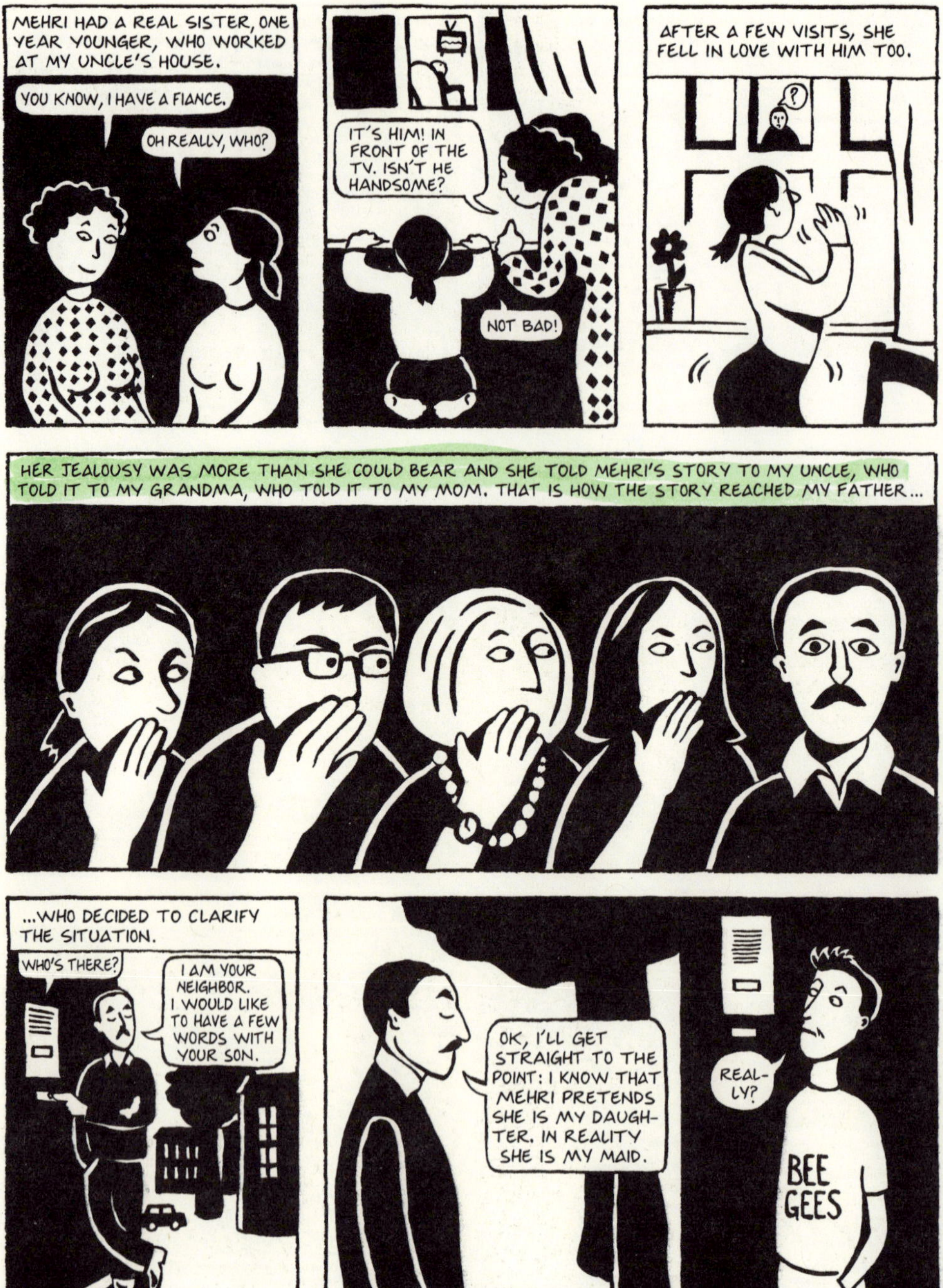

Not true love

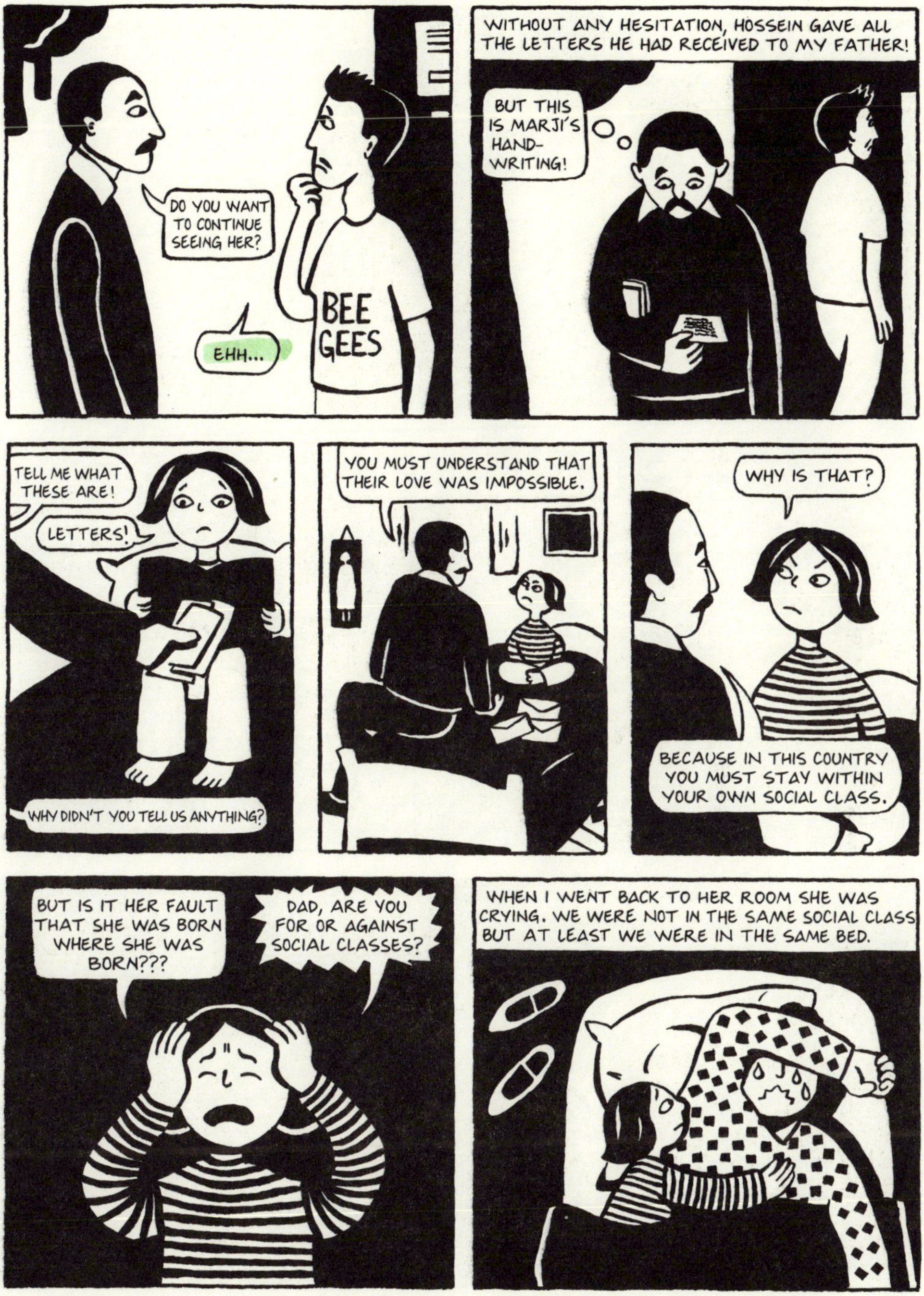
DO YOU WANT TO CONTINUE SEEING HER?
EHH...
BEE GEES
WITHOUT ANY HESITATION, HOSSEIN GAVE ALL THE LETTERS HE HAD RECEIVED TO MY FATHER!
BUT THIS IS MARJI'S HAND-WRITING!
TELL ME WHAT THESE ARE!
LETTERS!
WHY DIDN'T YOU TELL US ANYTHING?
YOU MUST UNDERSTAND THAT THEIR LOVE WAS IMPOSSIBLE.
WHY IS THAT?
BECAUSE IN THIS COUNTRY YOU MUST STAY WITHIN YOUR OWN SOCIAL CLASS.
BUT IS IT HER FAULT THAT SHE WAS BORN WHERE SHE WAS BORN???
DAD, ARE YOU FOR OR AGAINST SOCIAL CLASSES?
WHEN I WENT BACK TO HER ROOM SHE WAS CRYING. WE WERE NOT IN THE SAME SOCIAL CLASS BUT AT LEAST WE WERE IN THE SAME BED.

Shows Ethoe with her imagination

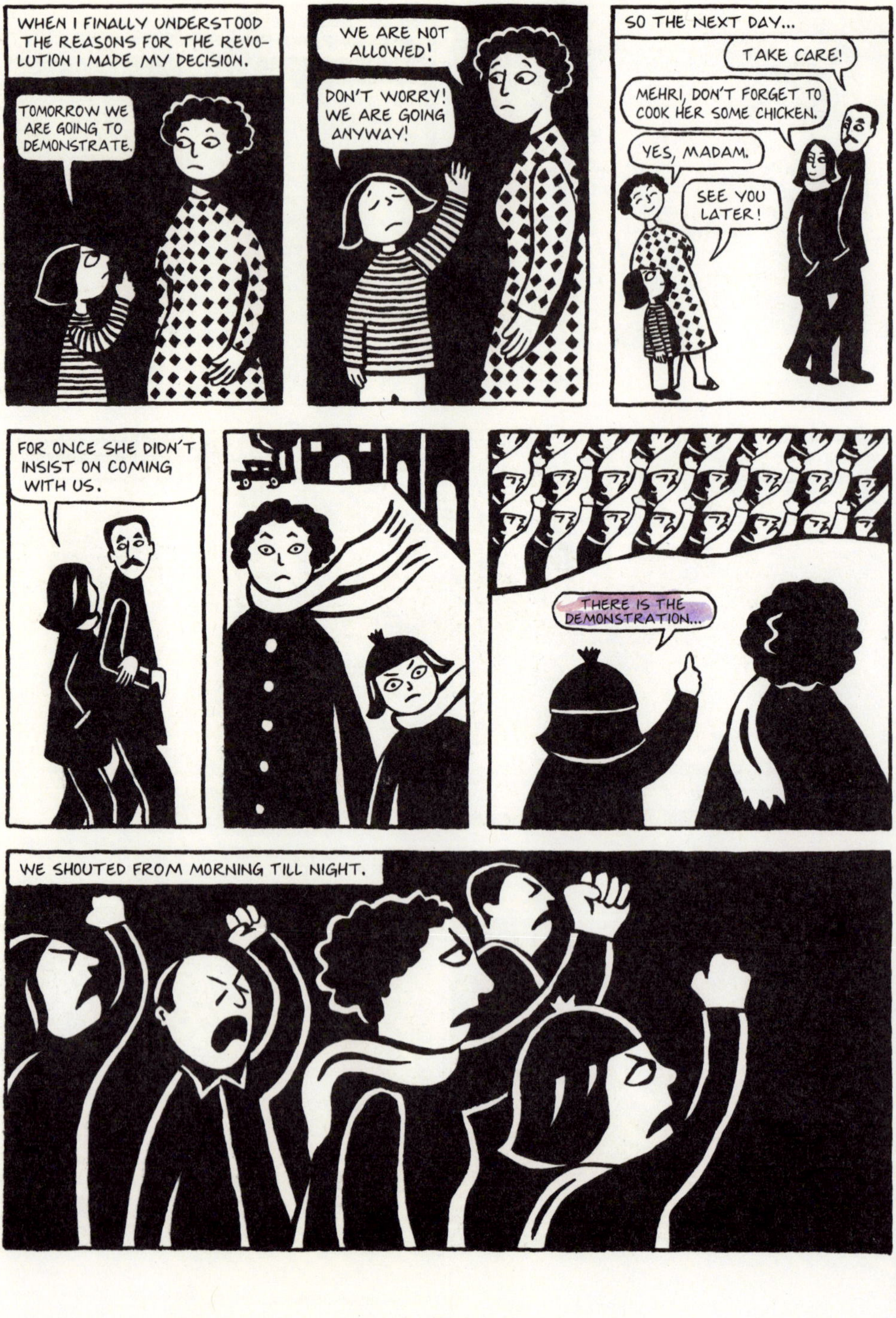

No dialogue and black to show shock

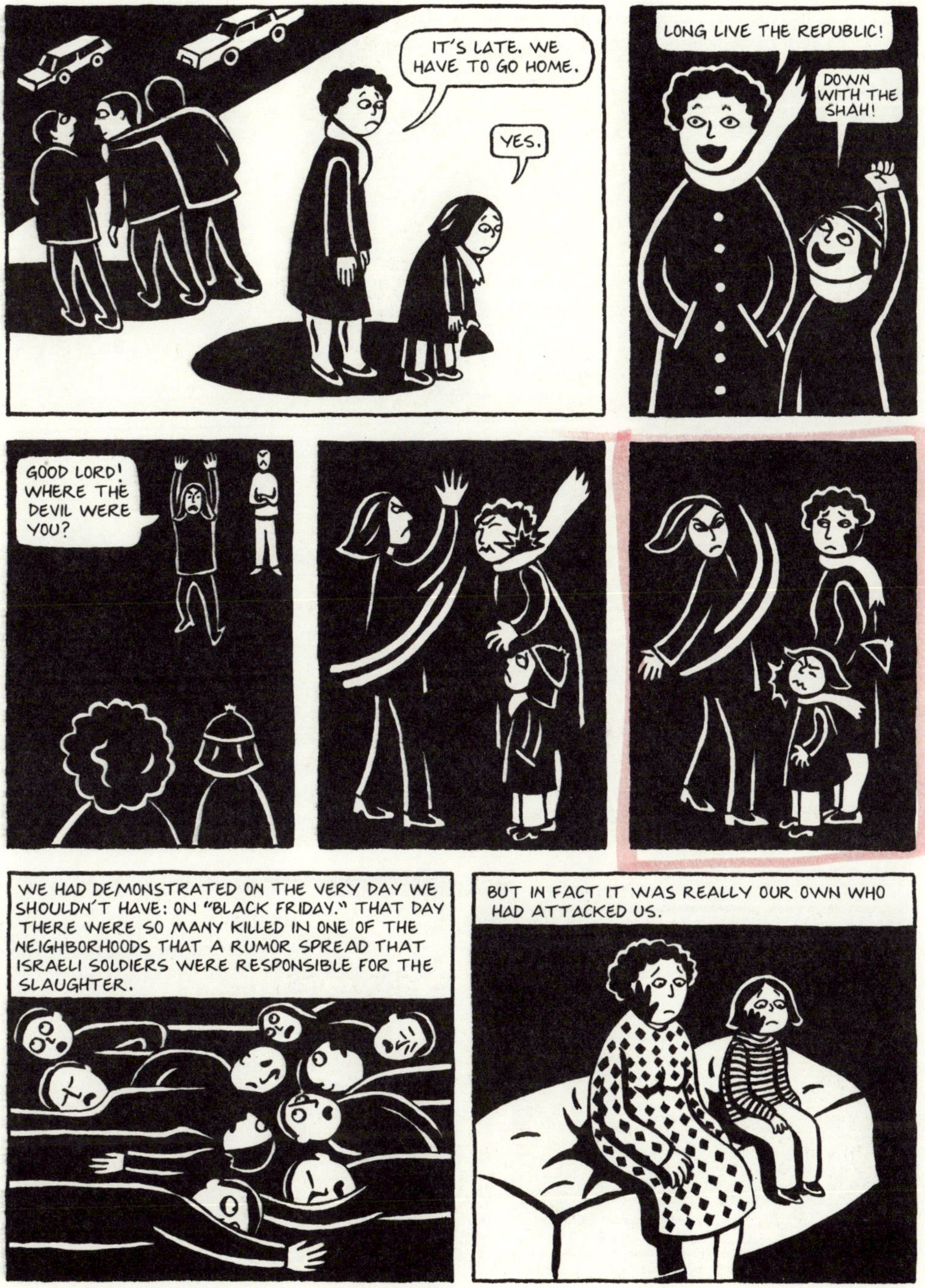

Hollowed faces to show effects of Shah

THE PARTY

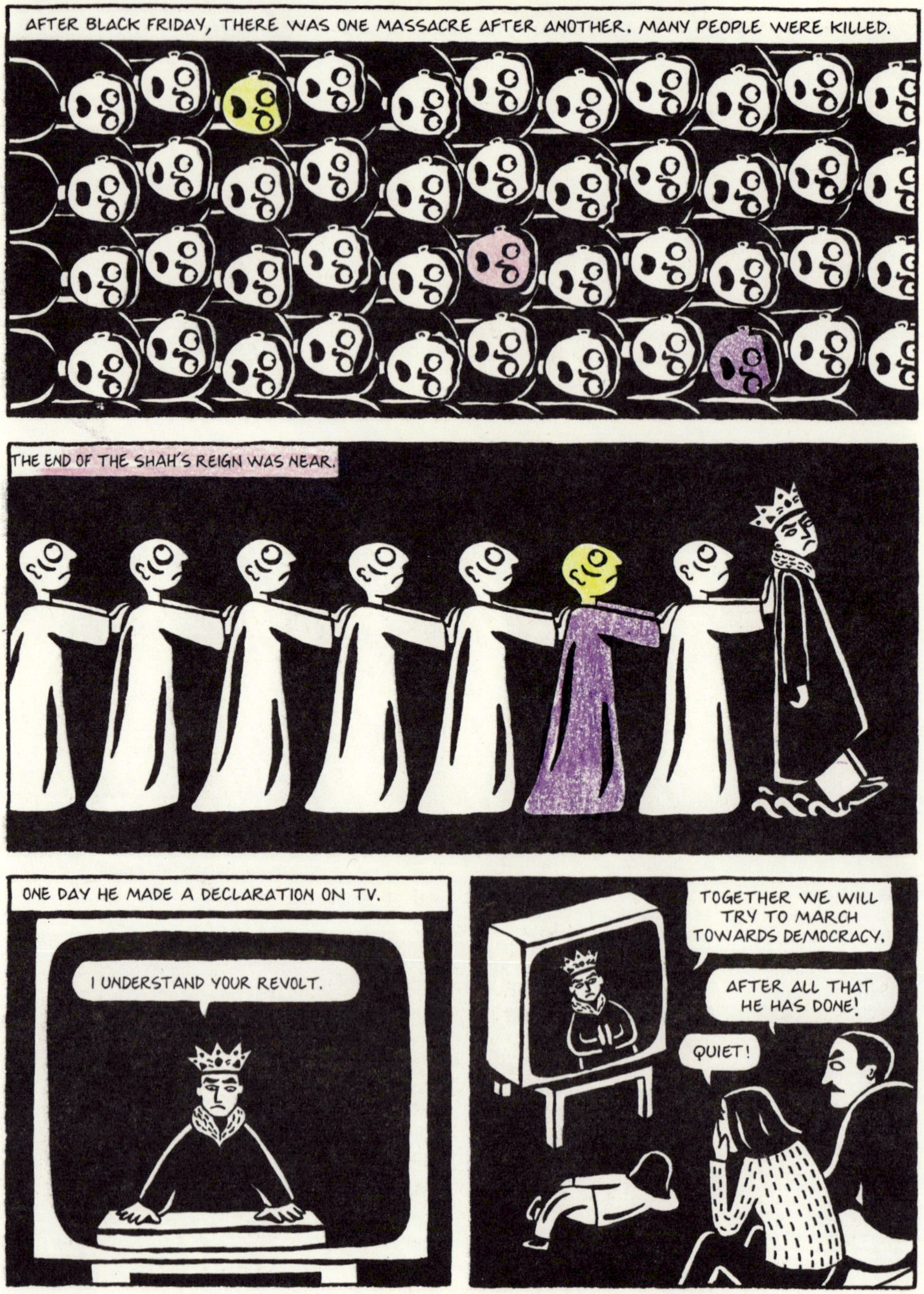
AFTER BLACK FRIDAY, THERE WAS ONE MASSACRE AFTER ANOTHER. MANY PEOPLE WERE KILLED.
THE END OF THE SHAH'S REIGN WAS NEAR.
ONE DAY HE MADE A DECLARATION ON TV.
I UNDERSTAND YOUR REVOLT.
TOGETHER WE WILL TRY TO MARCH TOWARDS DEMOCRACY.
AFTER ALL THAT HE HAS DONE!
QUIET!

Falling royality

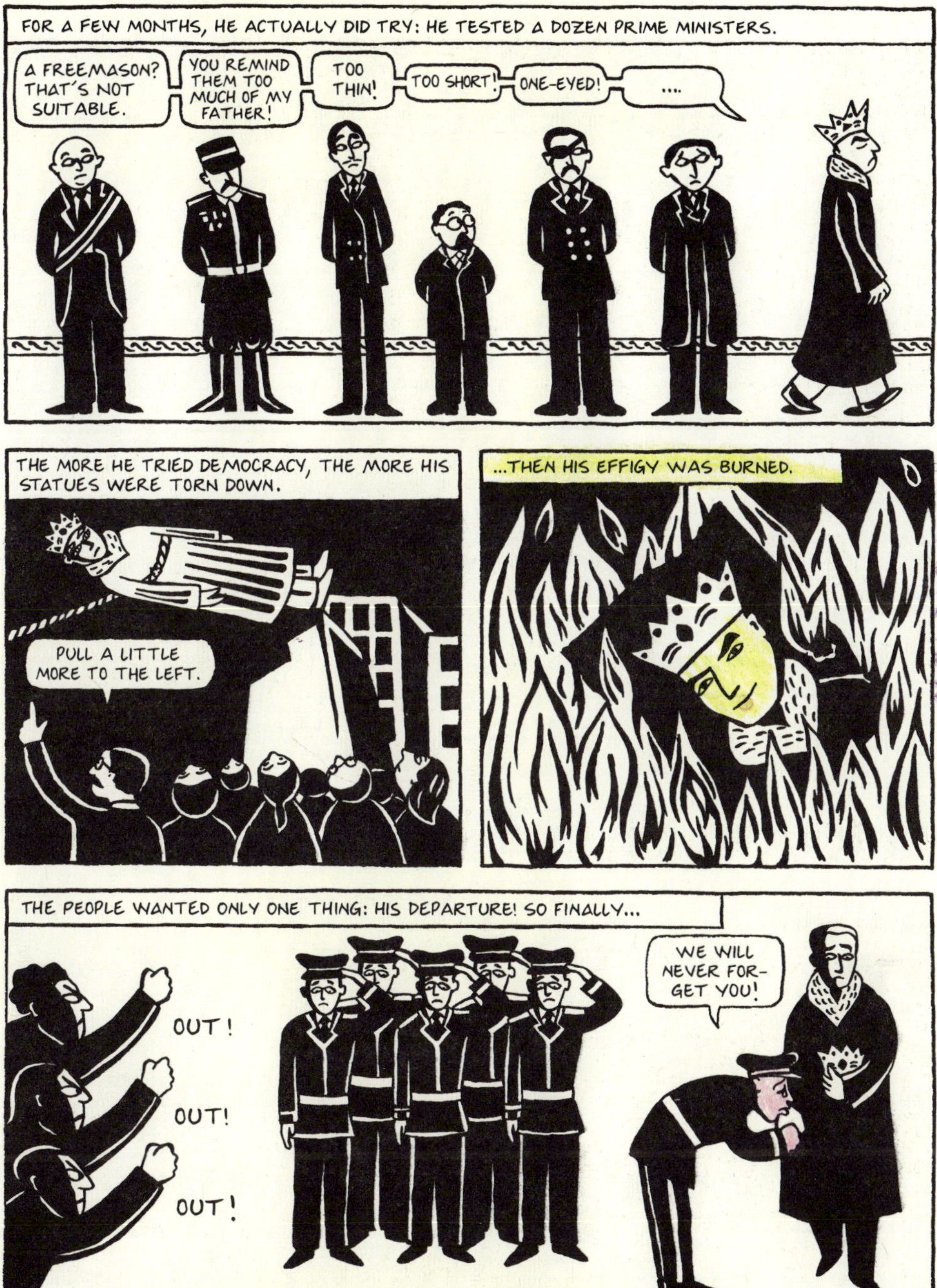

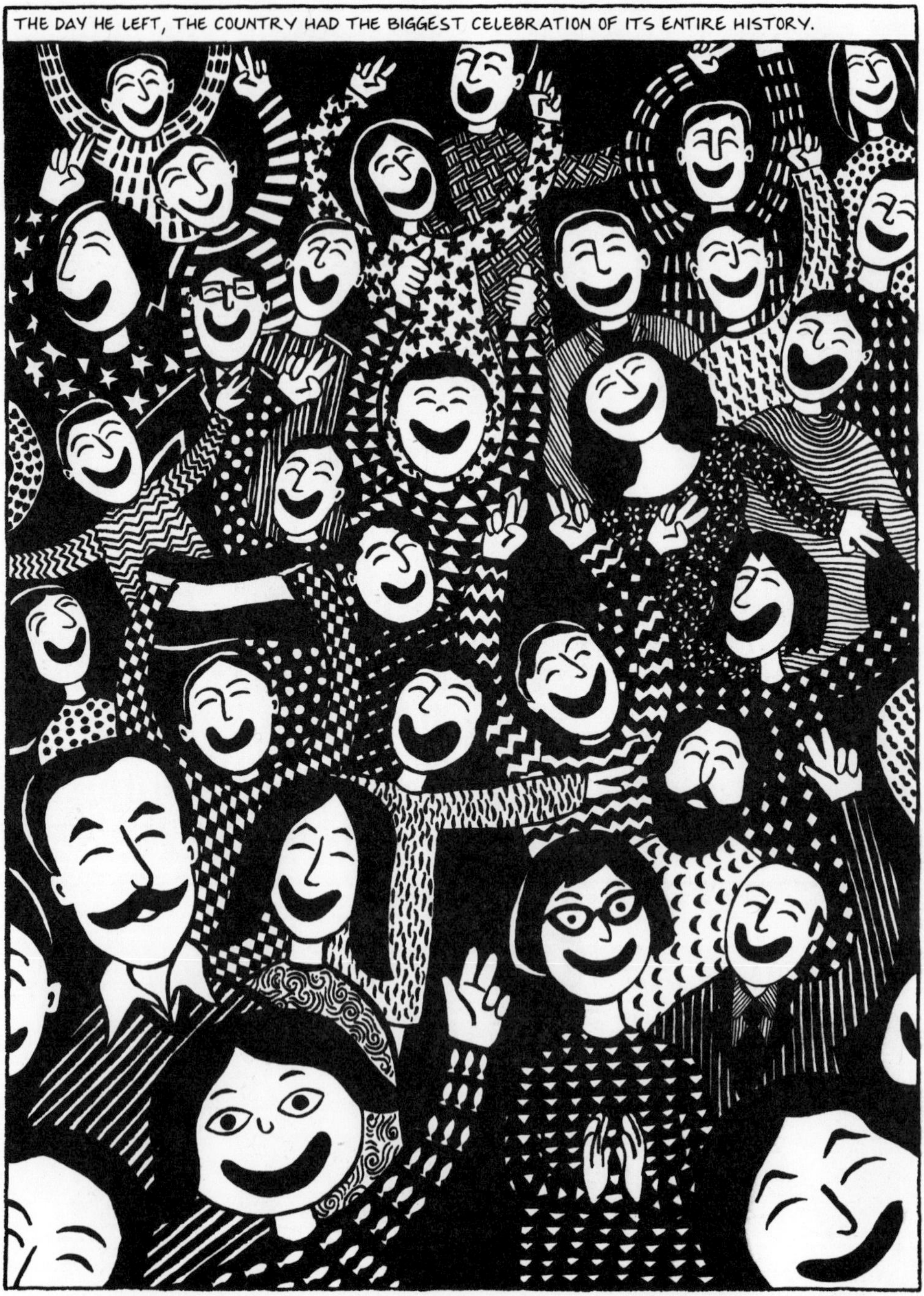
THE DAY HE LEFT, THE COUNTRY HAD THE BIGGEST CELEBRATION OF ITS ENTIRE HISTORY.

Demon appeals pathos

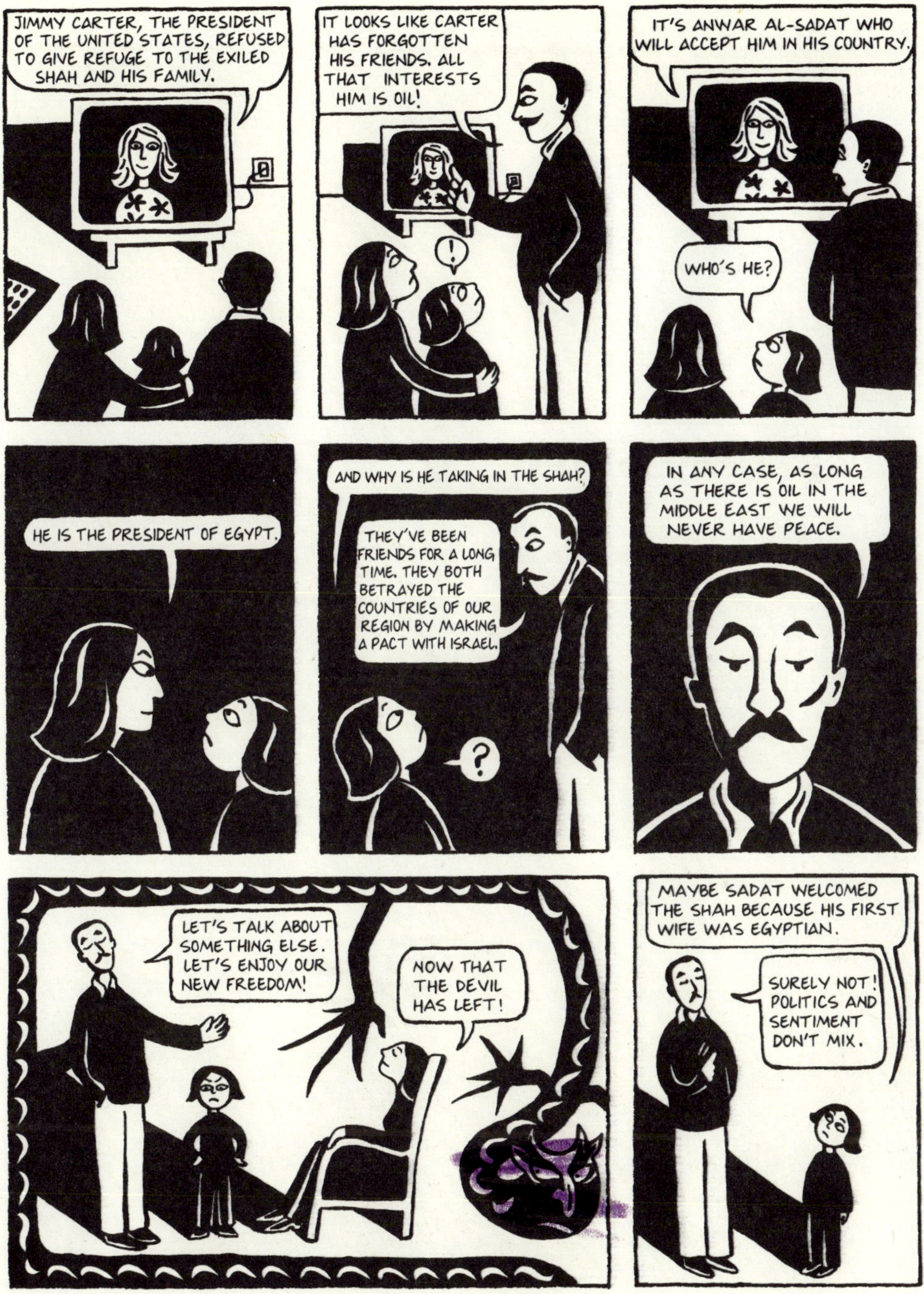

Children Gullible

hypocracy

irony

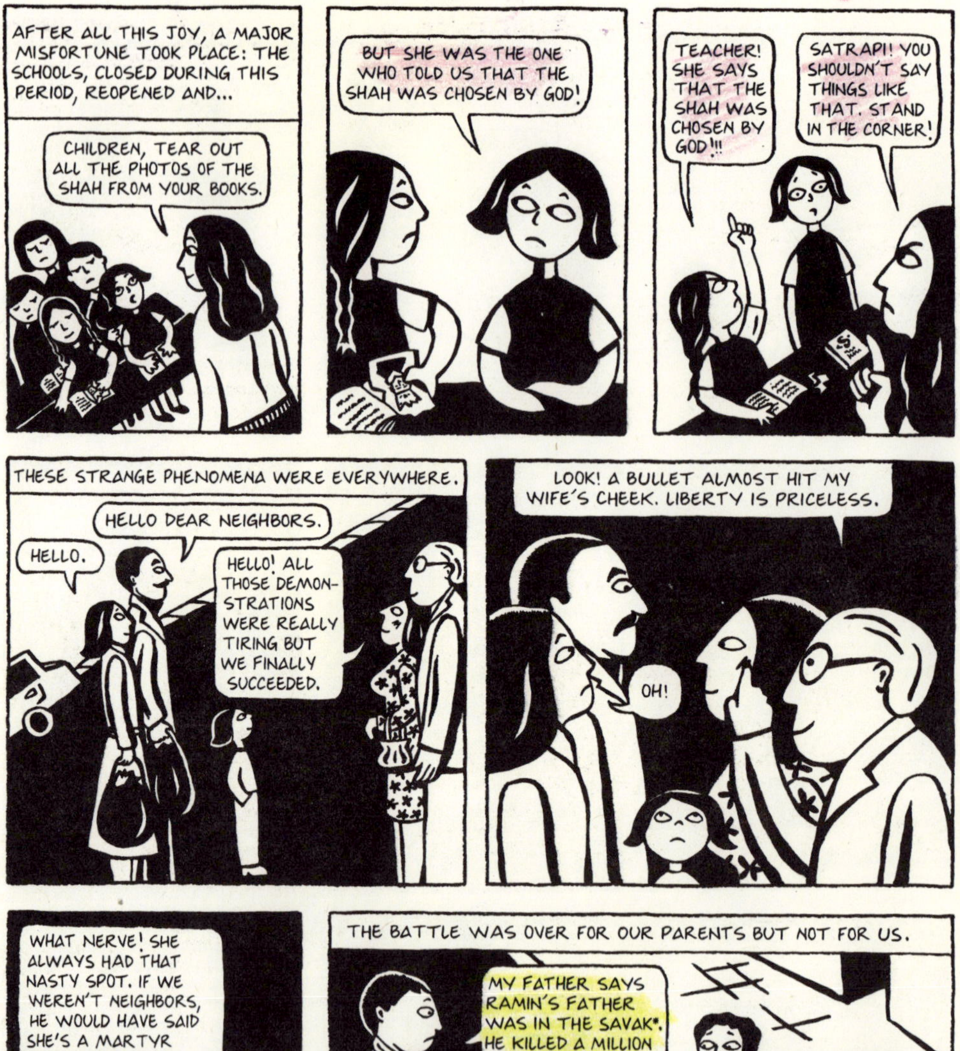

* SECRET POLICE OF THE SHAH'S REGIME.

-My father says

Copying what parents are saying

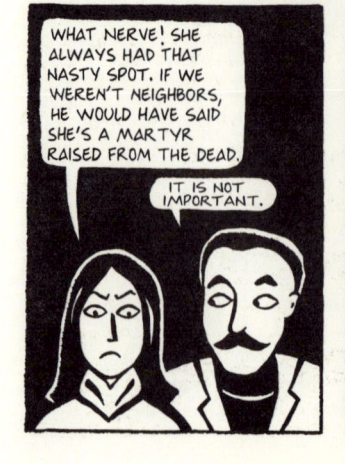

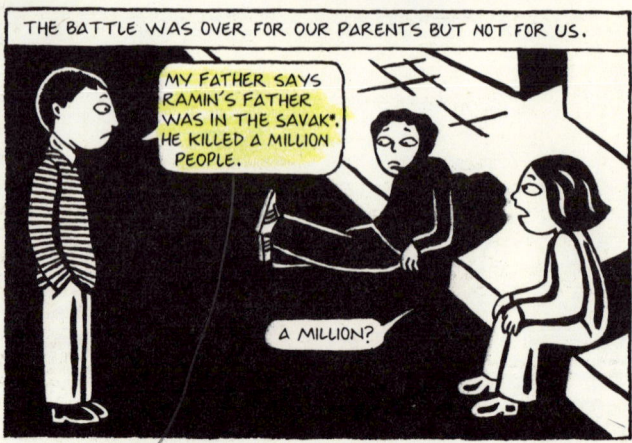

Appeals

ethos! trying to demonstrate like the adults

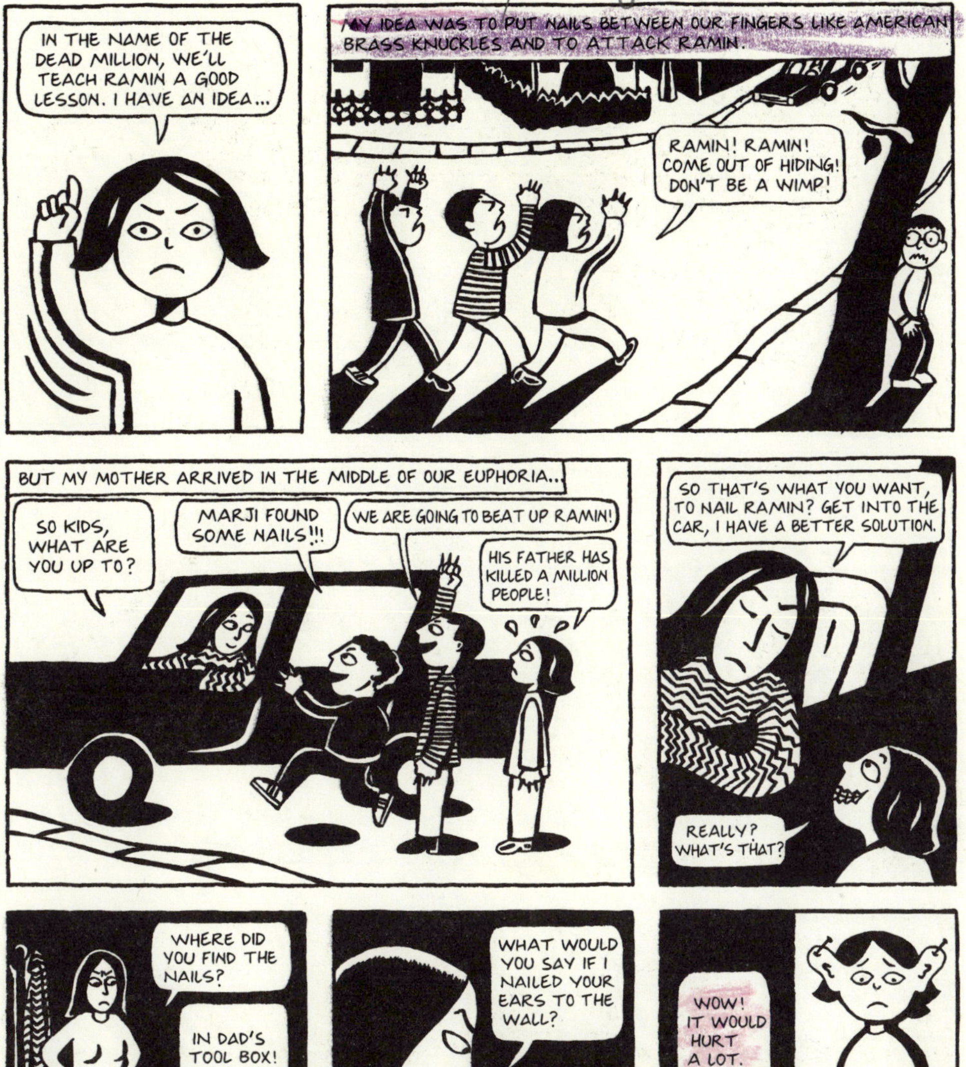

action to action

exaggeration

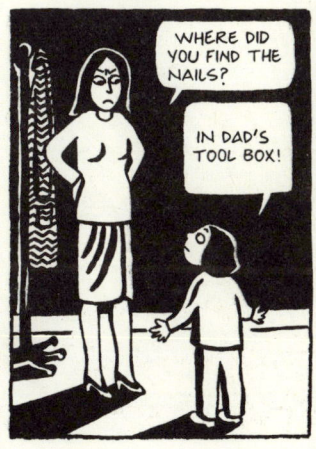

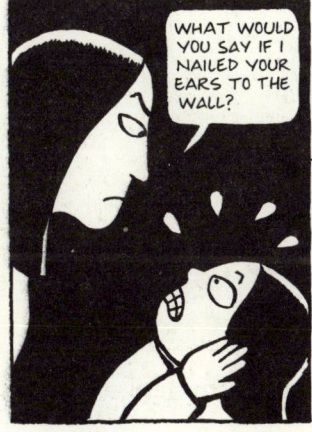

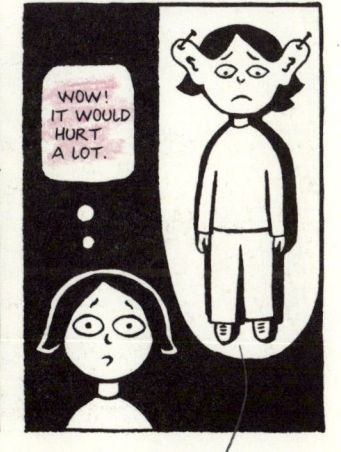

Guilt is not hereditary

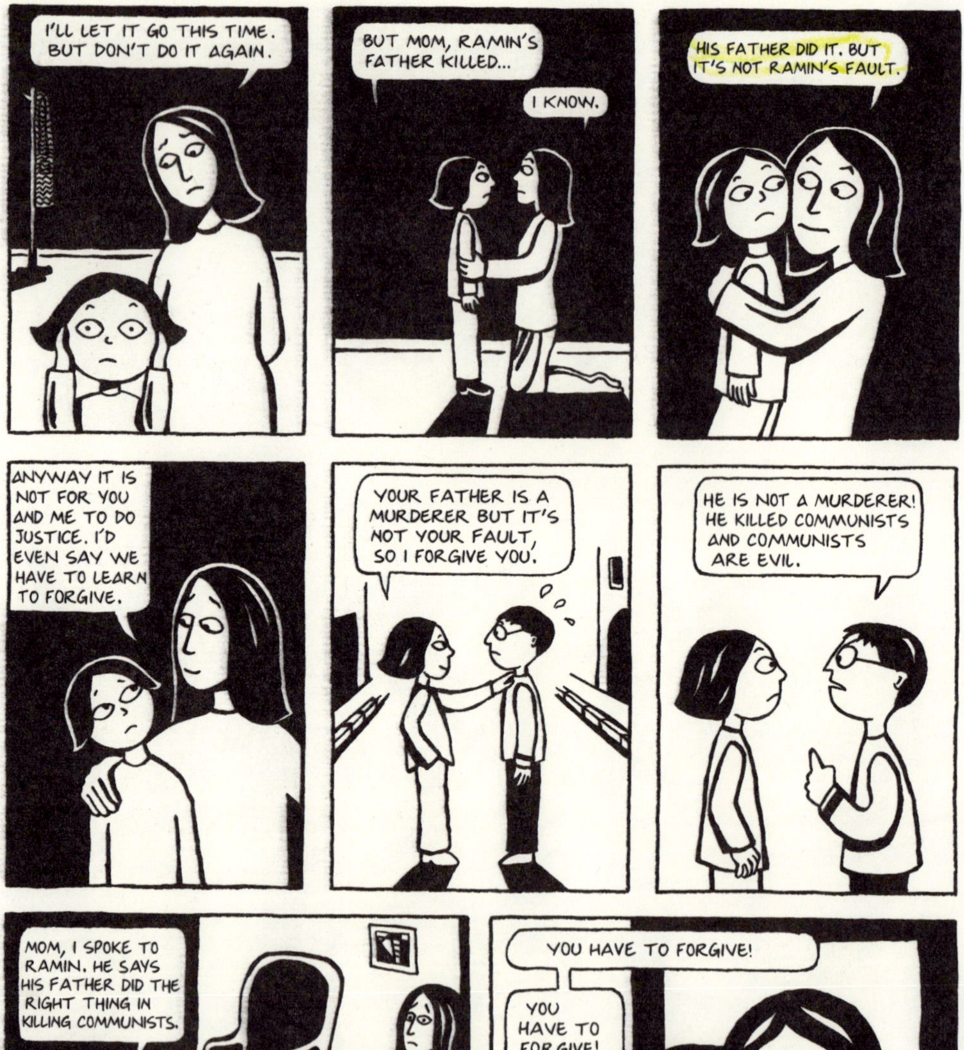
I'LL LET IT GO THIS TIME. BUT DON'T DO IT AGAIN.
BUT MOM, RAMIN'S FATHER KILLED...
I KNOW.
HIS FATHER DID IT. BUT IT'S NOT RAMIN'S FAULT.
ANYWAY IT IS NOT FOR YOU AND ME TO DO JUSTICE. I'D EVEN SAY WE HAVE TO LEARN TO FORGIVE.
YOUR FATHER IS A MURDERER BUT IT'S NOT YOUR FAULT, SO I FORGIVE YOU.
HE IS NOT A MURDERER! HE KILLED COMMUNISTS AND COMMUNISTS ARE EVIL.
MOM, I SPOKE TO RAMIN. HE SAYS HIS FATHER DID THE RIGHT THING IN KILLING COMMUNISTS.
MY GOD! HE REPEATS WHAT THEY TELL HIM. HE WILL UNDERSTAND LATER...
YOU HAVE TO FORGIVE!
YOU HAVE TO FORGIVE!
I HAD THE FEELING OF BEING SOMEONE REALLY, REALLY GOOD.

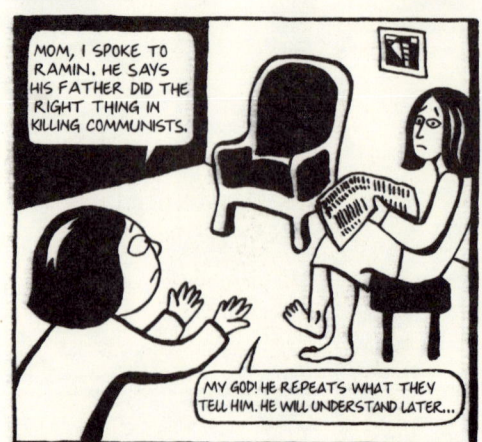

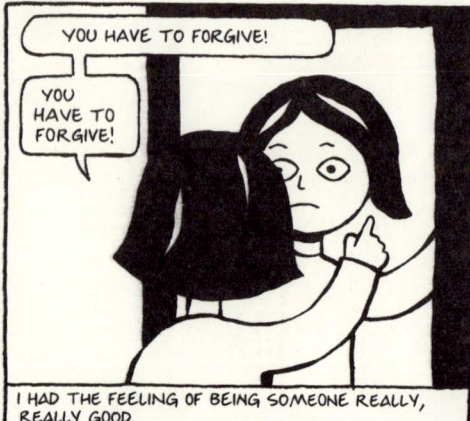

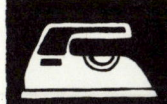

THE HEROES

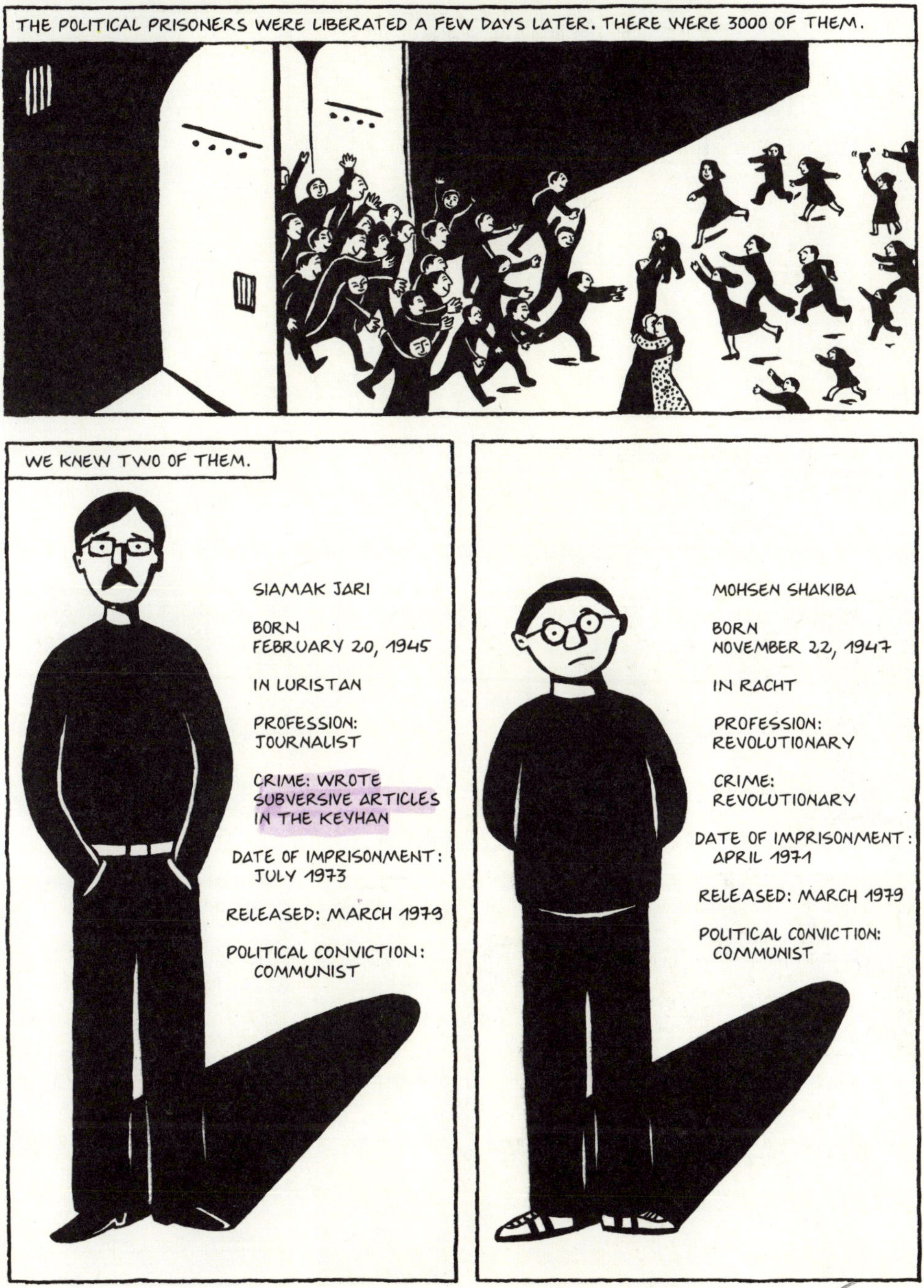
THE POLITICAL PRISONERS WERE LIBERATED A FEW DAYS LATER. THERE WERE 3000 OF THEM.
WE KNEW TWO OF THEM.
SIAMAK JARI
BORN
FEBRUARY 20, 1945
IN LURISTAN
PROFESSION:
JOURNALIST
CRIME: WROTE
SUBVERSIVE ARTICLES
IN THE KEYHAN
DATE OF IMPRISONMENT:
JULY 1973
RELEASED: MARCH 1979
POLITICAL CONVICTION:
COMMUNIST
MOHSEN SHAKIBA
BORN
NOVEMBER 22, 1947
IN RACHT
PROFESSION:
REVOLUTIONARY
CRIME:
REVOLUTIONARY
DATE OF IMPRISONMENT:
APRIL 1971
RELEASED: MARCH 1979
POLITICAL CONVICTION:
COMMUNIST

evokes anger, Freedom of speech should not be worth jailing a man.

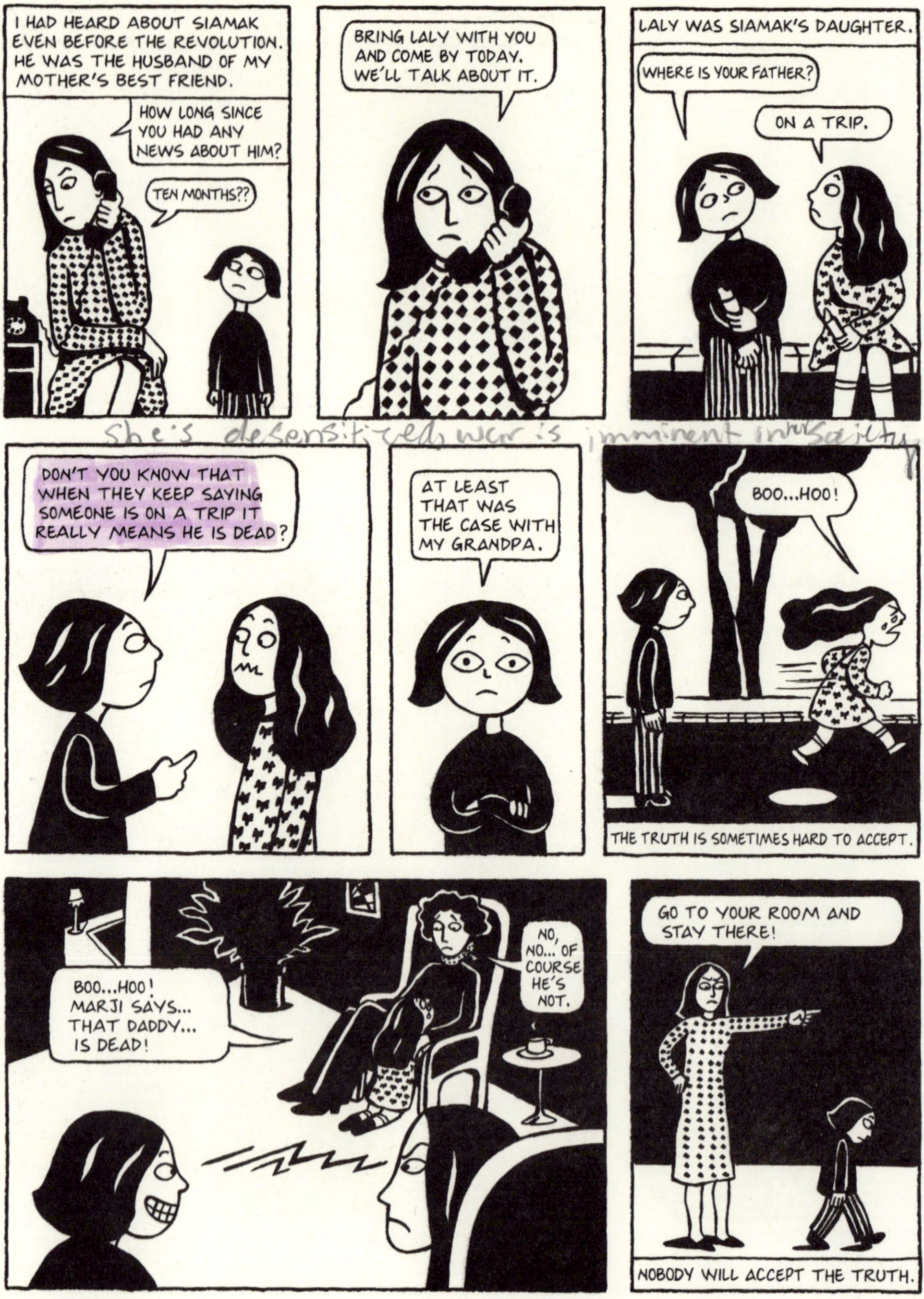
I HAD HEARD ABOUT SIAMAK EVEN BEFORE THE REVOLUTION. HE WAS THE HUSBAND OF MY MOTHER'S BEST FRIEND.
HOW LONG SINCE YOU HAD ANY NEWS ABOUT HIM?
TEN MONTHS??
BRING LALY WITH YOU AND COME BY TODAY. WE'LL TALK ABOUT IT.
LALY WAS SIAMAK'S DAUGHTER.
WHERE IS YOUR FATHER?
ON A TRIP.
DON'T YOU KNOW THAT WHEN THEY KEEP SAYING SOMEONE IS ON A TRIP IT REALLY MEANS HE IS DEAD?
AT LEAST THAT WAS THE CASE WITH MY GRANDPA.
BOO...HOO!
THE TRUTH IS SOMETIMES HARD TO ACCEPT.
BOO...HOO! MARJI SAYS... THAT DADDY... IS DEAD!
NO, NO... OF COURSE HE'S NOT.
GO TO YOUR ROOM AND STAY THERE!
NOBODY WILL ACCEPT THE TRUTH.

AFTER THE REVOLUTION I REALIZED THAT YOU COULD BE MISTAKEN.
TODAY IS A GREAT DAY, DARLING. WE'VE INVITED LALY'S FATHER AND MOHSEN. THEY BOTH JUST LEFT PRISON.
LALY'S FATHER?
WHAT DOES HE LOOK LIKE?
YOU'LL SOON FIND OUT.
DING! DONG!
SIAMAK!
I'M SO HAPPY THAT YOU ARE BACK...I DON'T KNOW WHAT TO SAY...
DON'T SAY ANYTHING. I KNOW!
OH TAJI! STILL A BEAUTY!
STILL A FLATTERER!
AND THIS MUST BE MARJI. LORD! THE LAST TIME I SAW HER SHE WAS ONLY THREE YEARS OLD.
TIME IS IRRETRIEVABLE. WHEN THEY ARRESTED ME, LALY BARELY SPOKE AND NOW SHE IS A REAL YOUNG LADY.
WELL, YES.
YES.
YOU WANT TO PLAY?
NO.
DING! DONG!
THAT MUST BE MOHSEN.

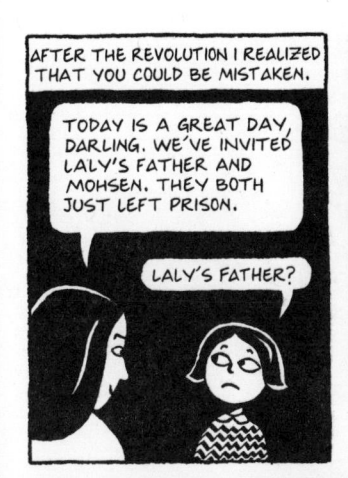

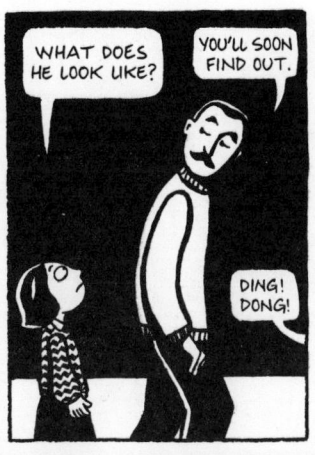

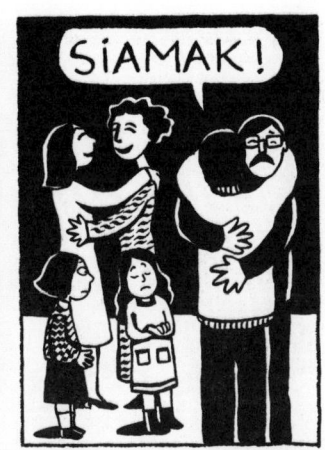

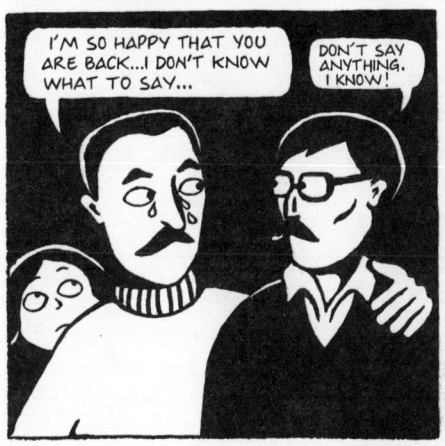

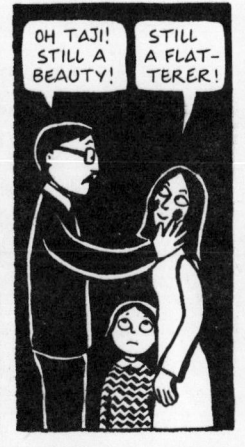

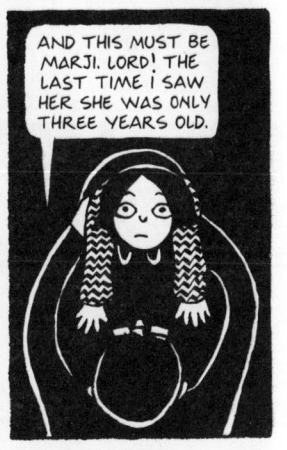

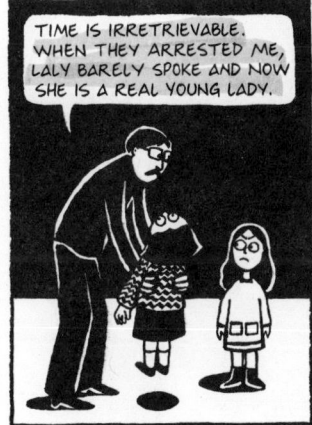

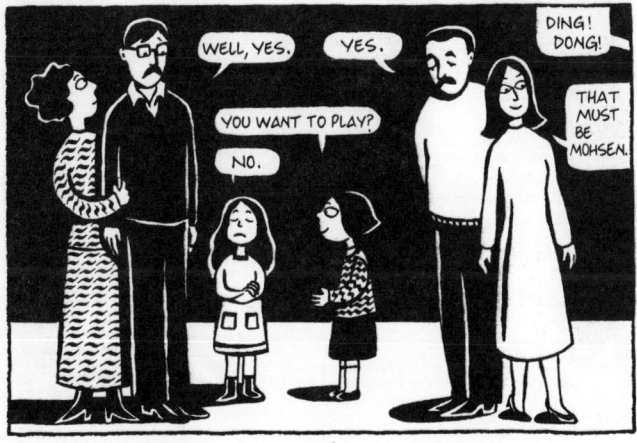

hes been gone so long Marji cant form an emotional attachment, a sense of sadness is formed

Words do not reflect tone, war is so prevelant in their society it is almost normalized

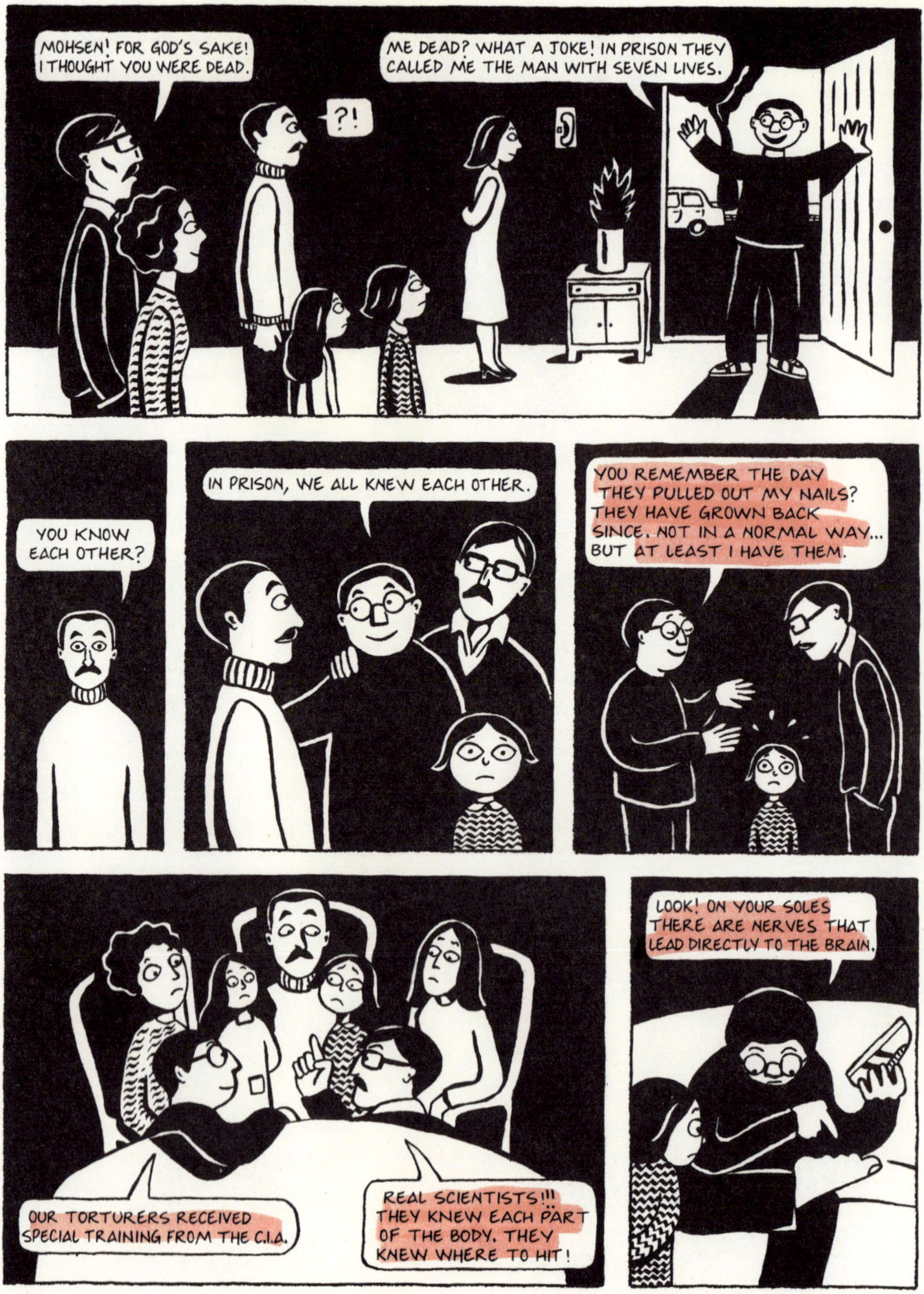
MOHSEN! FOR GOD'S SAKE! I THOUGHT YOU WERE DEAD.
?!
ME DEAD? WHAT A JOKE! IN PRISON THEY CALLED ME THE MAN WITH SEVEN LIVES.
YOU KNOW EACH OTHER?
IN PRISON, WE ALL KNEW EACH OTHER.
YOU REMEMBER THE DAY THEY PULLED OUT MY NAILS? THEY HAVE GROWN BACK SINCE. NOT IN A NORMAL WAY... BUT AT LEAST I HAVE THEM.
OUR TORTURERS RECEIVED SPECIAL TRAINING FROM THE C.I.A.
REAL SCIENTISTS!!! THEY KNEW EACH PART OF THE BODY. THEY KNEW WHERE TO HIT!
LOOK! ON YOUR SOLES THERE ARE NERVES THAT LEAD DIRECTLY TO THE BRAIN.

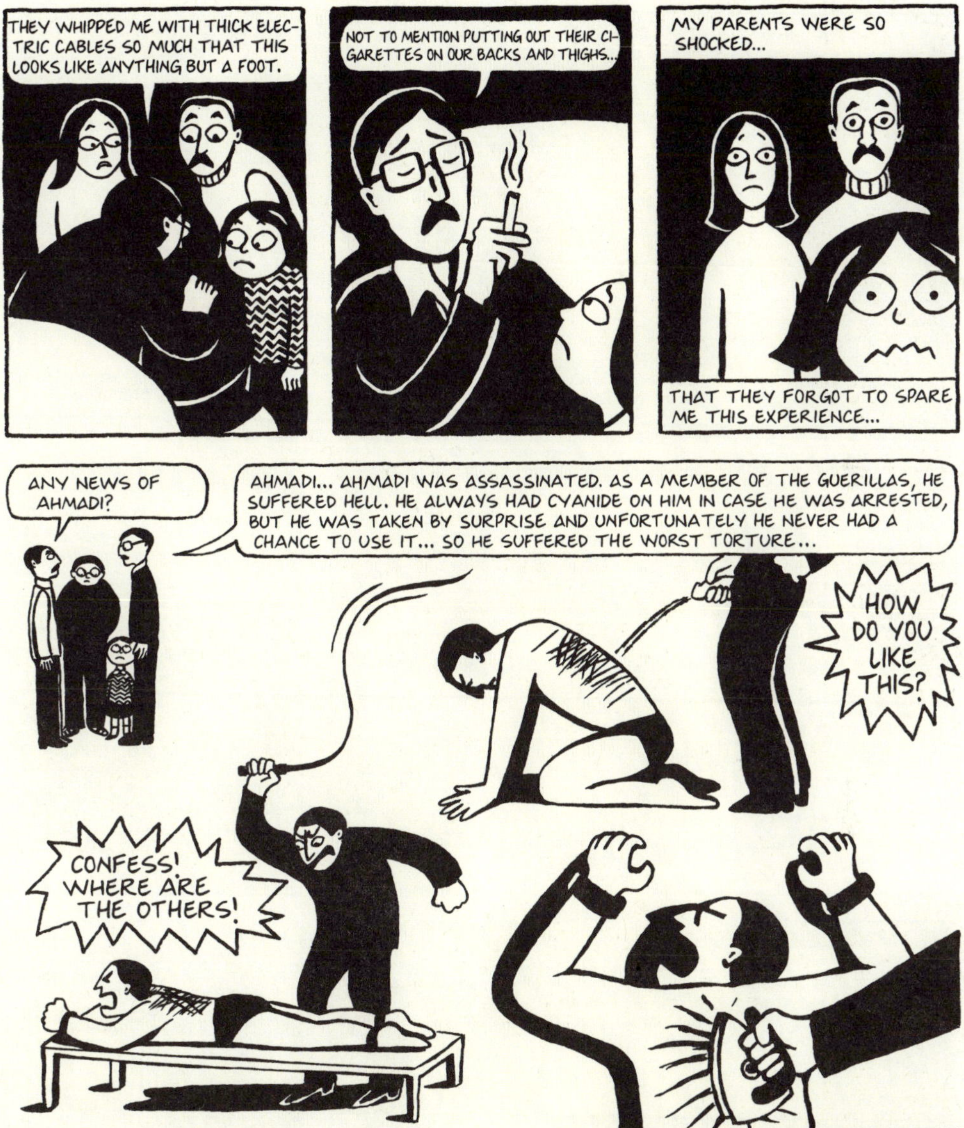

seeds of reality begin to set in

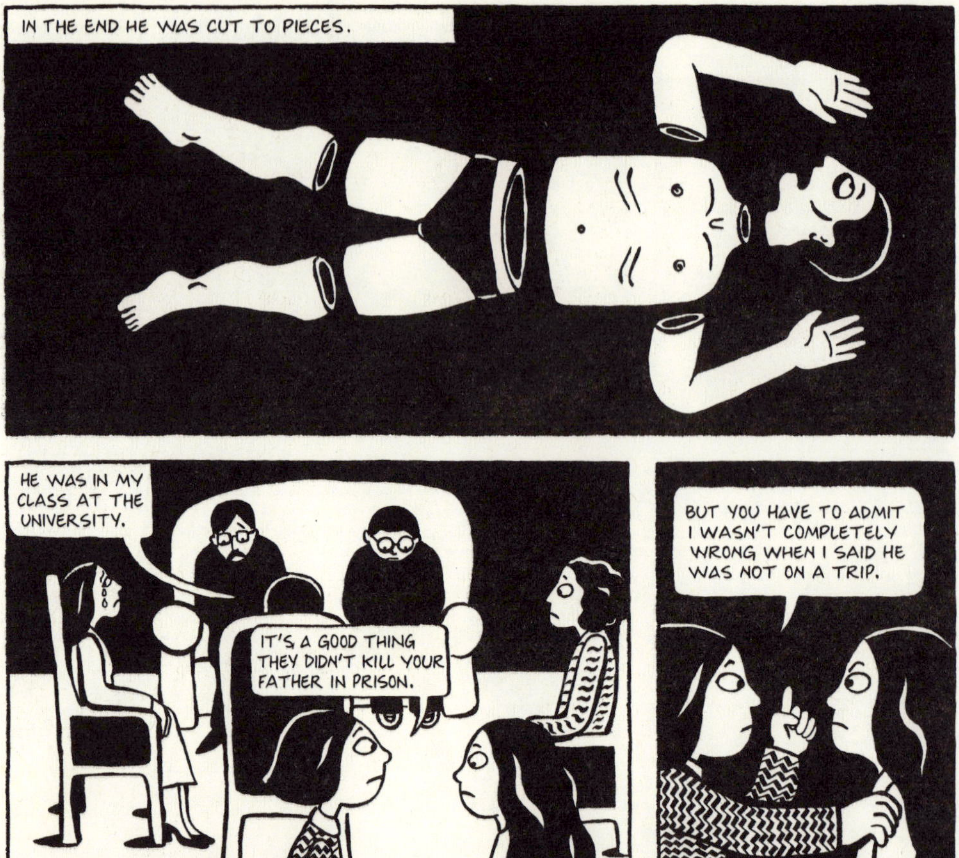

metaphorically she is bigger than her hero, shows her feelings of inferiority that leads to jealousy

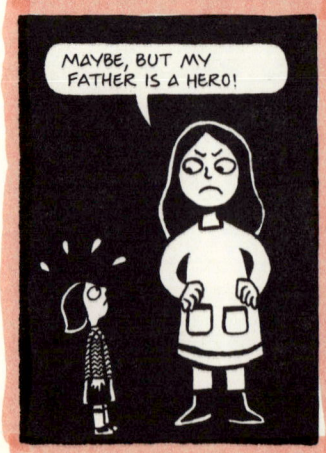

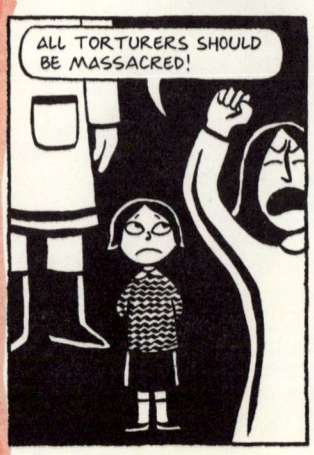

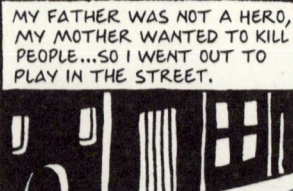

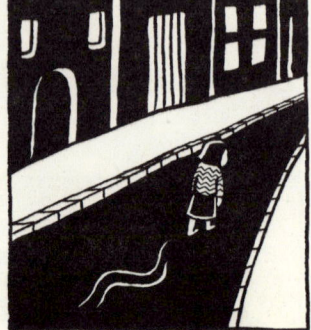

THOSE STORIES HAD GIVEN ME NEW IDEAS FOR GAMES. "THE ONE WHO LOSES WILL BE TORTURED." "YEAH!" "WHAT KIND OF TORTURE?"	I HAVE IMAGINATION TOO... THE MUSTACHE-ON-FIRE TORTURE CONSISTS OF PULLING ON THE TWO SIDES OF THE UPPER LIP.
THE TWISTED ARM.	THE MOUTH FILLED WITH GARBAGE.

BACK AT HOME THAT EVENING, I HAD THE DIABOLICAL FEELING OF POWER...

BUT IT DIDN'T LAST. I WAS OVERWHELMED.

"DON'T CRY DARLING. THEY WILL PAY FOR WHAT THEY HAVE DONE."

"BUT I THOUGHT ONE SHOULD FORGIVE."

"BAD PEOPLE ARE DANGEROUS BUT FORGIVING THEM IS TOO. DON'T WORRY, THERE IS JUSTICE ON EARTH."

I DIDN'T KNOW WHAT JUSTICE WAS. NOW THAT THE REVOLUTION WAS FINALLY OVER ONCE AND FOR ALL, I ABANDONED THE DIALECTIC MATERIALISM OF MY COMIC STRIPS. THE ONLY PLACE I FELT SAFE WAS IN THE ARMS OF MY FRIEND.

Justice is a balance, one must have empathy for others while also being able to achieve self-preservation

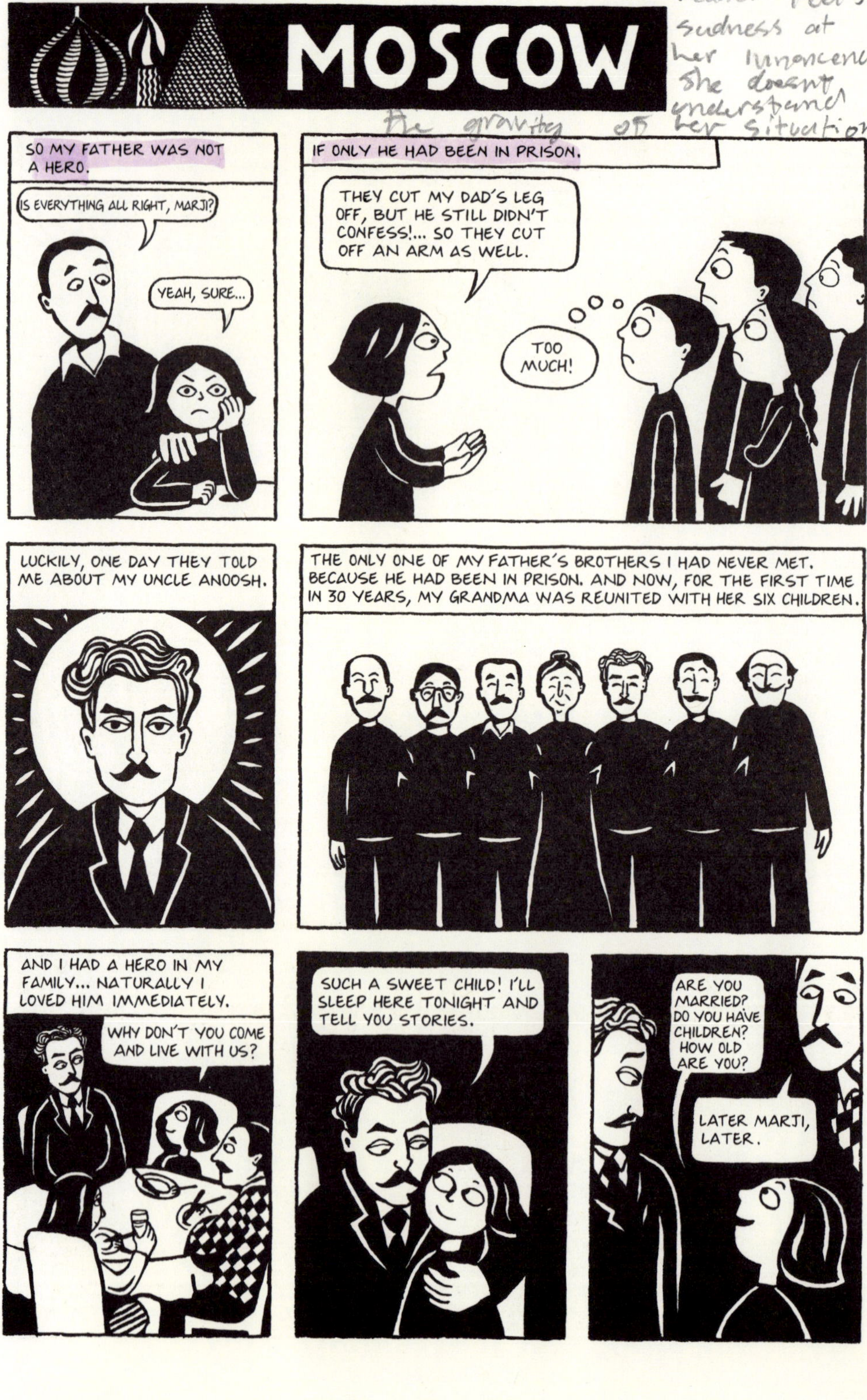

reader feels sadness at her innocence, she doesn't understand the gravity of her situation

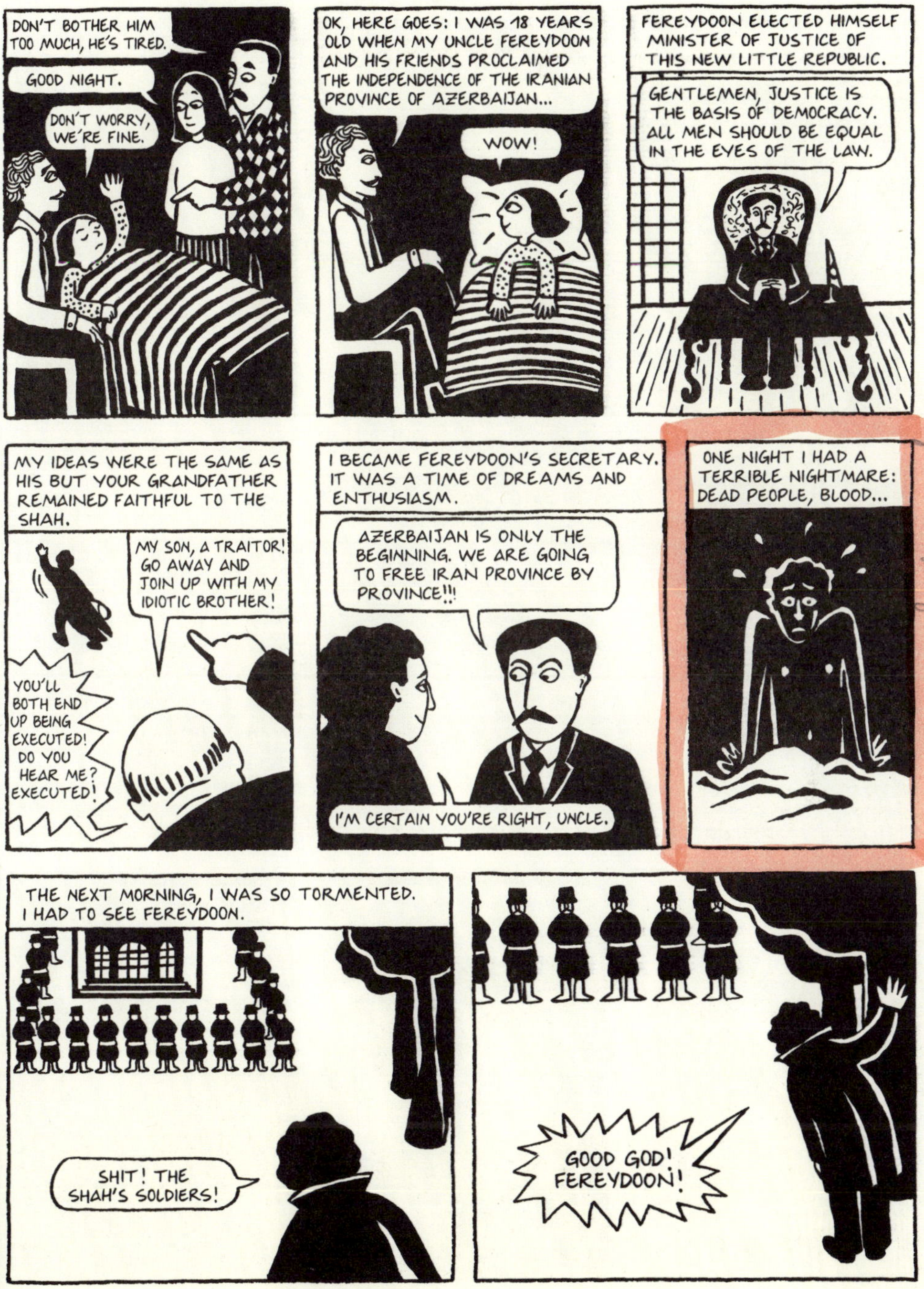
DON'T BOTHER HIM TOO MUCH, HE'S TIRED.
GOOD NIGHT.
DON'T WORRY, WE'RE FINE.
OK, HERE GOES: I WAS 18 YEARS OLD WHEN MY UNCLE FEREYDOON AND HIS FRIENDS PROCLAIMED THE INDEPENDENCE OF THE IRANIAN PROVINCE OF AZERBAIJAN...
WOW!
FEREYDOON ELECTED HIMSELF MINISTER OF JUSTICE OF THIS NEW LITTLE REPUBLIC.
GENTLEMEN, JUSTICE IS THE BASIS OF DEMOCRACY. ALL MEN SHOULD BE EQUAL IN THE EYES OF THE LAW.
MY IDEAS WERE THE SAME AS HIS BUT YOUR GRANDFATHER REMAINED FAITHFUL TO THE SHAH.
MY SON, A TRAITOR! GO AWAY AND JOIN UP WITH MY IDIOTIC BROTHER!
YOU'LL BOTH END UP BEING EXECUTED! DO YOU HEAR ME? EXECUTED!
I BECAME FEREYDOON'S SECRETARY. IT WAS A TIME OF DREAMS AND ENTHUSIASM.
AZERBAIJAN IS ONLY THE BEGINNING. WE ARE GOING TO FREE IRAN PROVINCE BY PROVINCE!!!
I'M CERTAIN YOU'RE RIGHT, UNCLE.
ONE NIGHT I HAD A TERRIBLE NIGHTMARE: DEAD PEOPLE, BLOOD...
THE NEXT MORNING, I WAS SO TORMENTED. I HAD TO SEE FEREYDOON.
SHIT! THE SHAH'S SOLDIERS!
GOOD GOD! FEREYDOON!

reader begins to root for him, as his determination to survive creates high stakes

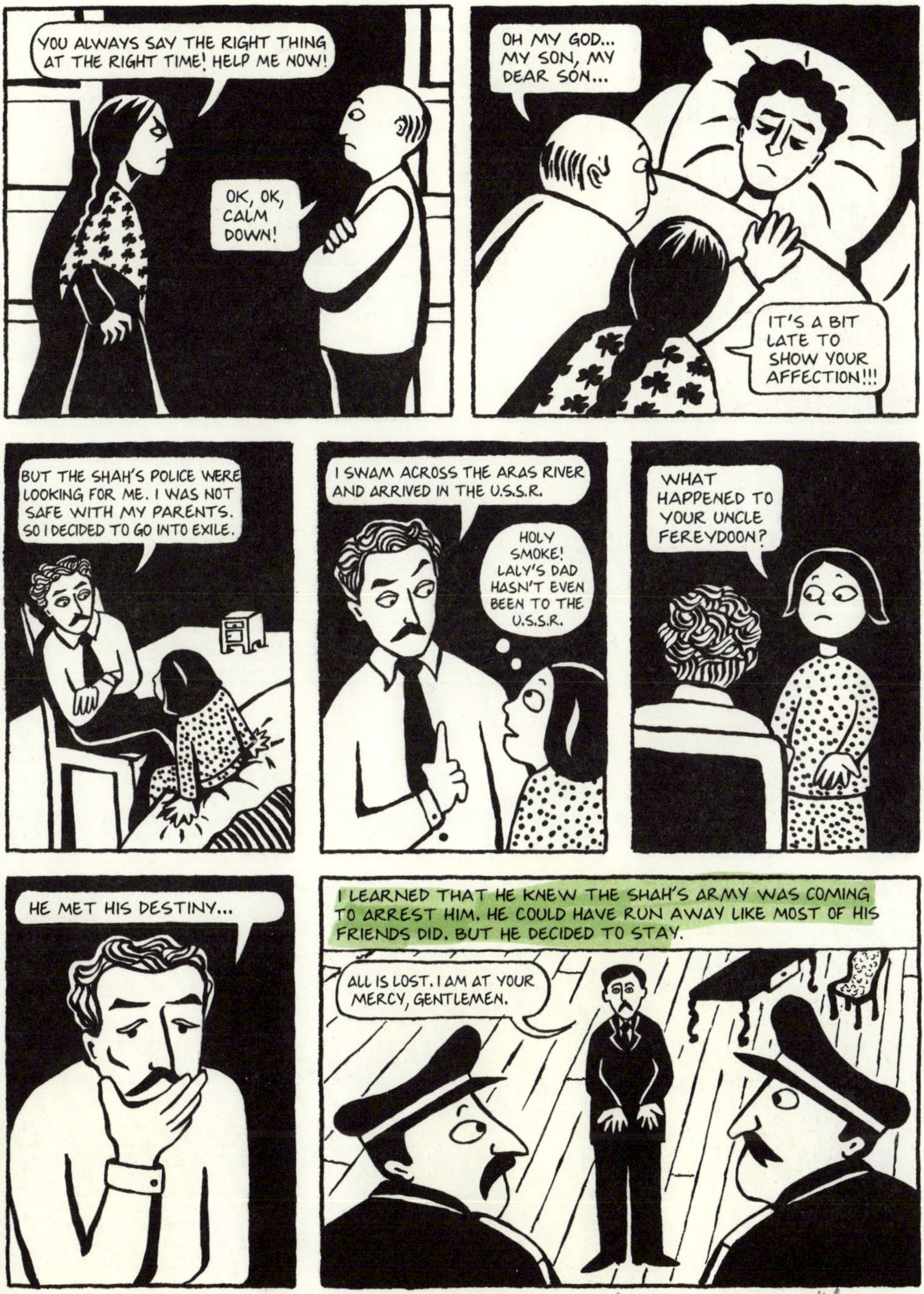

be brave and have integrity even in death.

after reality sets in, she is going to lose him and is desperate for any semblance of him in the future

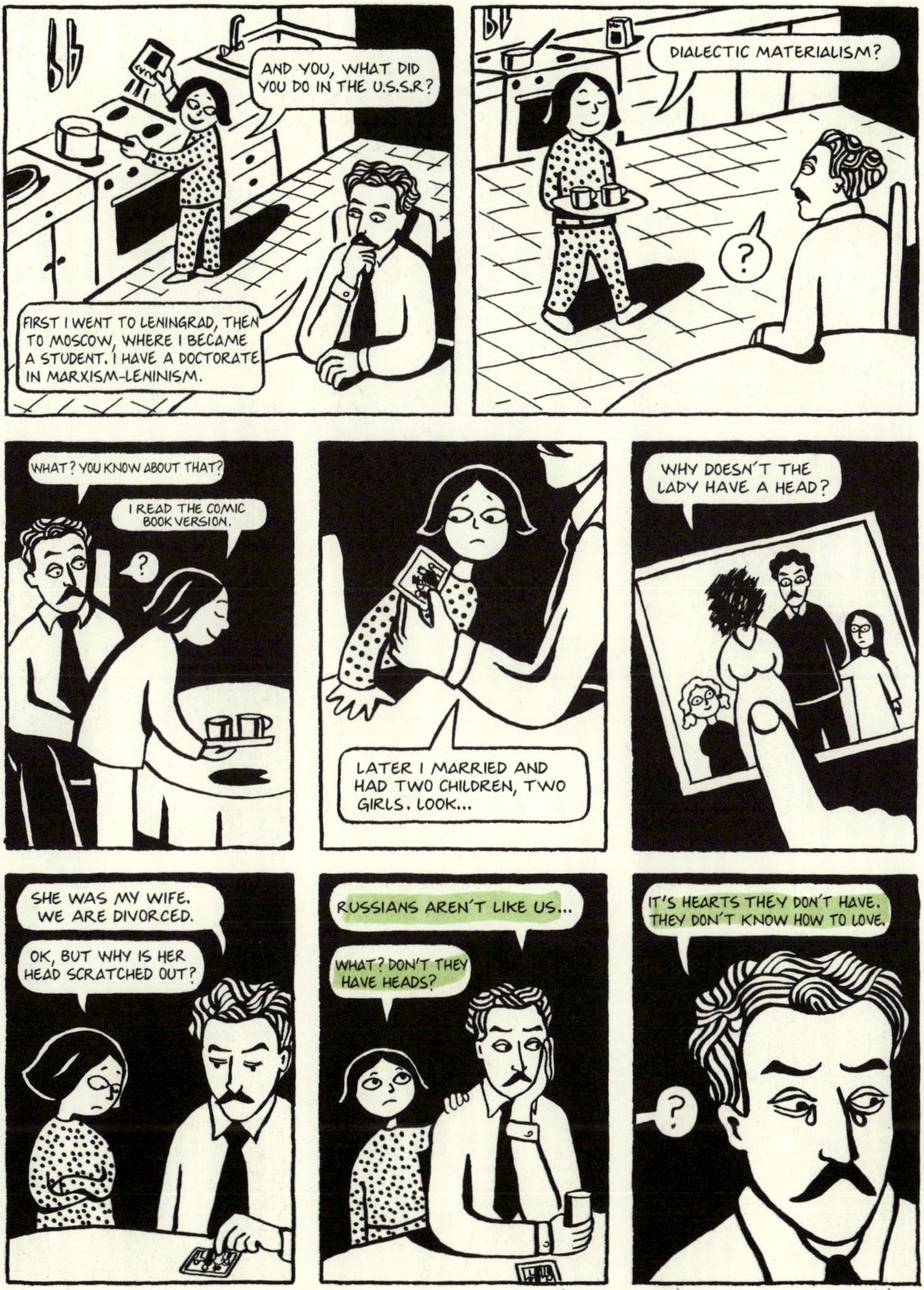

innocence vs. wisdom directly correlates to happiness vs. sadness

9 years later and he still has perfect recollection, he'll never forget

shadow can symbolize that his past is behind him now

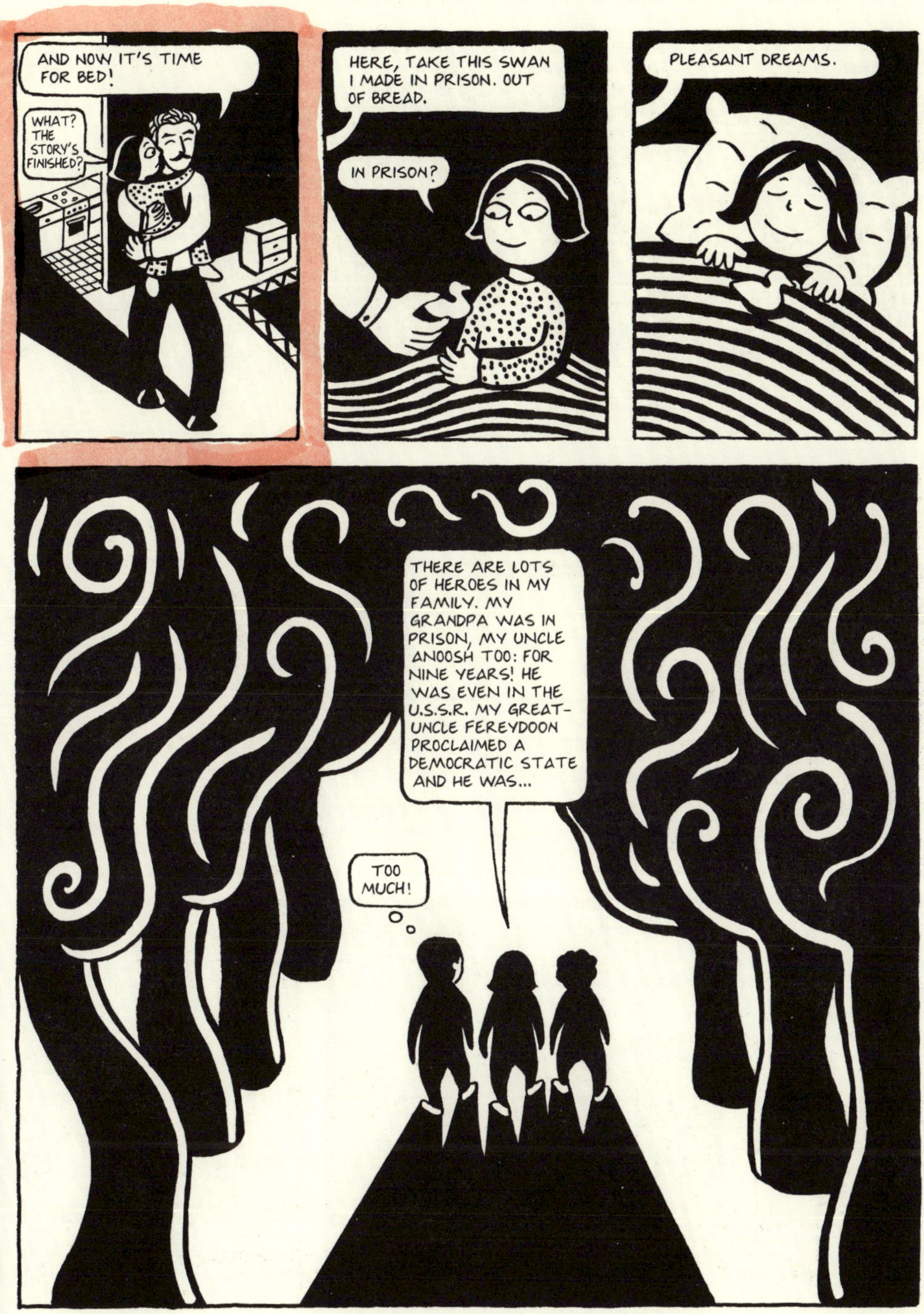

THE SHEEP

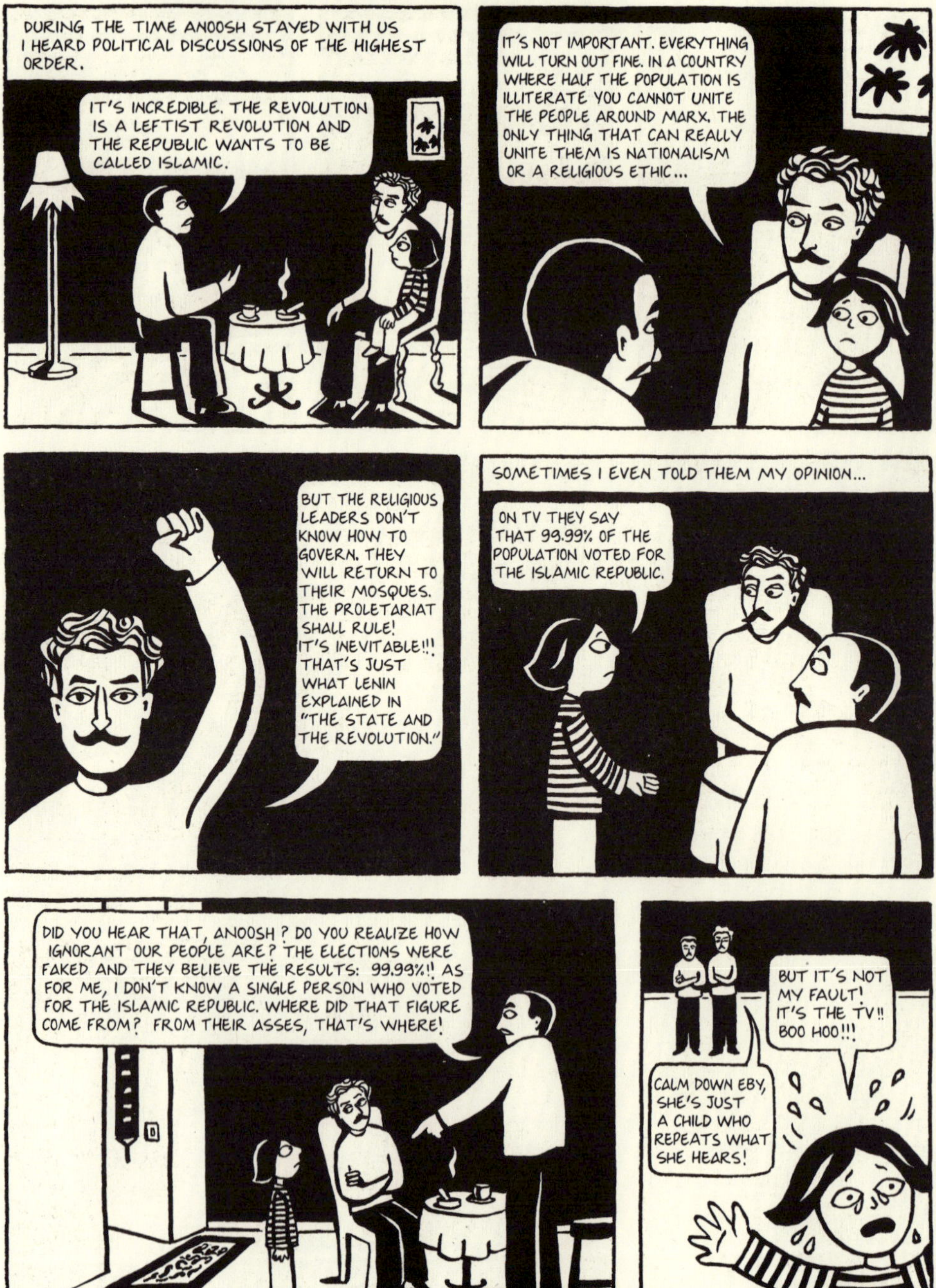

DURING THE TIME ANOOSH STAYED WITH US I HEARD POLITICAL DISCUSSIONS OF THE HIGHEST ORDER.
IT'S INCREDIBLE. THE REVOLUTION IS A LEFTIST REVOLUTION AND THE REPUBLIC WANTS TO BE CALLED ISLAMIC.
IT'S NOT IMPORTANT. EVERYTHING WILL TURN OUT FINE. IN A COUNTRY WHERE HALF THE POPULATION IS ILLITERATE YOU CANNOT UNITE THE PEOPLE AROUND MARX. THE ONLY THING THAT CAN REALLY UNITE THEM IS NATIONALISM OR A RELIGIOUS ETHIC...
BUT THE RELIGIOUS LEADERS DON'T KNOW HOW TO GOVERN. THEY WILL RETURN TO THEIR MOSQUES. THE PROLETARIAT SHALL RULE! IT'S INEVITABLE!!! THAT'S JUST WHAT LENIN EXPLAINED IN "THE STATE AND THE REVOLUTION."
SOMETIMES I EVEN TOLD THEM MY OPINION...
ON TV THEY SAY THAT 99.99% OF THE POPULATION VOTED FOR THE ISLAMIC REPUBLIC.
DID YOU HEAR THAT, ANOOSH? DO YOU REALIZE HOW IGNORANT OUR PEOPLE ARE? THE ELECTIONS WERE FAKED AND THEY BELIEVE THE RESULTS: 99.99%!! AS FOR ME, I DON'T KNOW A SINGLE PERSON WHO VOTED FOR THE ISLAMIC REPUBLIC. WHERE DID THAT FIGURE COME FROM? FROM THEIR ASSES, THAT'S WHERE!
BUT IT'S NOT MY FAULT! IT'S THE TV!! BOO HOO!!!
CALM DOWN EBY, SHE'S JUST A CHILD WHO REPEATS WHAT SHE HEARS!

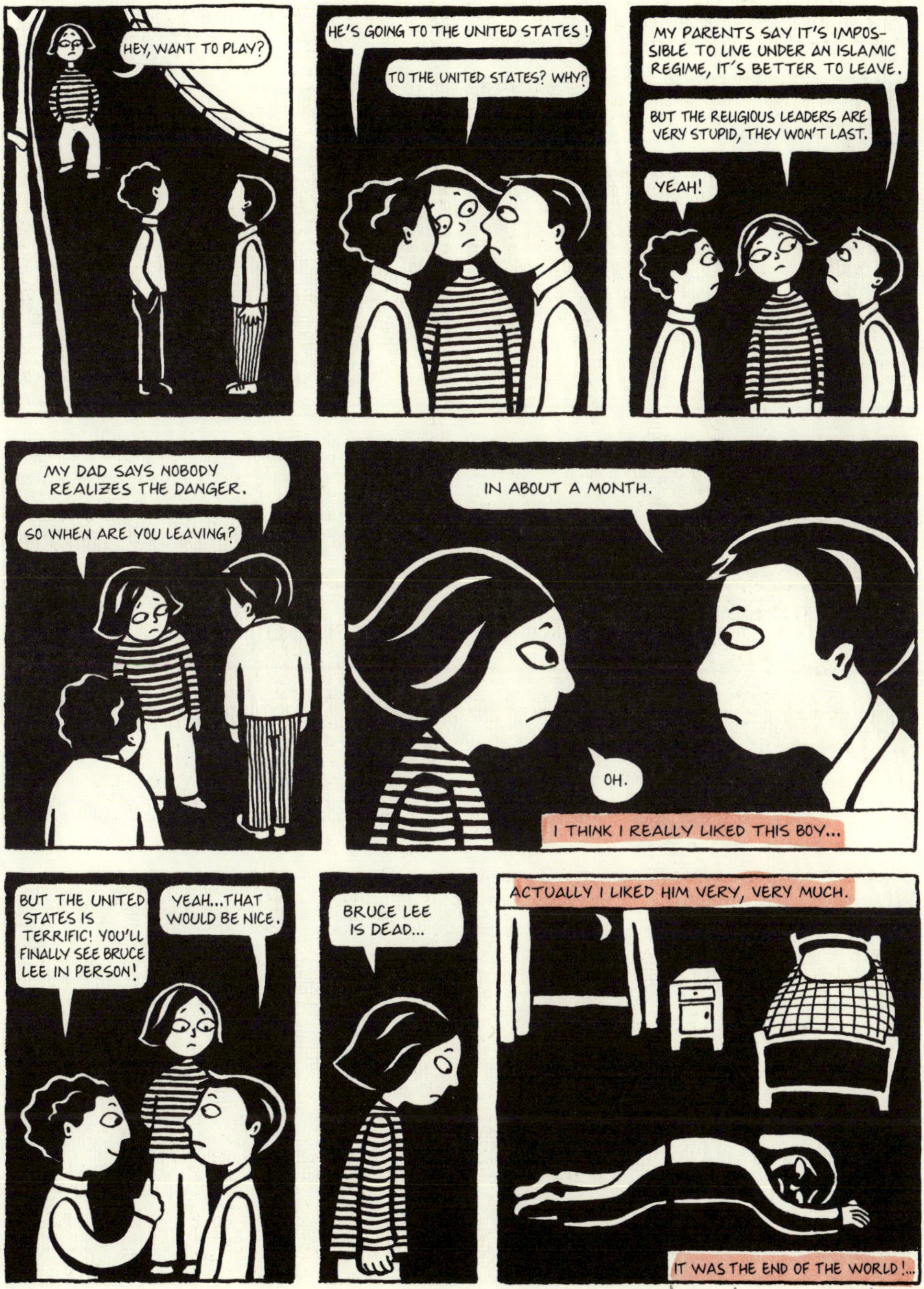

Sentence structure and where information is revealed creates a sense of despair.

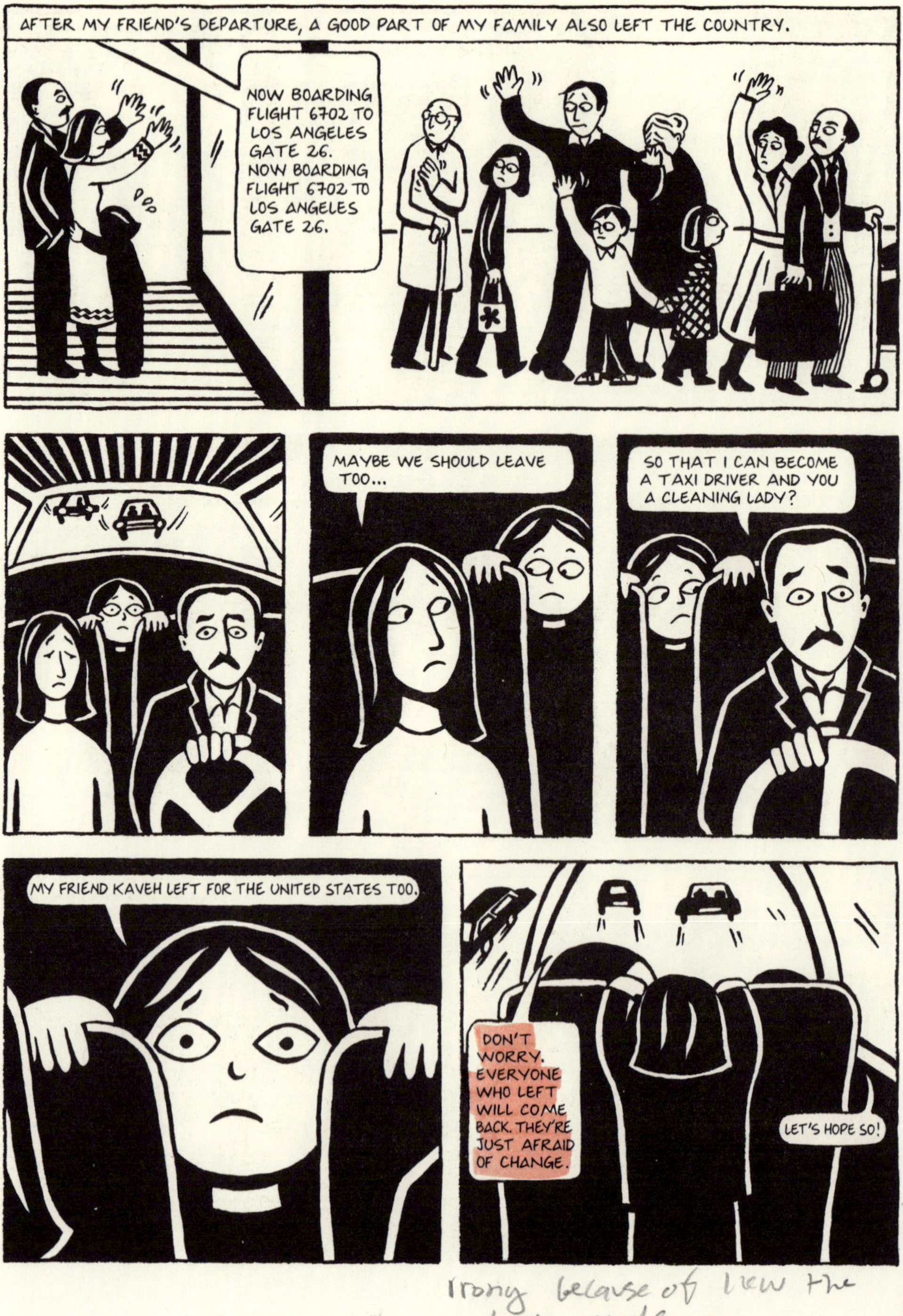

Irony because of how the book ends

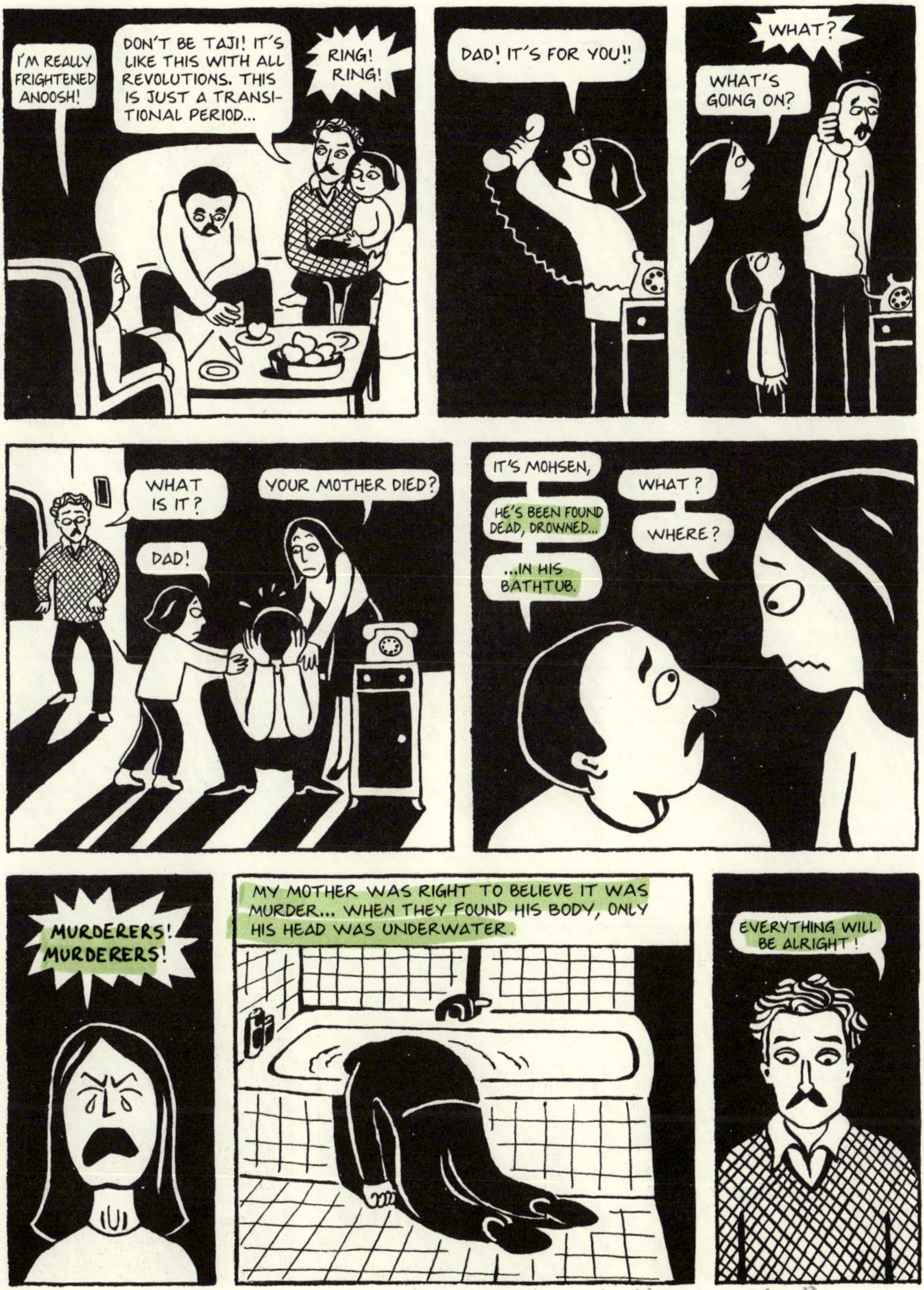

there is no Justice, yet the only choice is to carry on

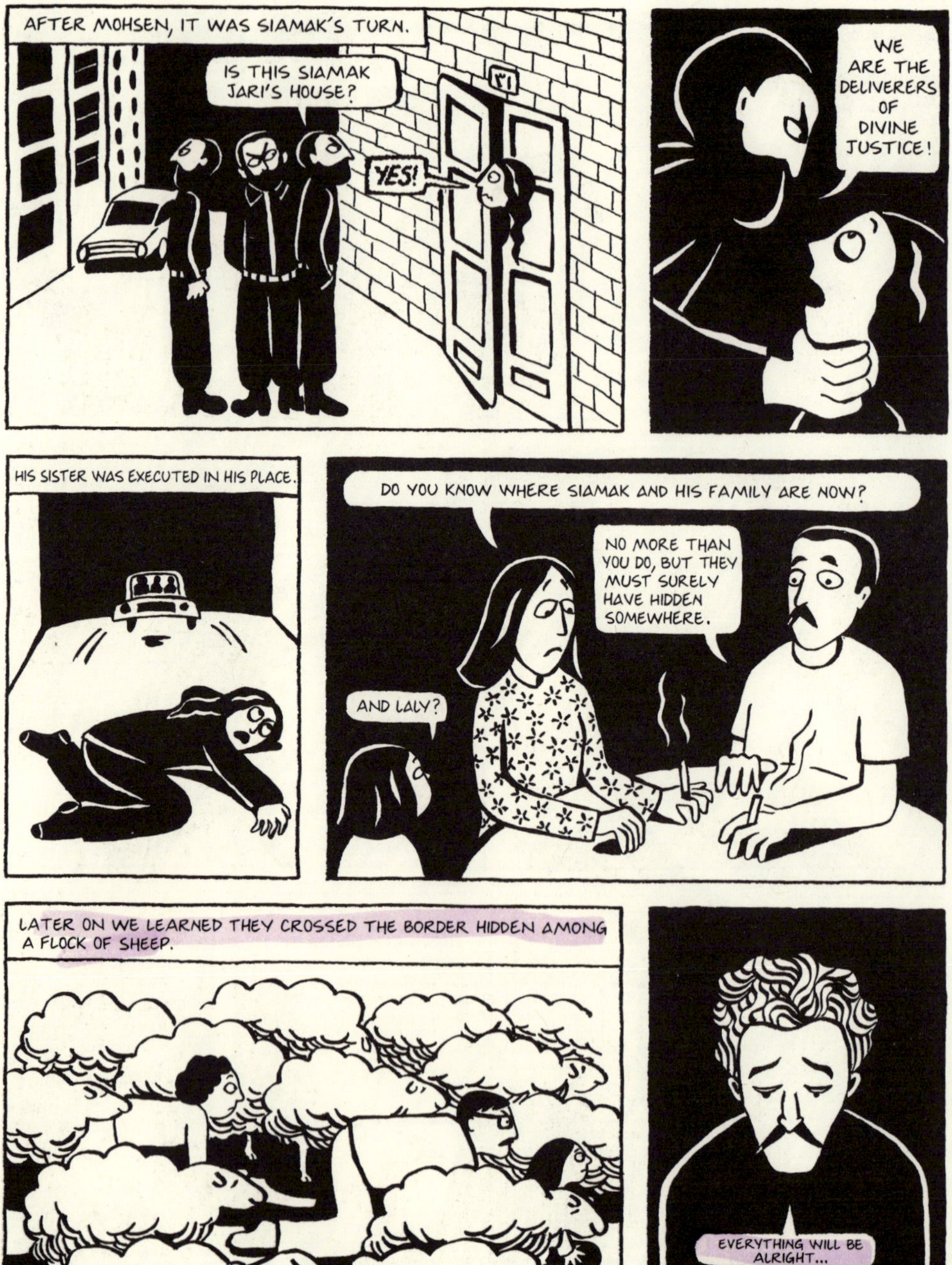
AFTER MOHSEN, IT WAS SIAMAK'S TURN.
IS THIS SIAMAK JARI'S HOUSE?
YES!
WE ARE THE DELIVERERS OF DIVINE JUSTICE!
HIS SISTER WAS EXECUTED IN HIS PLACE.
DO YOU KNOW WHERE SIAMAK AND HIS FAMILY ARE NOW?
NO MORE THAN YOU DO, BUT THEY MUST SURELY HAVE HIDDEN SOMEWHERE.
AND LALY?
LATER ON WE LEARNED THEY CROSSED THE BORDER HIDDEN AMONG A FLOCK OF SHEEP.
EVERYTHING WILL BE ALRIGHT...

Face zoom shows her progress in slowly losing her innocence, reality sets in

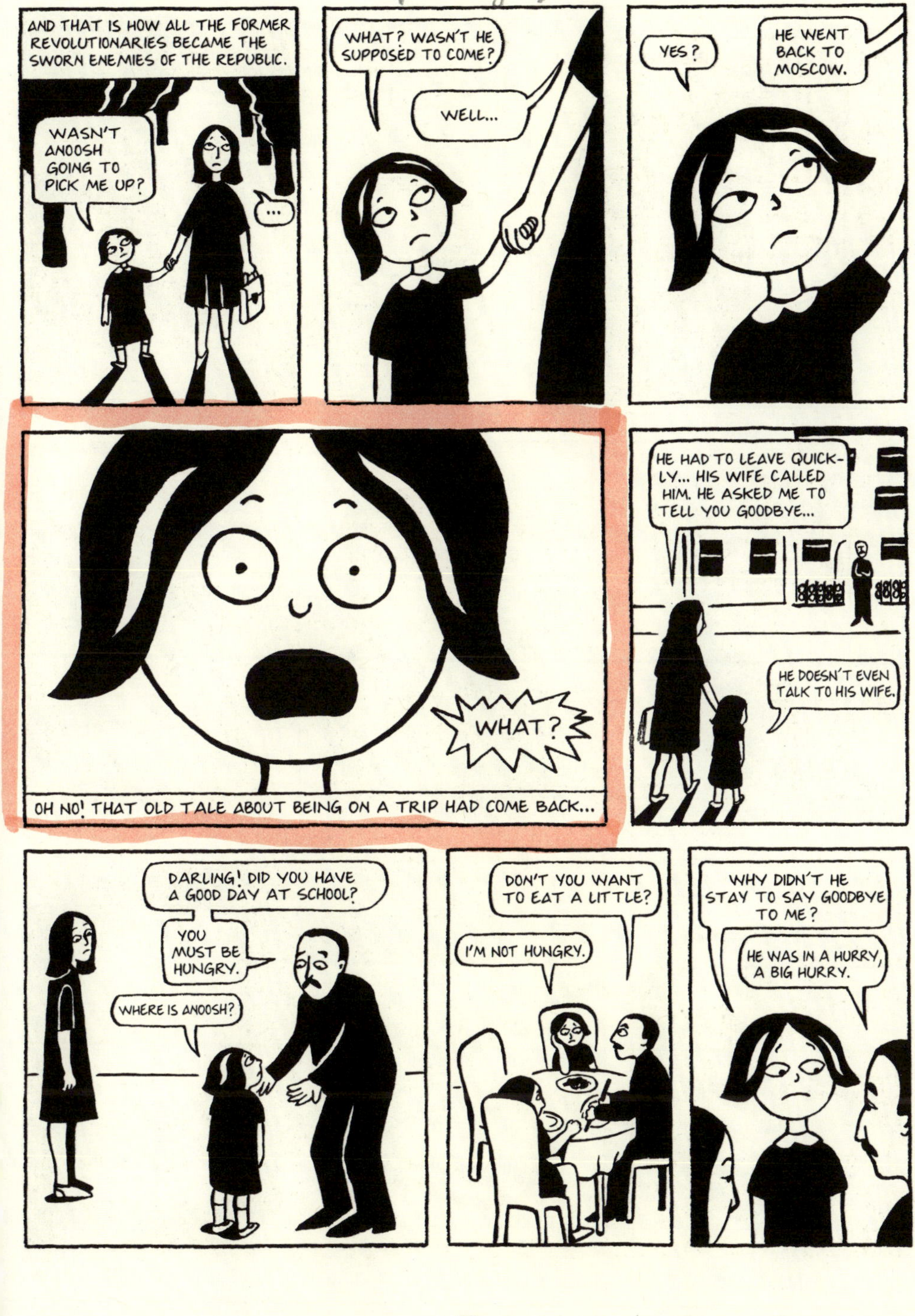

Shes the daughter he never had, one that doesnt remind him of his past

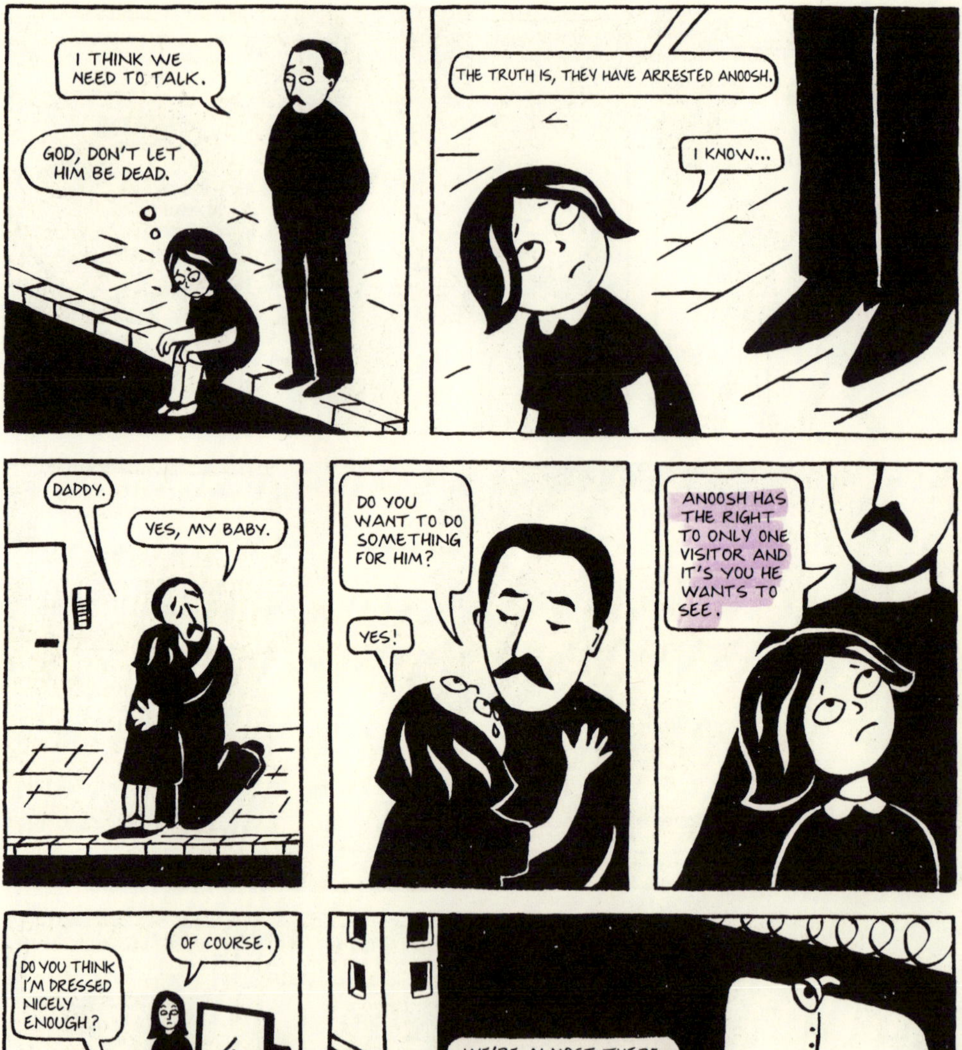
I THINK WE NEED TO TALK.
GOD, DON'T LET HIM BE DEAD.
THE TRUTH IS, THEY HAVE ARRESTED ANOOSH.
I KNOW...
DADDY.
YES, MY BABY.
DO YOU WANT TO DO SOMETHING FOR HIM?
YES!
ANOOSH HAS THE RIGHT TO ONLY ONE VISITOR AND IT'S YOU HE WANTS TO SEE.
DO YOU THINK I'M DRESSED NICELY ENOUGH?
OF COURSE.
WE'RE ALMOST THERE.

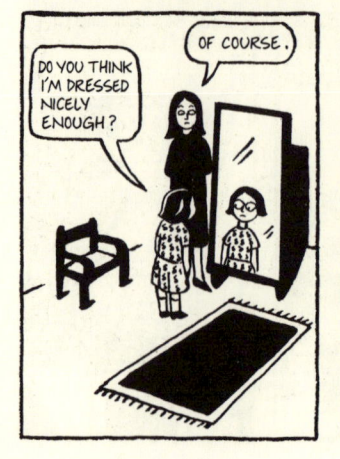

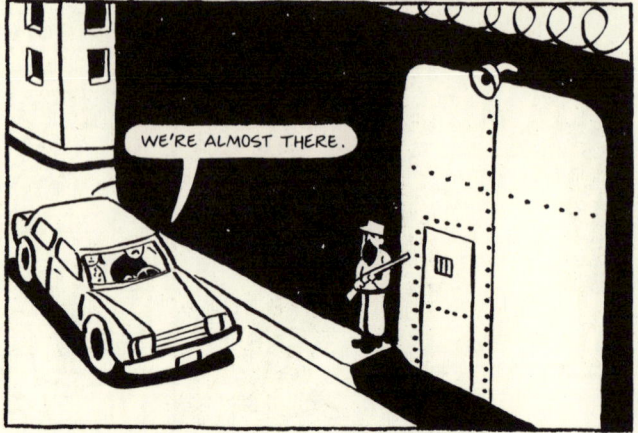

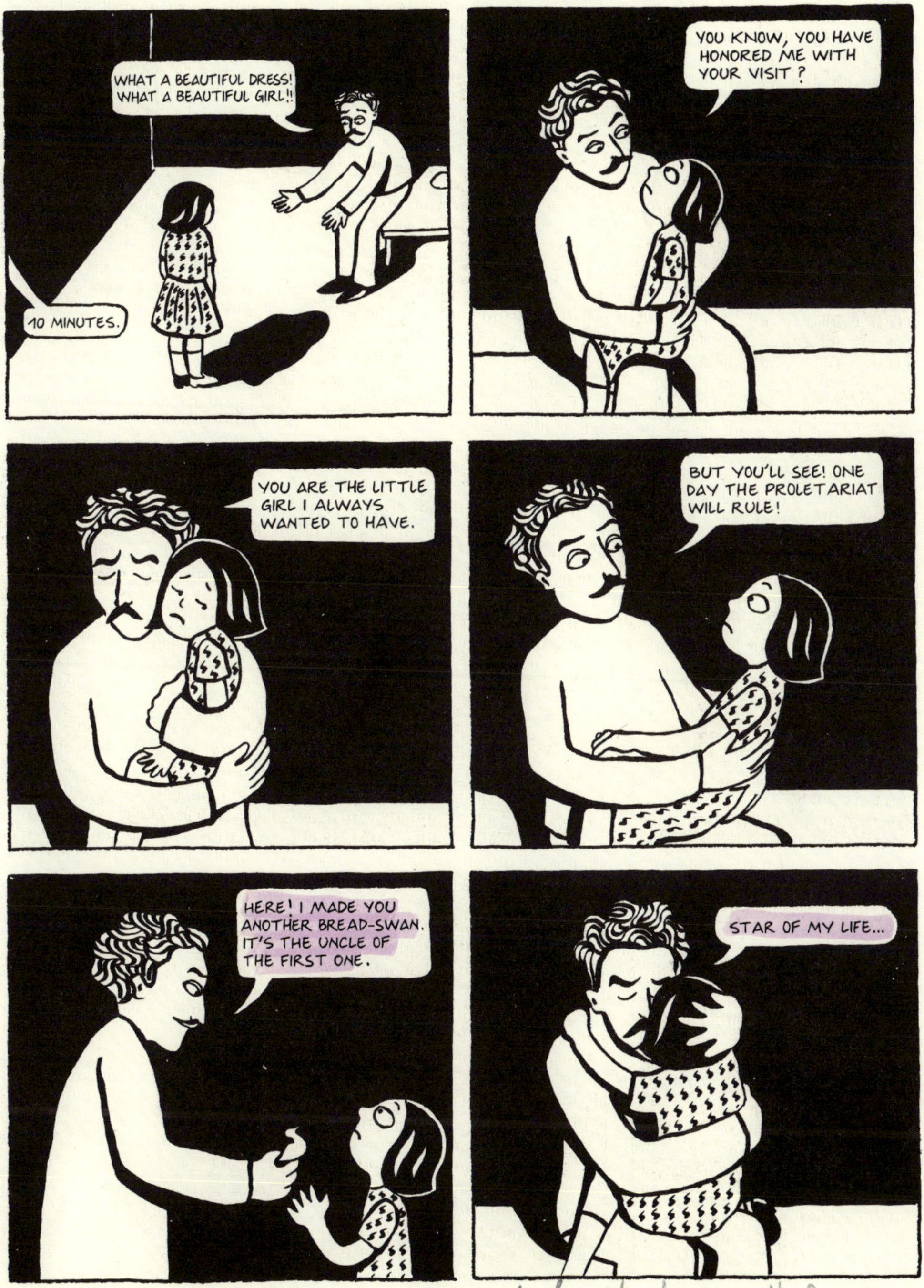

a call back to earlier, there is truly no hope for him

call back to what her uncle always says> she has to move on

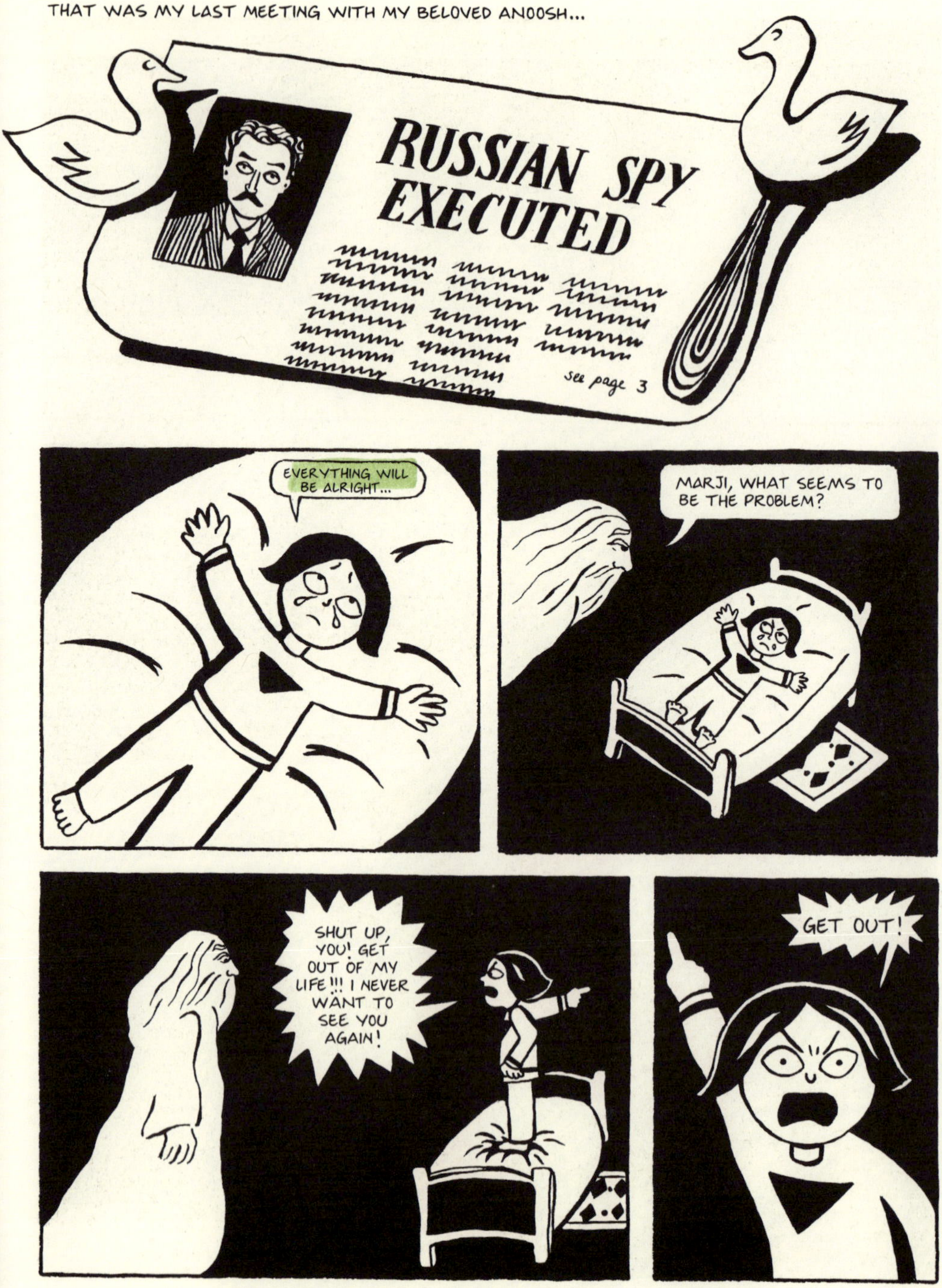
THAT WAS MY LAST MEETING WITH MY BELOVED ANOOSH...
RUSSIAN SPY EXECUTED
see page 3
EVERYTHING WILL BE ALRIGHT...
MARJI, WHAT SEEMS TO BE THE PROBLEM?
SHUT UP, YOU! GET OUT OF MY LIFE!!! I NEVER WANT TO SEE YOU AGAIN!
GET OUT!

Space symoblizes how shes truly lost, there is no gods and for the first time shes truly alone

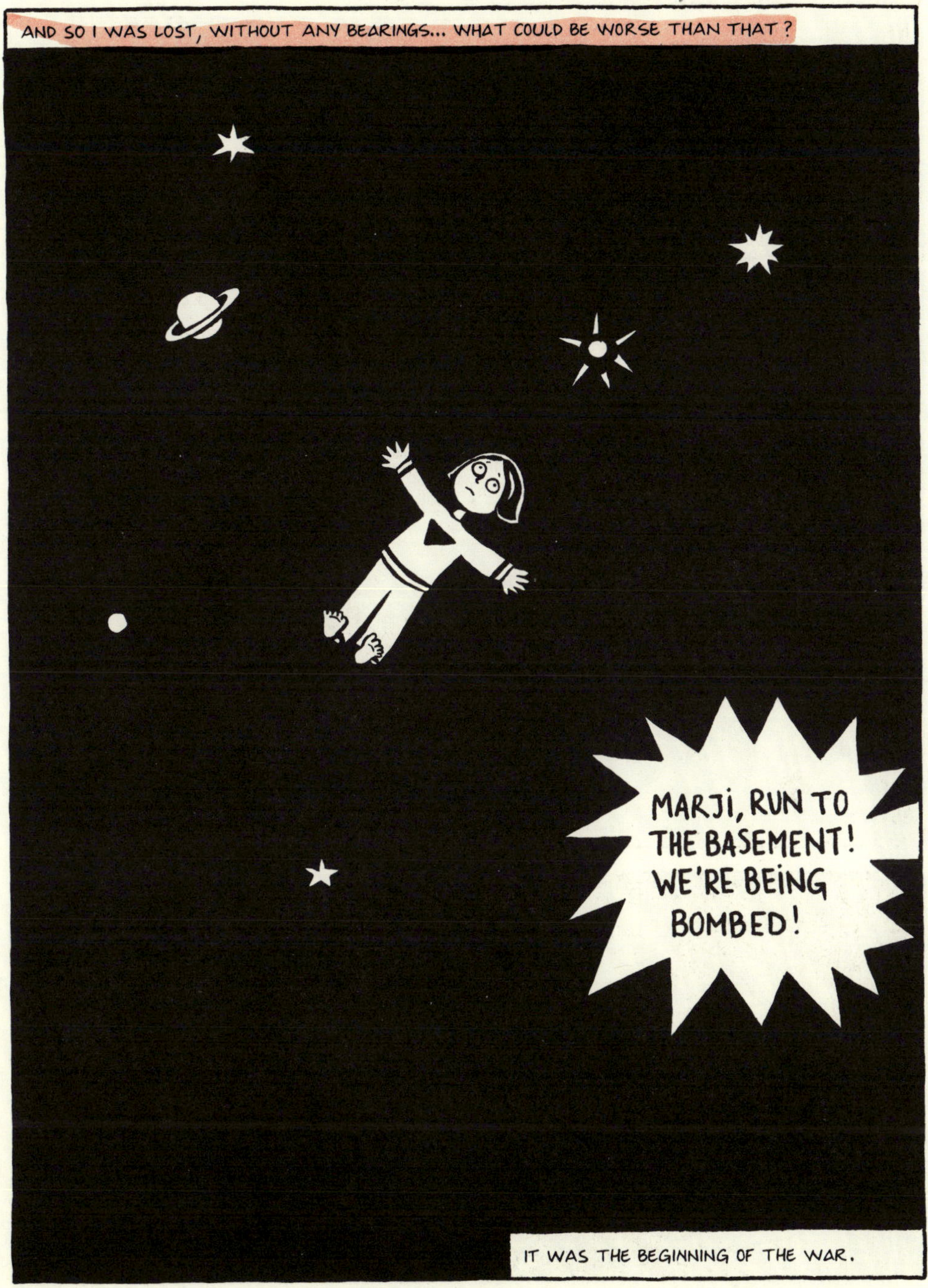
AND SO I WAS LOST, WITHOUT ANY BEARINGS... WHAT COULD BE WORSE THAN THAT?
MARJI, RUN TO THE BASEMENT! WE'RE BEING BOMBED!
IT WAS THE BEGINNING OF THE WAR.

THE TRIP

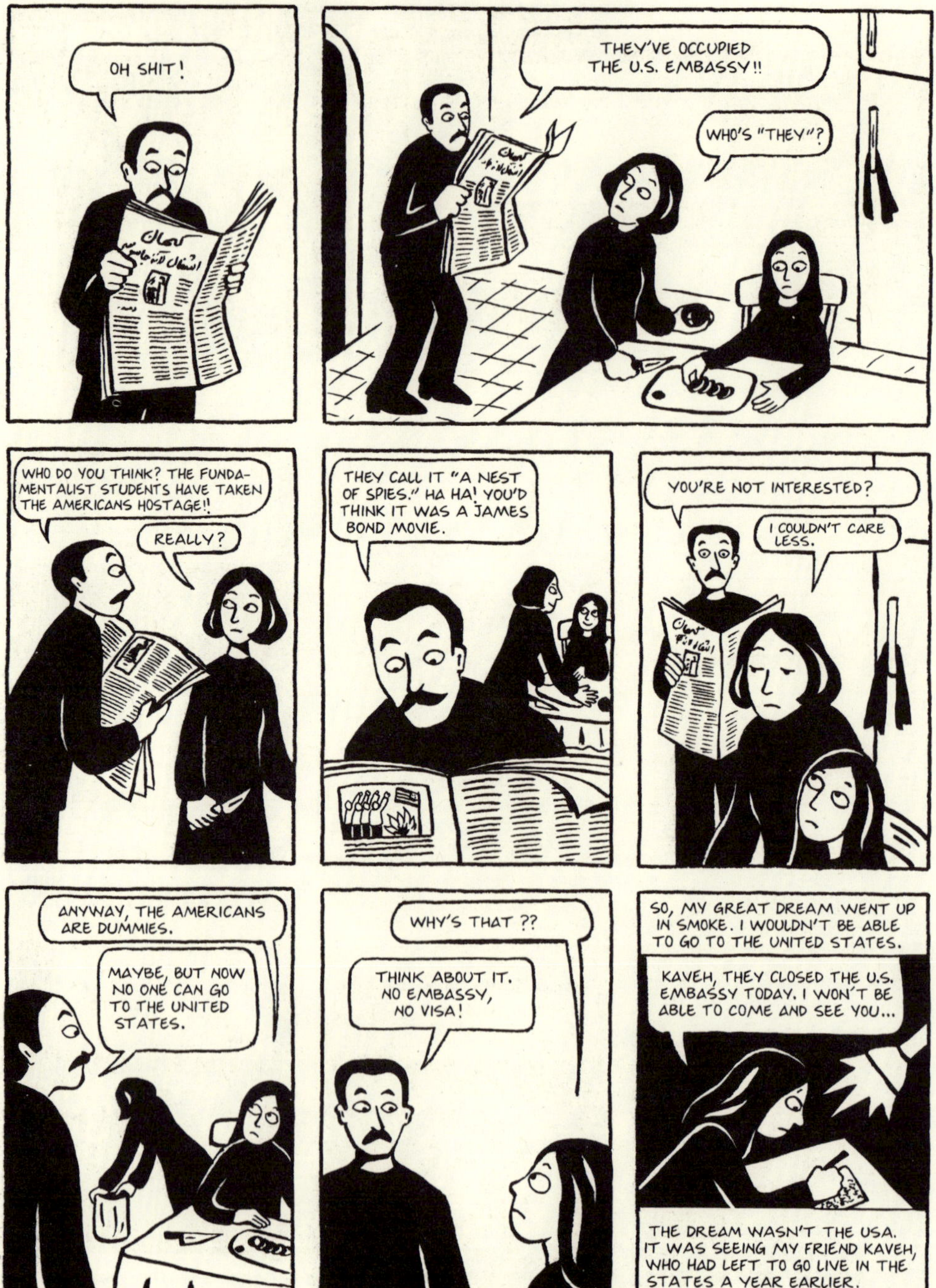
OH SHIT!
THEY'VE OCCUPIED THE U.S. EMBASSY!!
WHO'S "THEY"?
WHO DO YOU THINK? THE FUNDA-MENTALIST STUDENTS HAVE TAKEN THE AMERICANS HOSTAGE!!
REALLY?
THEY CALL IT "A NEST OF SPIES." HA HA! YOU'D THINK IT WAS A JAMES BOND MOVIE.
YOU'RE NOT INTERESTED?
I COULDN'T CARE LESS.
ANYWAY, THE AMERICANS ARE DUMMIES.
MAYBE, BUT NOW NO ONE CAN GO TO THE UNITED STATES.
WHY'S THAT ??
THINK ABOUT IT. NO EMBASSY, NO VISA!
SO, MY GREAT DREAM WENT UP IN SMOKE. I WOULDN'T BE ABLE TO GO TO THE UNITED STATES.
KAVEH, THEY CLOSED THE U.S. EMBASSY TODAY. I WON'T BE ABLE TO COME AND SEE YOU...
THE DREAM WASN'T THE USA. IT WAS SEEING MY FRIEND KAVEH, WHO HAD LEFT TO GO LIVE IN THE STATES A YEAR EARLIER.

what one means vs. what they say. Irony

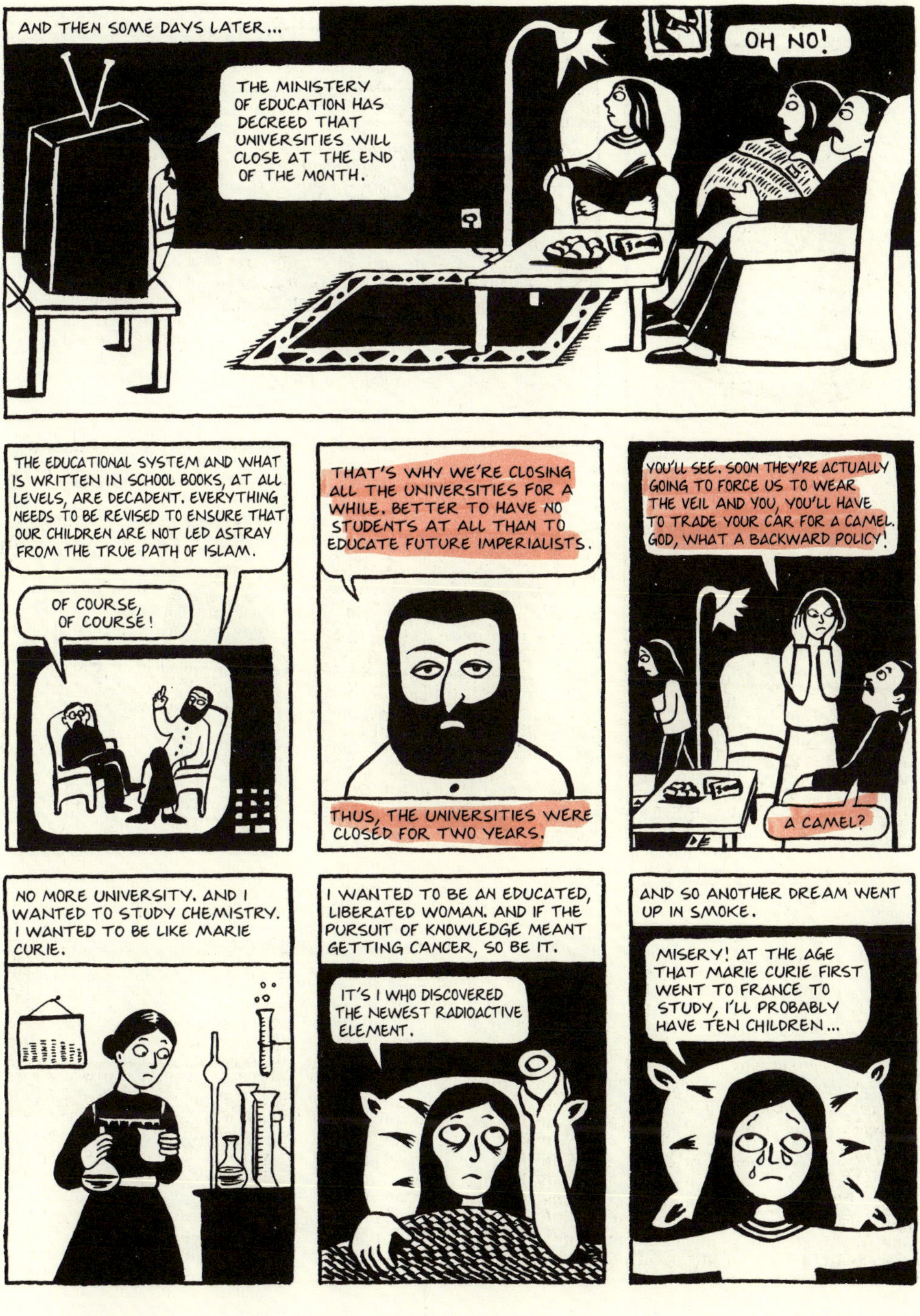

policies are to "save" women but they do more harm than good

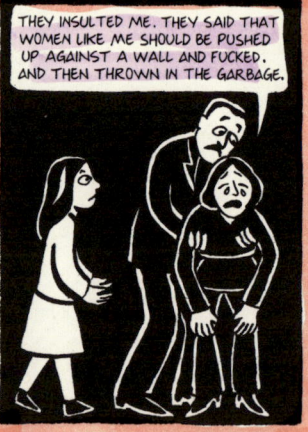

Irony, as the amount of Freedom taken away is equal

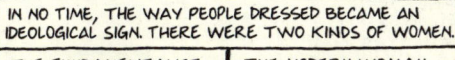

everyone has to join together if they want to achieve their goal

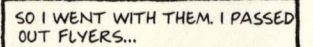

fly away From their problems

THINGS GOT WORSE FROM ONE DAY TO THE NEXT. IN SEPTEMBER 1980, MY PARENTS ABRUPTLY PLANNED A VACATION. I THINK THEY REALIZED THAT SOON SUCH THINGS WOULD NO LONGER BE POSSIBLE. AS IT HAPPENED, THEY WERE RIGHT. AND SO WE WENT TO ITALY AND SPAIN FOR THREE WEEKS...
...IT WAS WONDERFUL.

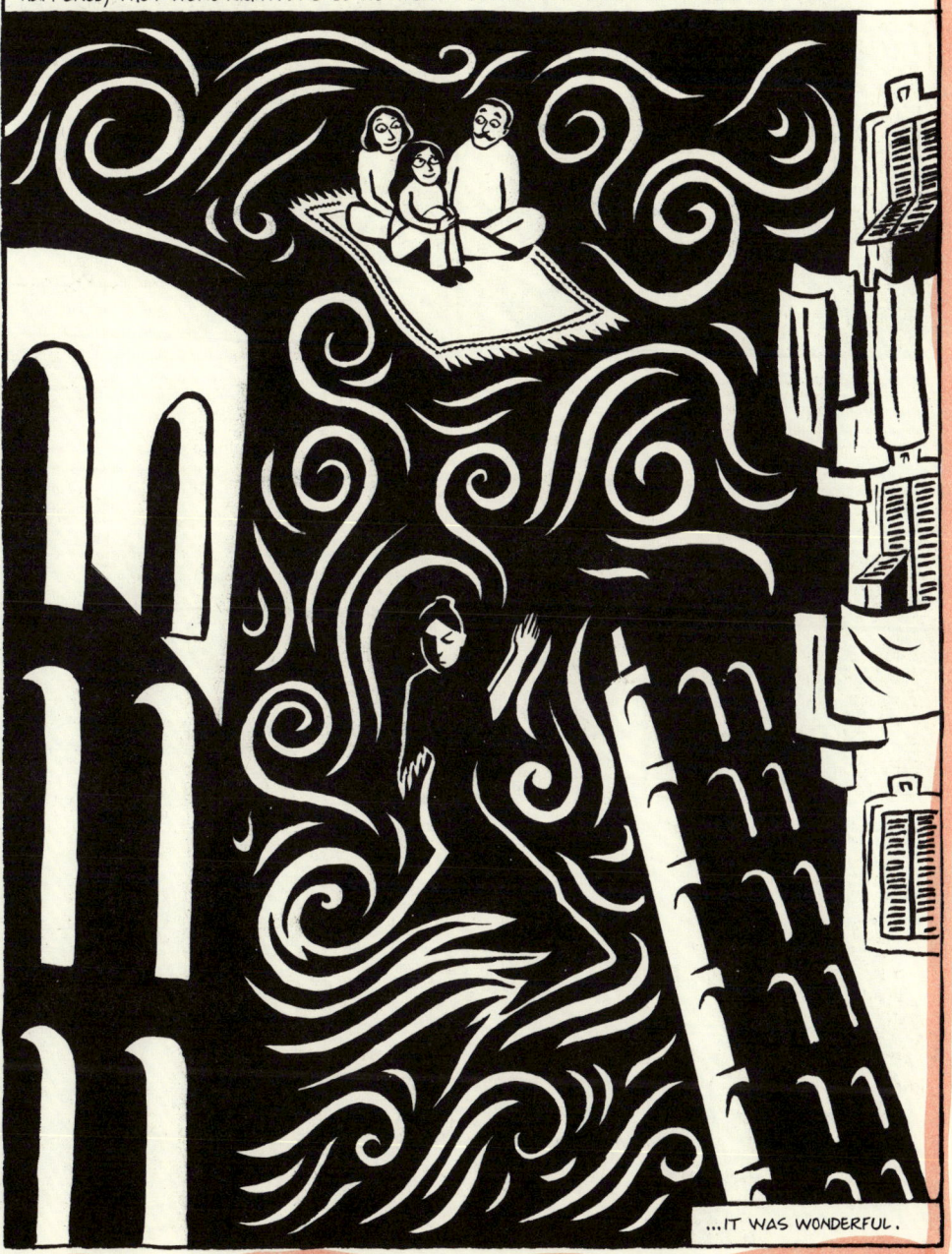

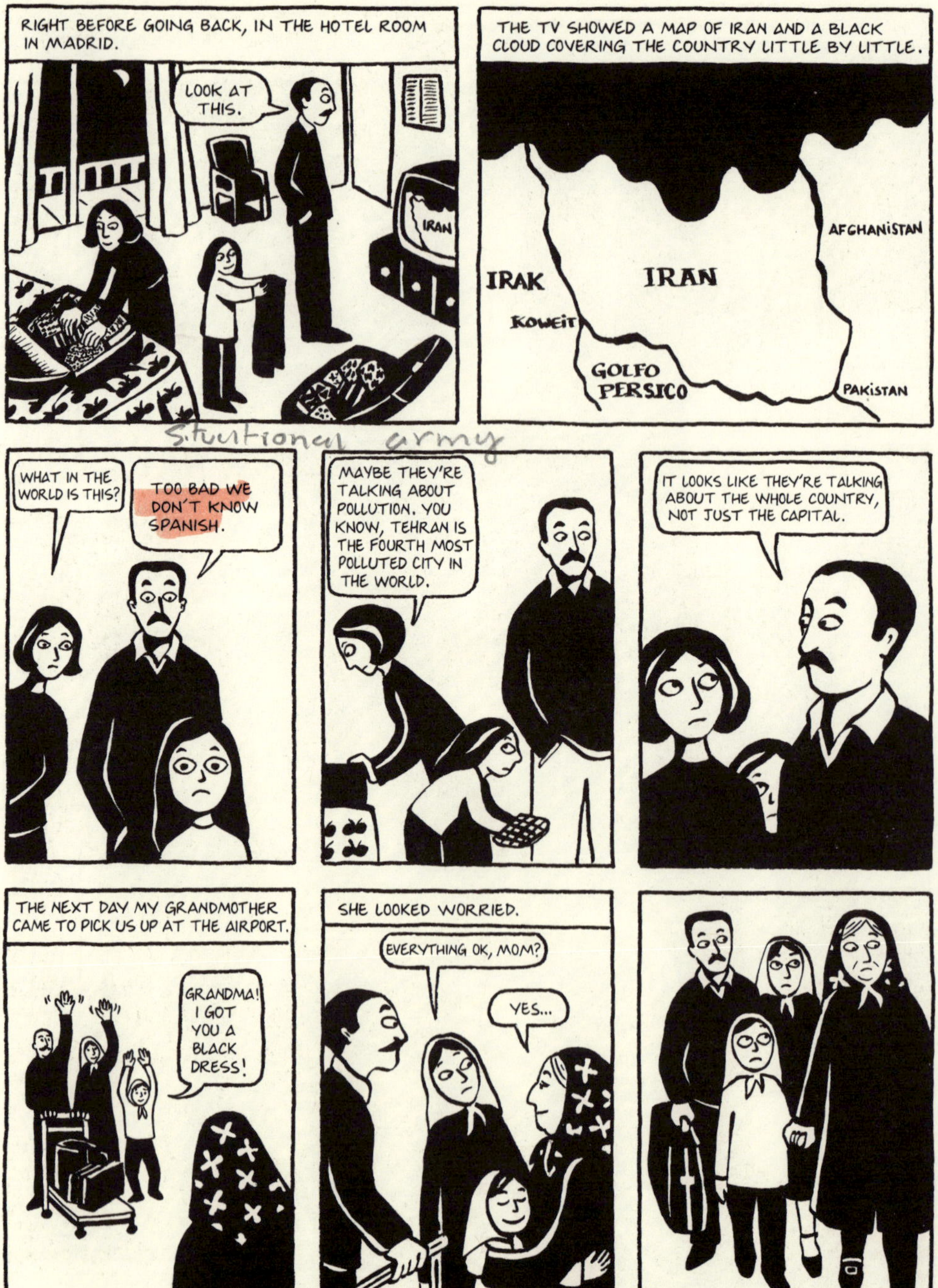
RIGHT BEFORE GOING BACK, IN THE HOTEL ROOM IN MADRID.
LOOK AT THIS.
IRAN
THE TV SHOWED A MAP OF IRAN AND A BLACK CLOUD COVERING THE COUNTRY LITTLE BY LITTLE.
AFGHANISTAN
IRAK
IRAN
KOWEIT
GOLFO PERSICO
PAKISTAN
WHAT IN THE WORLD IS THIS?
TOO BAD WE DON'T KNOW SPANISH.
MAYBE THEY'RE TALKING ABOUT POLLUTION. YOU KNOW, TEHRAN IS THE FOURTH MOST POLLUTED CITY IN THE WORLD.
IT LOOKS LIKE THEY'RE TALKING ABOUT THE WHOLE COUNTRY, NOT JUST THE CAPITAL.
THE NEXT DAY MY GRANDMOTHER CAME TO PICK US UP AT THE AIRPORT.
GRANDMA! I GOT YOU A BLACK DRESS!
SHE LOOKED WORRIED.
EVERYTHING OK, MOM?
YES...

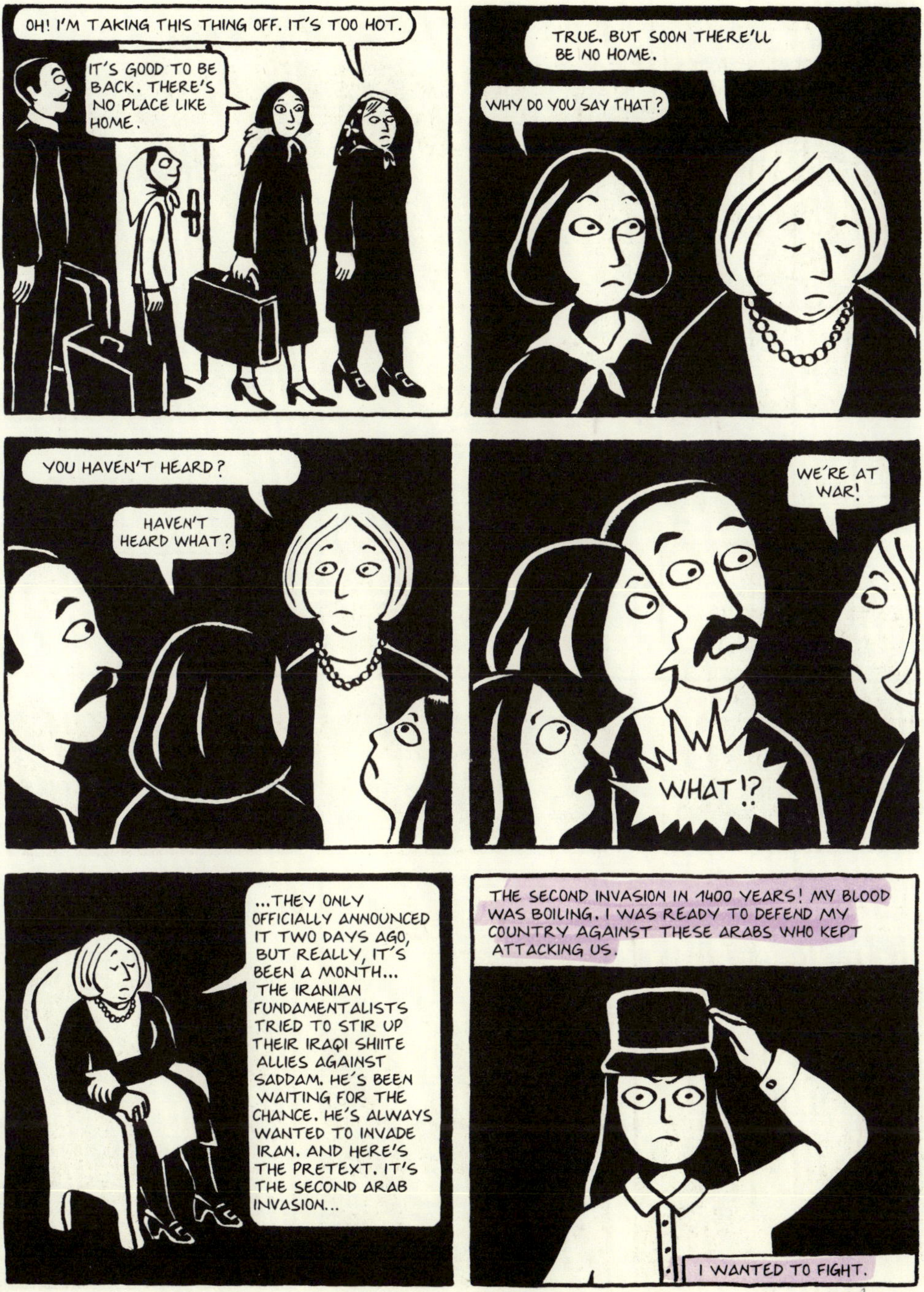

more innocence lost
she is ready to die

THE F-14s

their world goes dark

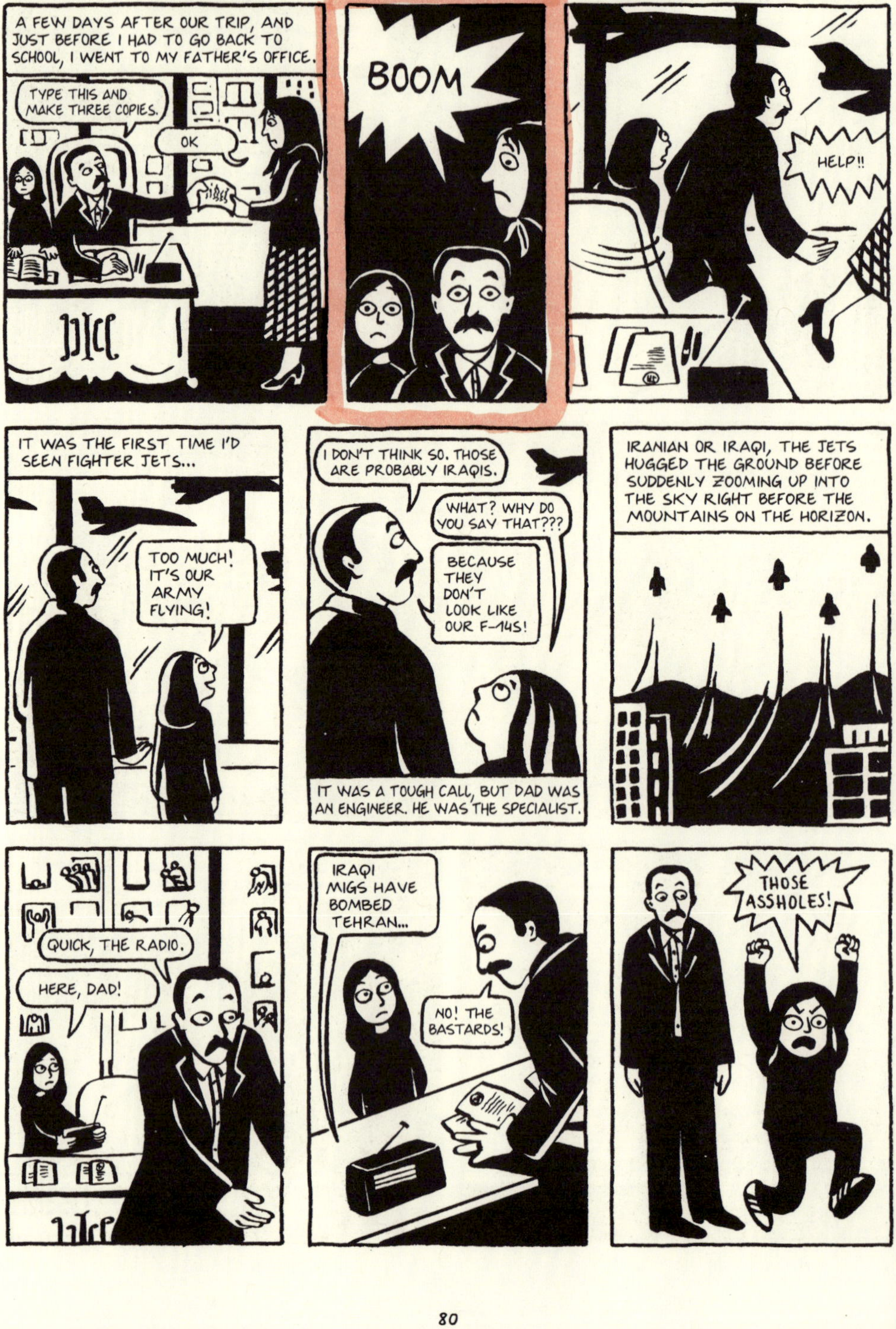

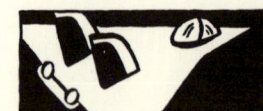

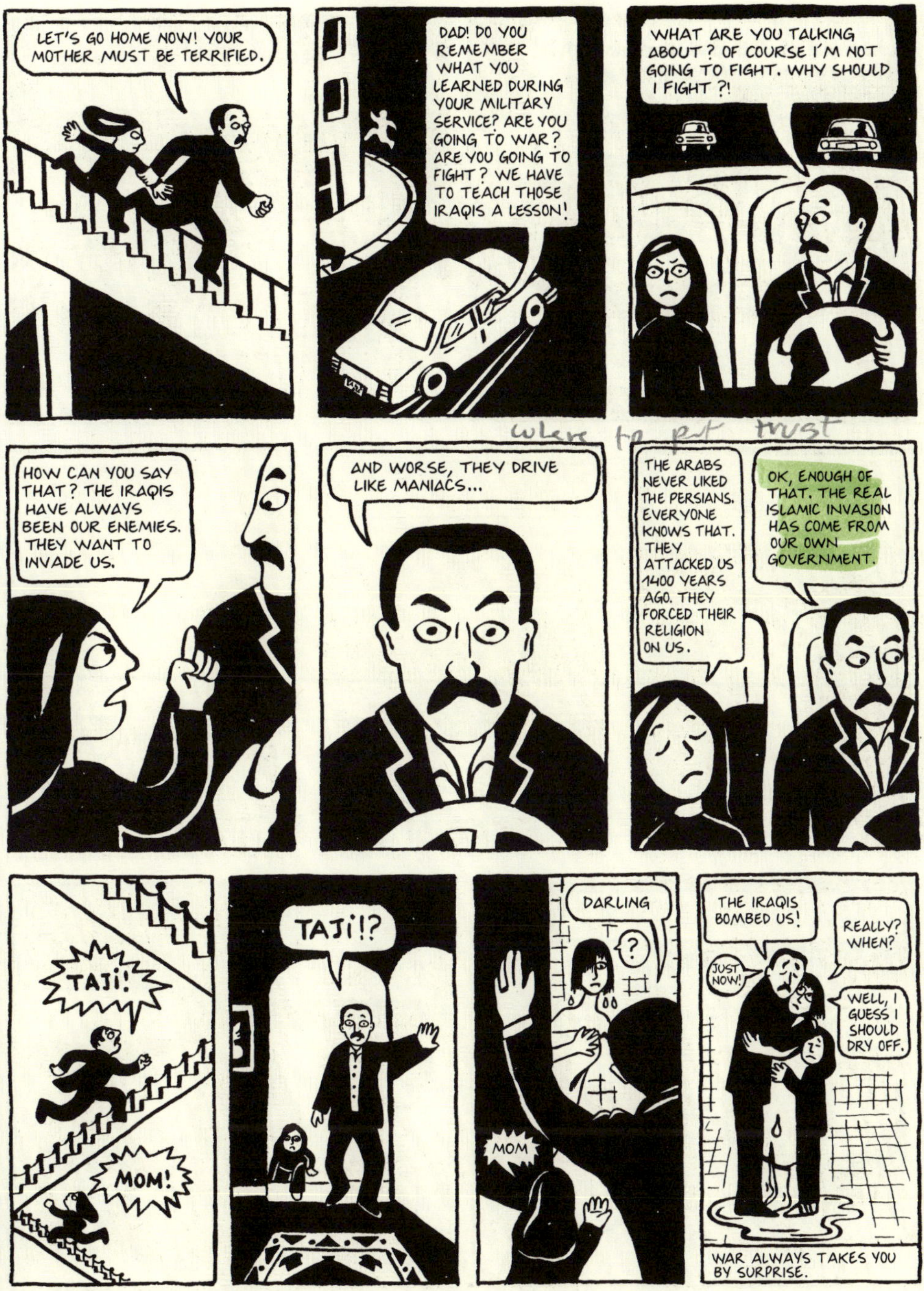
LET'S GO HOME NOW! YOUR MOTHER MUST BE TERRIFIED.
DAD! DO YOU REMEMBER WHAT YOU LEARNED DURING YOUR MILITARY SERVICE? ARE YOU GOING TO WAR? ARE YOU GOING TO FIGHT? WE HAVE TO TEACH THOSE IRAQIS A LESSON!
WHAT ARE YOU TALKING ABOUT? OF COURSE I'M NOT GOING TO FIGHT. WHY SHOULD I FIGHT?!
HOW CAN YOU SAY THAT? THE IRAQIS HAVE ALWAYS BEEN OUR ENEMIES. THEY WANT TO INVADE US.
AND WORSE, THEY DRIVE LIKE MANIACS...
THE ARABS NEVER LIKED THE PERSIANS. EVERYONE KNOWS THAT. THEY ATTACKED US 1400 YEARS AGO. THEY FORCED THEIR RELIGION ON US.
OK, ENOUGH OF THAT. THE REAL ISLAMIC INVASION HAS COME FROM OUR OWN GOVERNMENT.
TAJI!
MOM!
TAJI!?
DARLING
?
MOM
THE IRAQIS BOMBED US!
JUST NOW!
REALLY? WHEN?
WELL, I GUESS I SHOULD DRY OFF.
WAR ALWAYS TAKES YOU BY SURPRISE.

War is personal

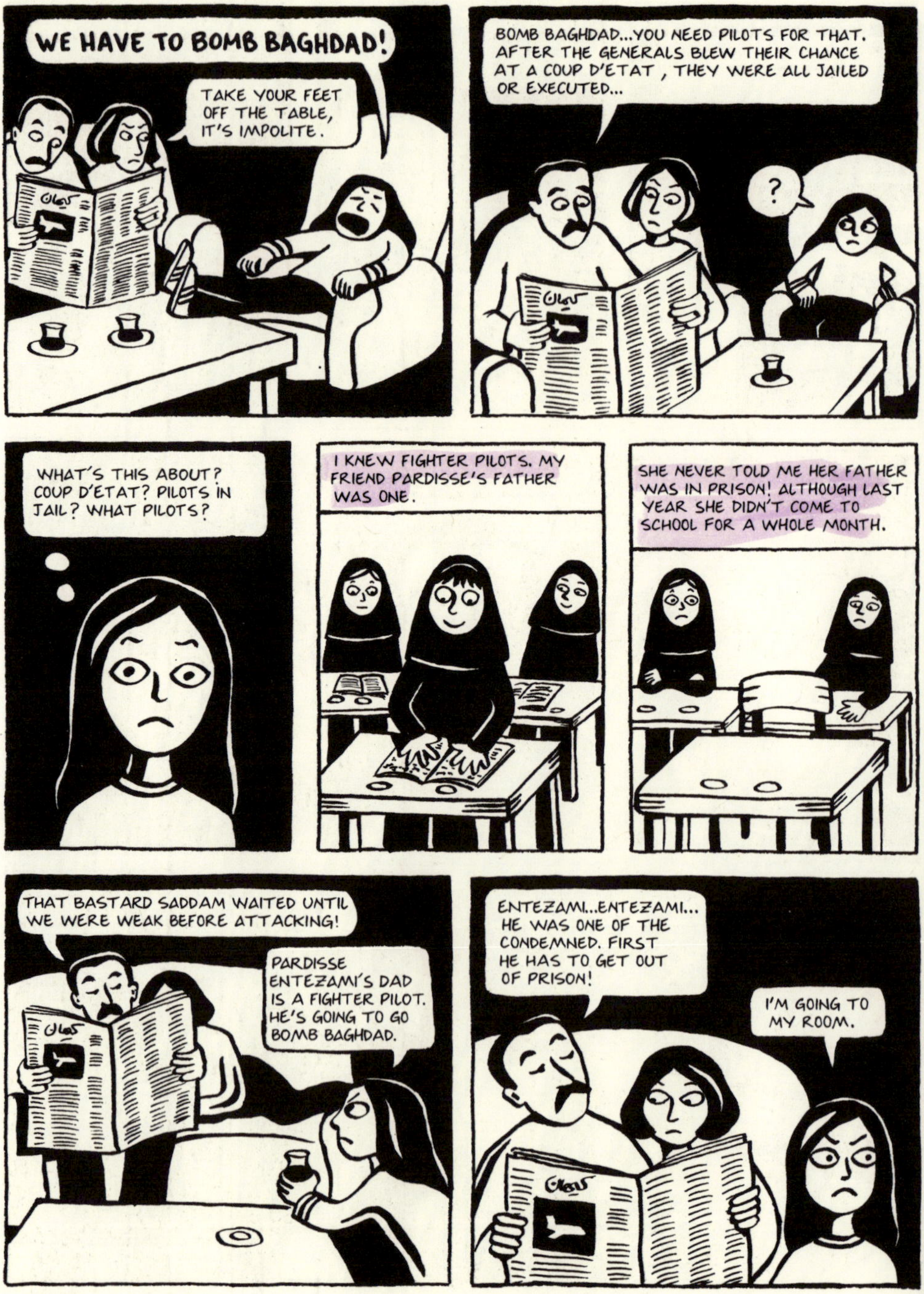
WE HAVE TO BOMB BAGHDAD!
TAKE YOUR FEET OFF THE TABLE, IT'S IMPOLITE.
BOMB BAGHDAD...YOU NEED PILOTS FOR THAT. AFTER THE GENERALS BLEW THEIR CHANCE AT A COUP D'ETAT , THEY WERE ALL JAILED OR EXECUTED...
?
WHAT'S THIS ABOUT? COUP D'ETAT? PILOTS IN JAIL? WHAT PILOTS?
I KNEW FIGHTER PILOTS. MY FRIEND PARDISSE'S FATHER WAS ONE.
SHE NEVER TOLD ME HER FATHER WAS IN PRISON! ALTHOUGH LAST YEAR SHE DIDN'T COME TO SCHOOL FOR A WHOLE MONTH.
THAT BASTARD SADDAM WAITED UNTIL WE WERE WEAK BEFORE ATTACKING!
PARDISSE ENTEZAMI'S DAD IS A FIGHTER PILOT. HE'S GOING TO GO BOMB BAGHDAD.
ENTEZAMI...ENTEZAMI... HE WAS ONE OF THE CONDEMNED. FIRST HE HAS TO GET OUT OF PRISON!
I'M GOING TO MY ROOM.

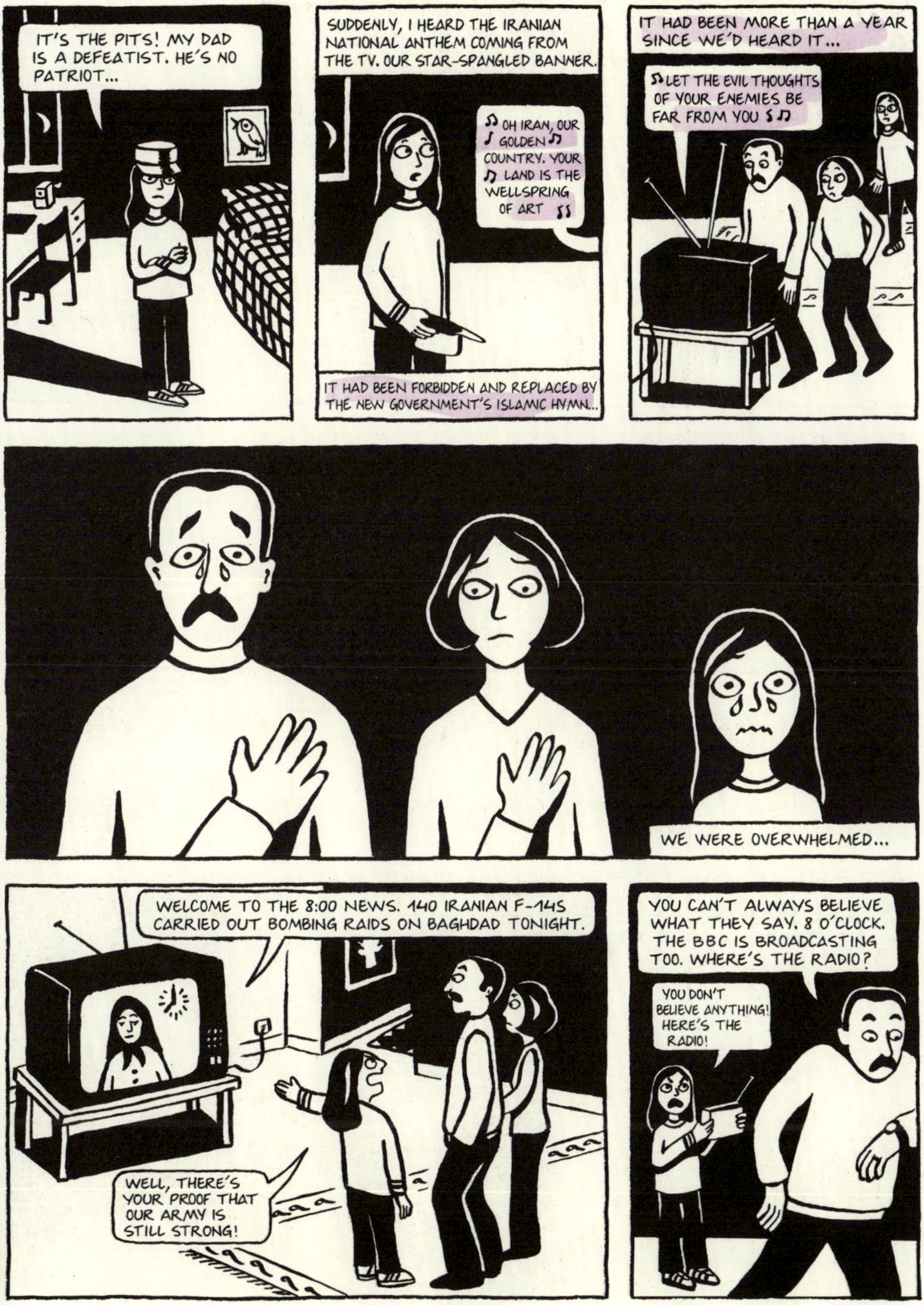
IT'S THE PITS! MY DAD IS A DEFEATIST. HE'S NO PATRIOT...
SUDDENLY, I HEARD THE IRANIAN NATIONAL ANTHEM COMING FROM THE TV. OUR STAR-SPANGLED BANNER.
OH IRAN, OUR GOLDEN COUNTRY. YOUR LAND IS THE WELLSPRING OF ART
IT HAD BEEN FORBIDDEN AND REPLACED BY THE NEW GOVERNMENT'S ISLAMIC HYMN...
IT HAD BEEN MORE THAN A YEAR SINCE WE'D HEARD IT...
LET THE EVIL THOUGHTS OF YOUR ENEMIES BE FAR FROM YOU
WE WERE OVERWHELMED...
WELCOME TO THE 8:00 NEWS. 140 IRANIAN F-14S CARRIED OUT BOMBING RAIDS ON BAGHDAD TONIGHT.
WELL, THERE'S YOUR PROOF THAT OUR ARMY IS STILL STRONG!
YOU CAN'T ALWAYS BELIEVE WHAT THEY SAY. 8 O'CLOCK. THE BBC IS BROADCASTING TOO. WHERE'S THE RADIO?
YOU DON'T BELIEVE ANYTHING! HERE'S THE RADIO!

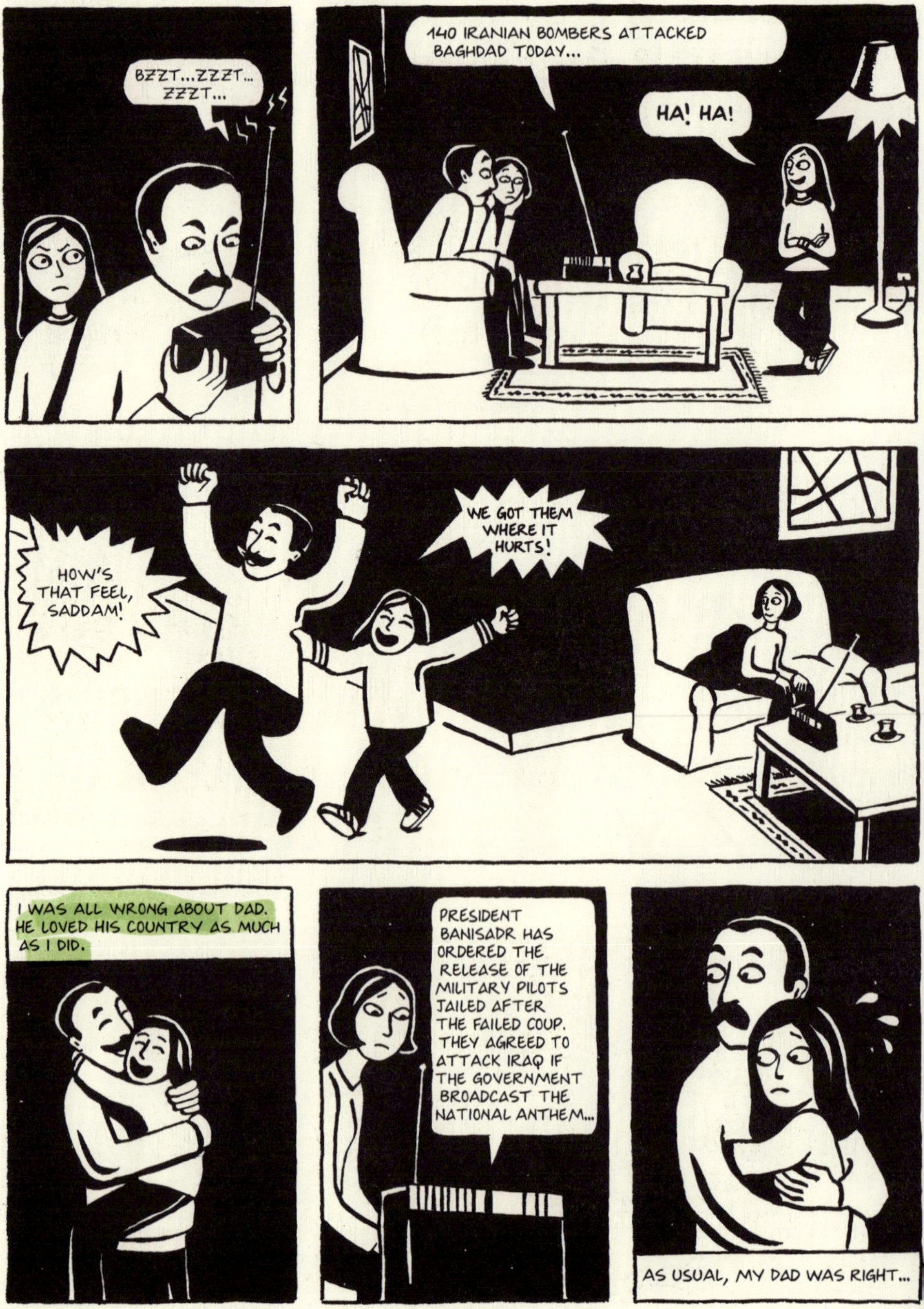

Realism vs. Idealism

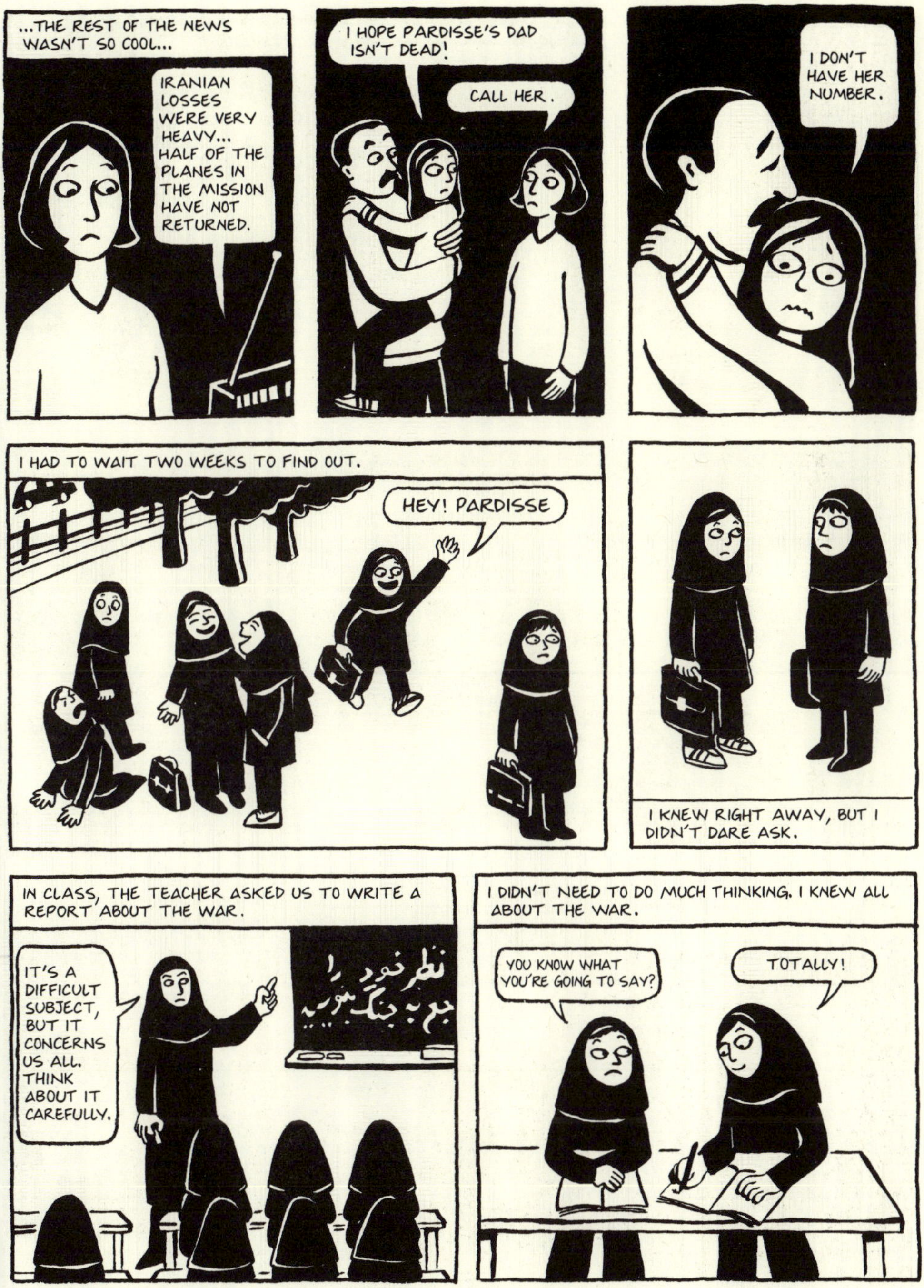
...THE REST OF THE NEWS WASN'T SO COOL...
IRANIAN LOSSES WERE VERY HEAVY... HALF OF THE PLANES IN THE MISSION HAVE NOT RETURNED.
I HOPE PARDISSE'S DAD ISN'T DEAD!
CALL HER.
I DON'T HAVE HER NUMBER.
I HAD TO WAIT TWO WEEKS TO FIND OUT.
HEY! PARDISSE
I KNEW RIGHT AWAY, BUT I DIDN'T DARE ASK.
IN CLASS, THE TEACHER ASKED US TO WRITE A REPORT ABOUT THE WAR.
IT'S A DIFFICULT SUBJECT, BUT IT CONCERNS US ALL. THINK ABOUT IT CAREFULLY.
I DIDN'T NEED TO DO MUCH THINKING. I KNEW ALL ABOUT THE WAR.
YOU KNOW WHAT YOU'RE GOING TO SAY?
TOTALLY!

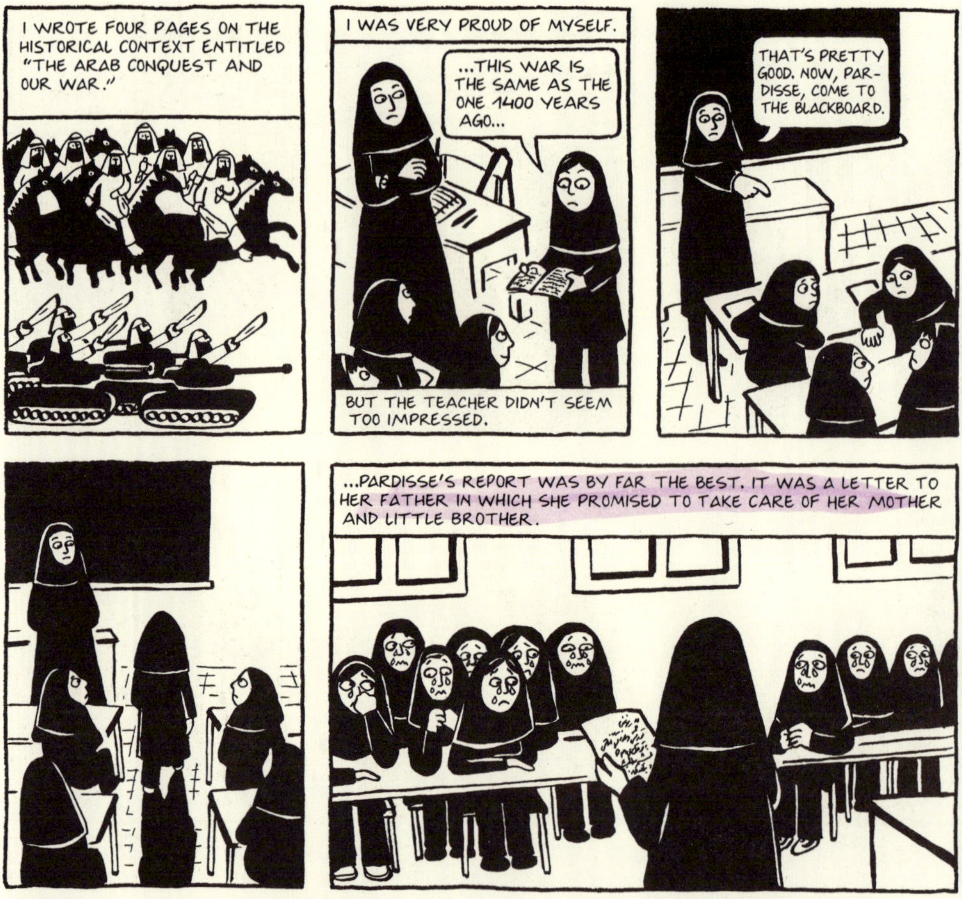

war gets closer to home, more than just one person she knows has been effected

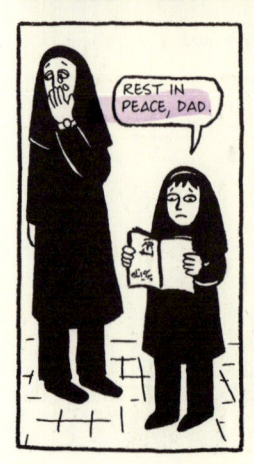

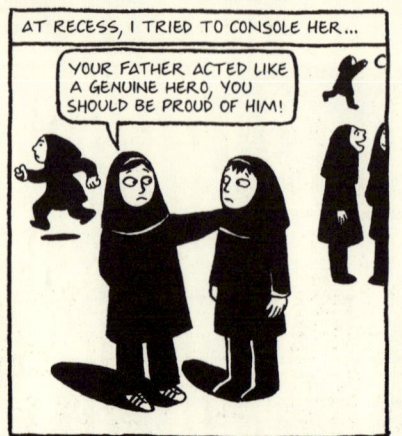

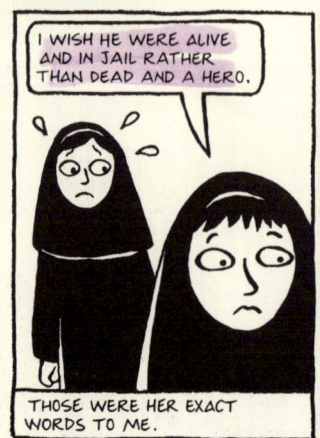

THE JEWELS

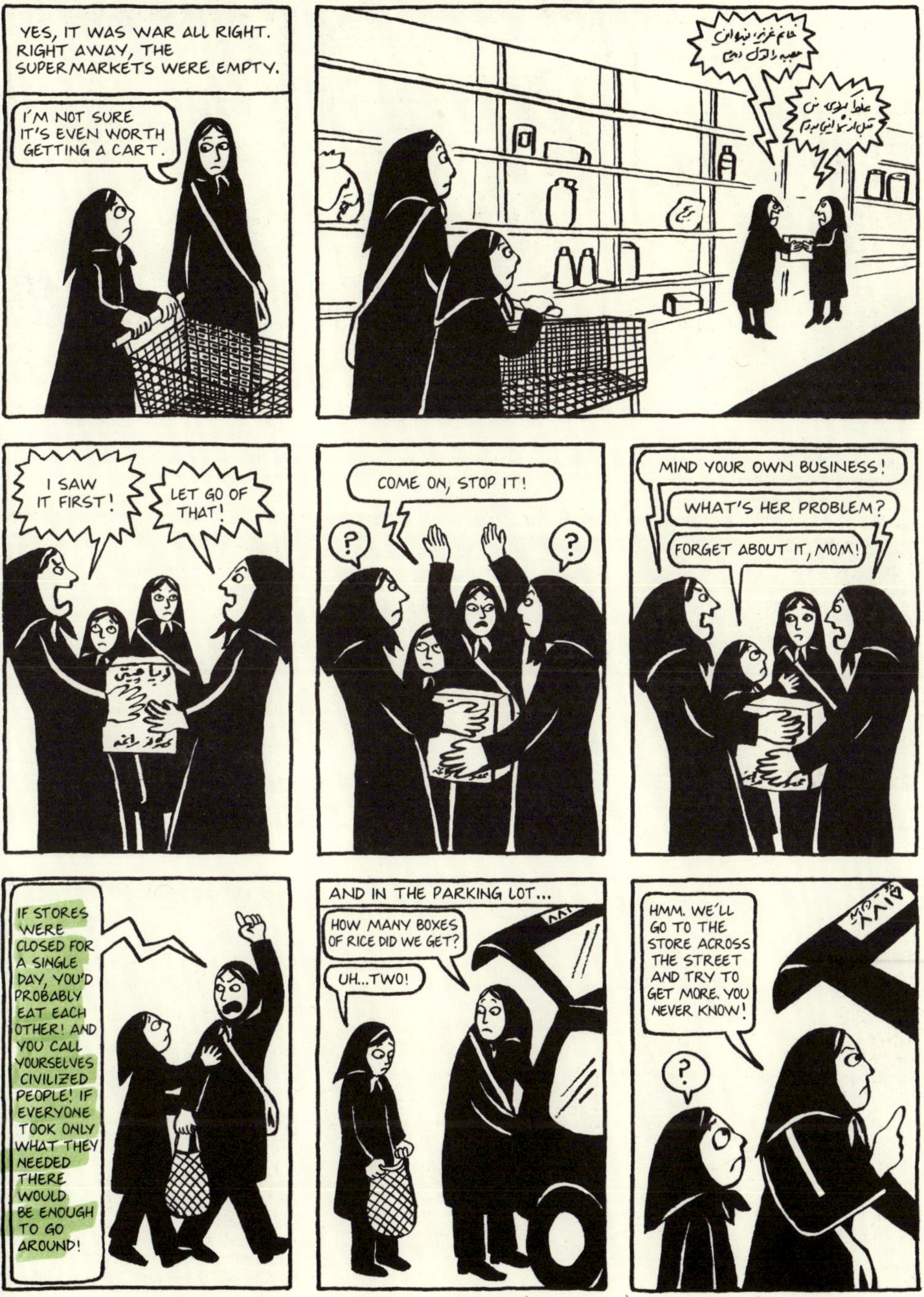

unity is too expensive

Fear changes
people

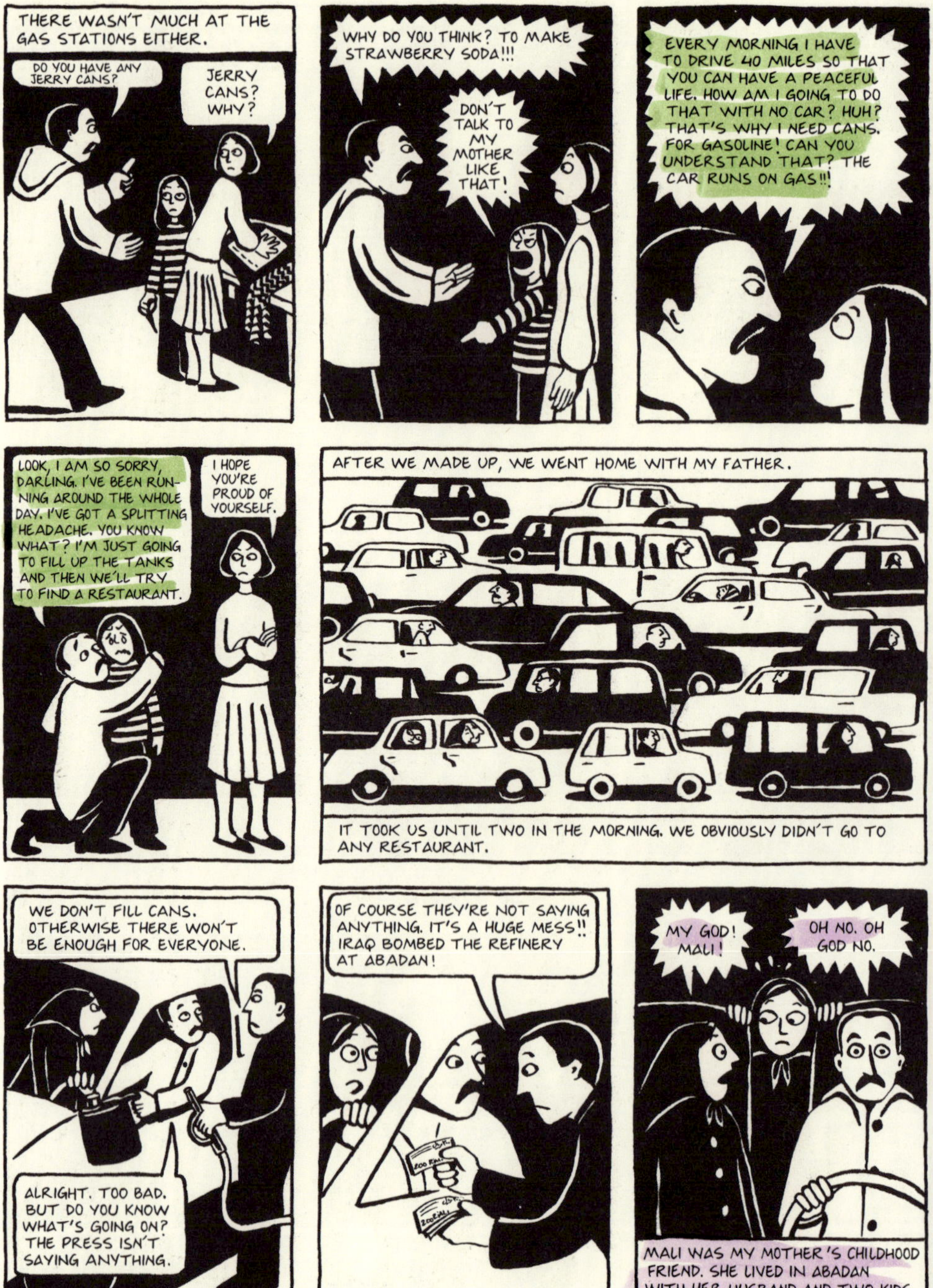

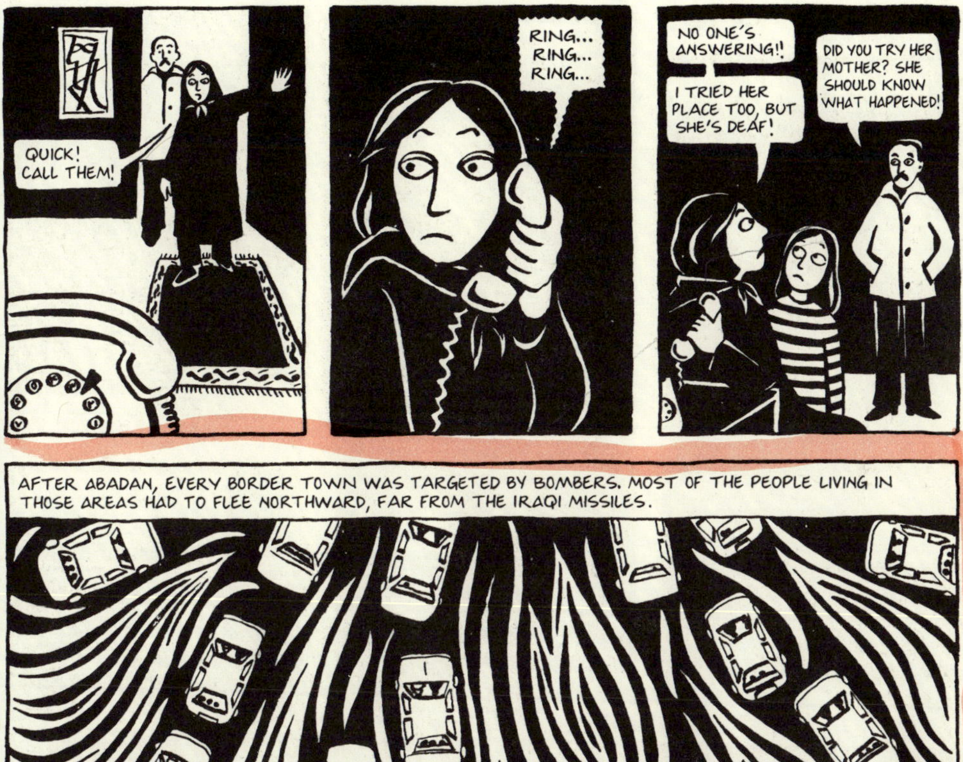

escape the growing fire that is their reality as citizens of their government

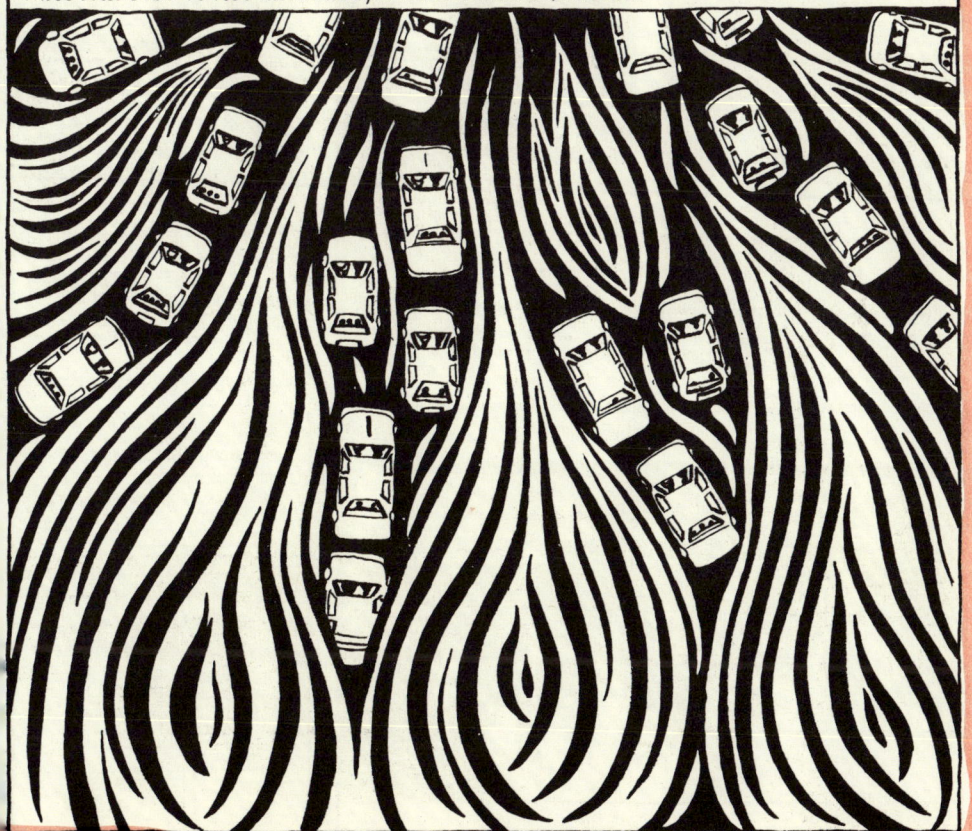

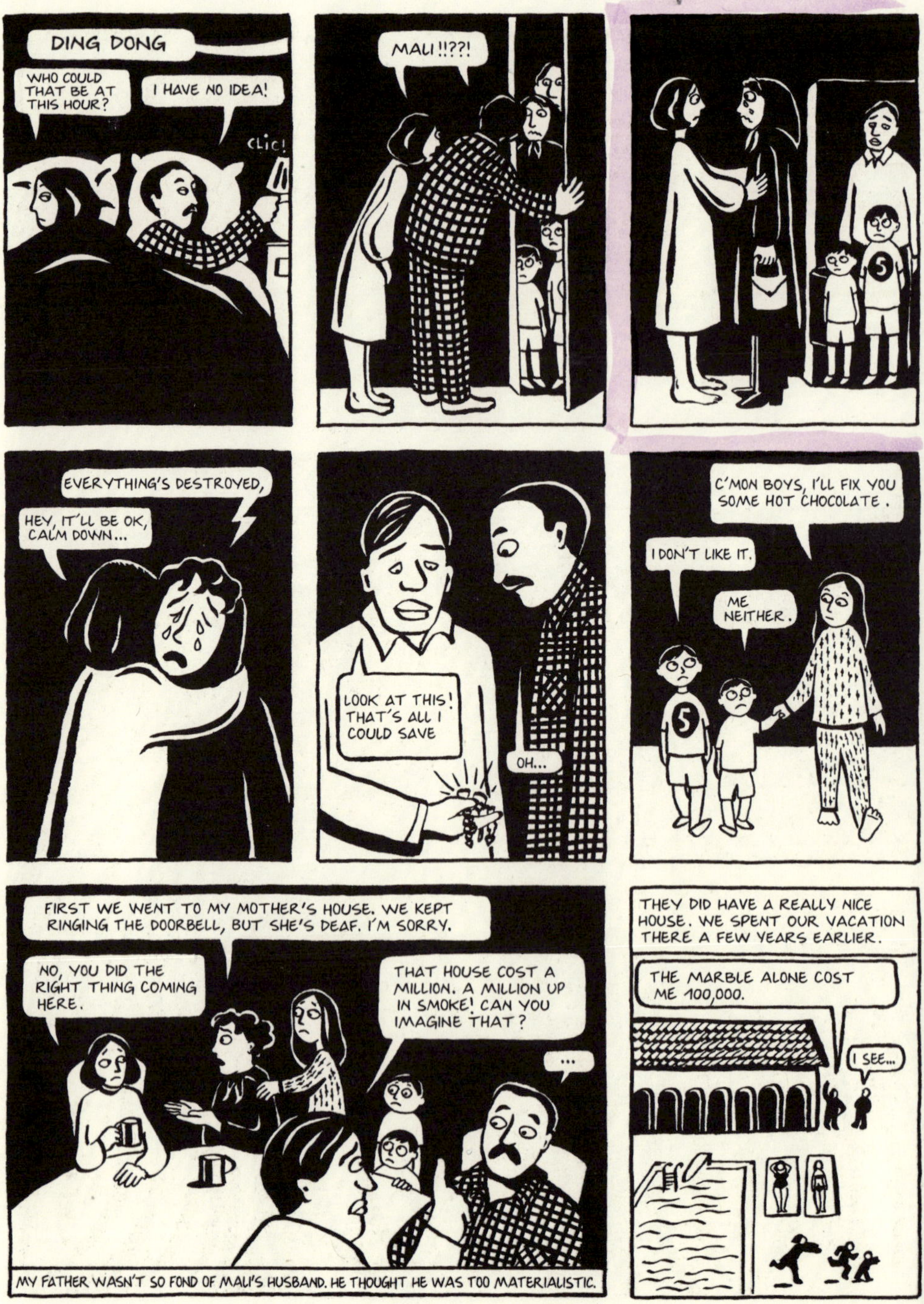

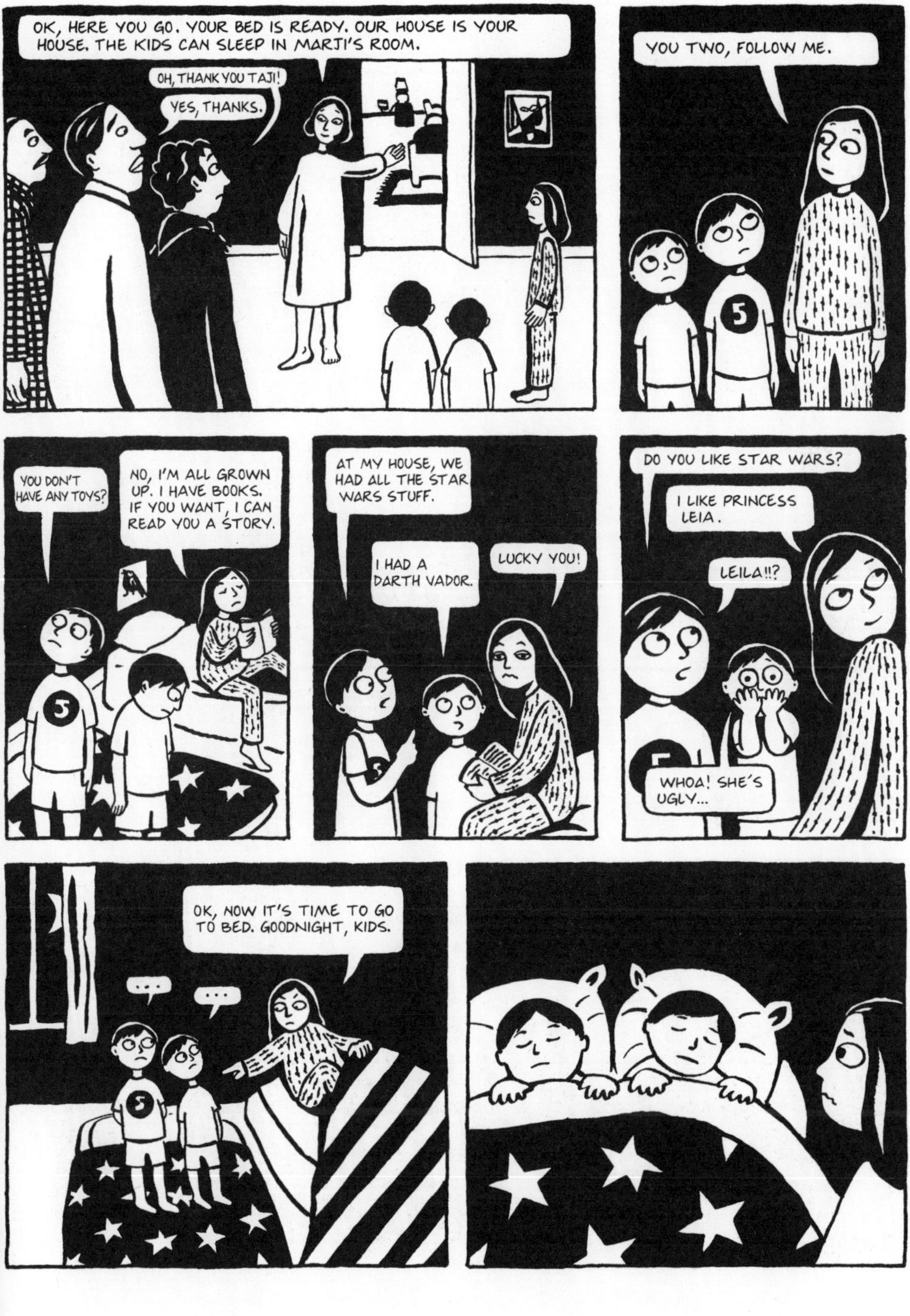
OK, HERE YOU GO. YOUR BED IS READY. OUR HOUSE IS YOUR HOUSE. THE KIDS CAN SLEEP IN MARJI'S ROOM.
OH, THANK YOU TAJI!
YES, THANKS.
YOU TWO, FOLLOW ME.
YOU DON'T HAVE ANY TOYS?
NO, I'M ALL GROWN UP. I HAVE BOOKS. IF YOU WANT, I CAN READ YOU A STORY.
AT MY HOUSE, WE HAD ALL THE STAR WARS STUFF.
I HAD A DARTH VADOR.
LUCKY YOU!
DO YOU LIKE STAR WARS?
I LIKE PRINCESS LEIA.
LEILA!!?
WHOA! SHE'S UGLY...
OK, NOW IT'S TIME TO GO TO BED. GOODNIGHT, KIDS.
...
...

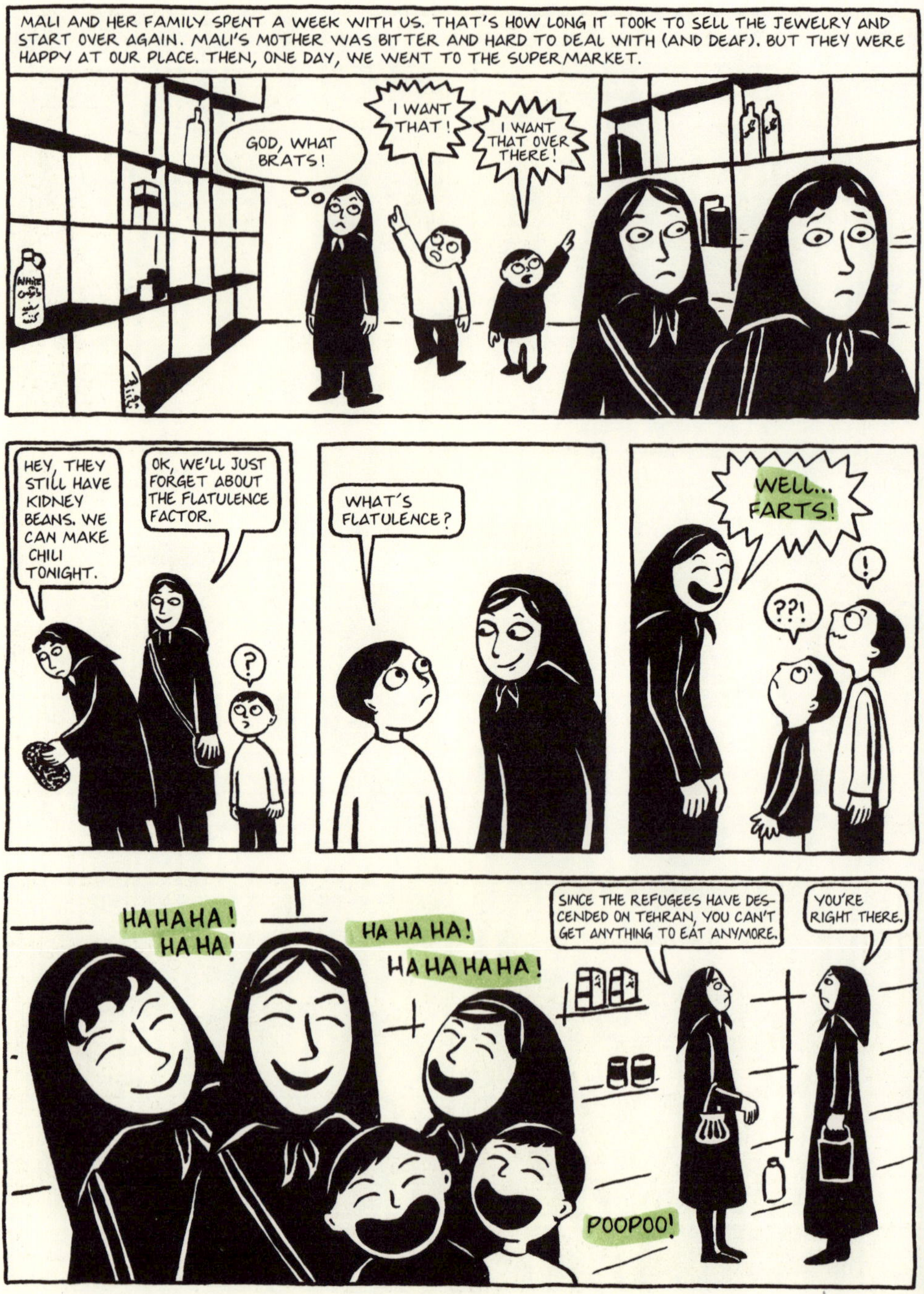

Find happiness even when times are hard, make a reason to keep going

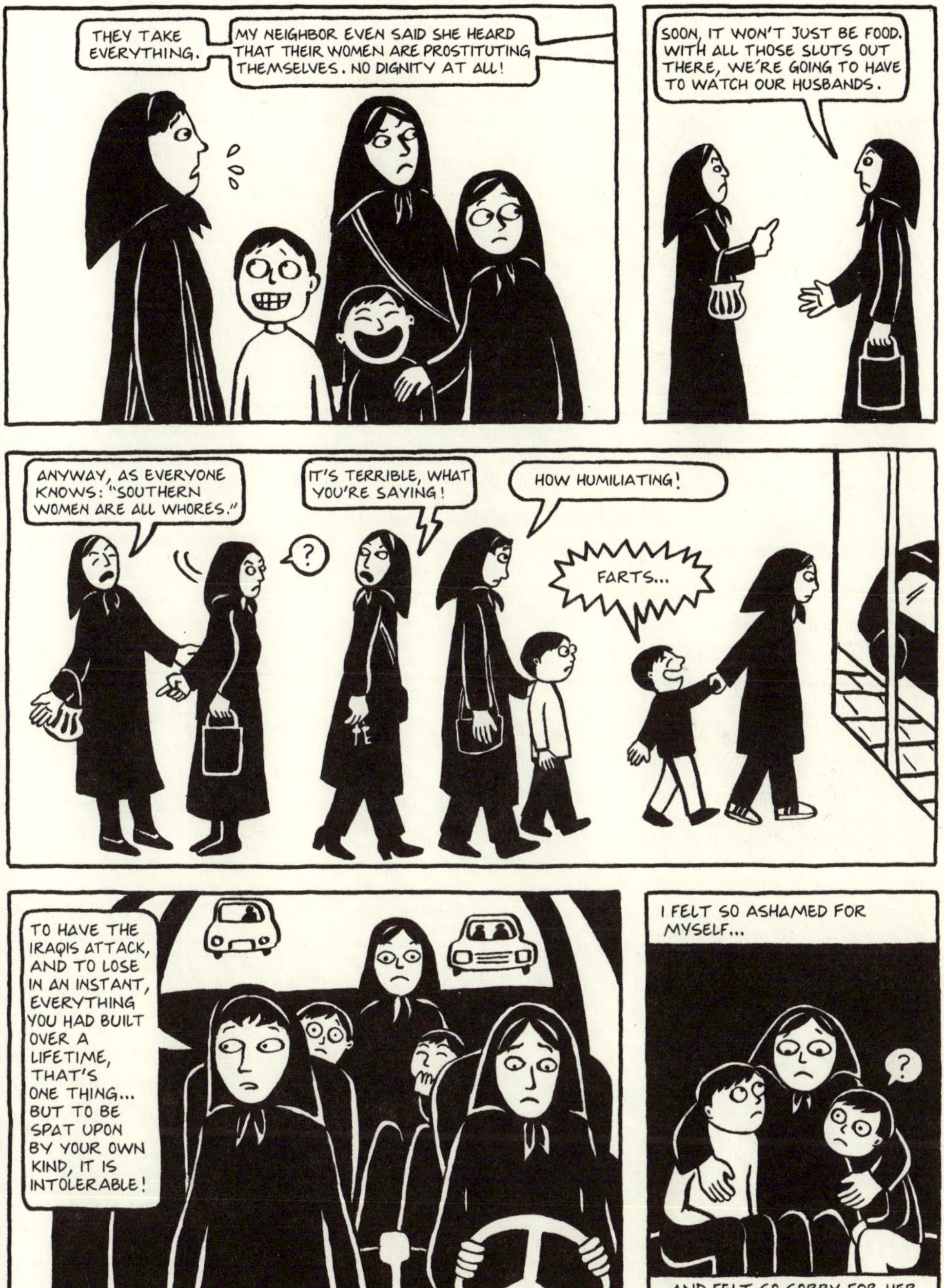
THEY TAKE EVERYTHING.
MY NEIGHBOR EVEN SAID SHE HEARD THAT THEIR WOMEN ARE PROSTITUTING THEMSELVES. NO DIGNITY AT ALL!
SOON, IT WON'T JUST BE FOOD. WITH ALL THOSE SLUTS OUT THERE, WE'RE GOING TO HAVE TO WATCH OUR HUSBANDS.
ANYWAY, AS EVERYONE KNOWS: "SOUTHERN WOMEN ARE ALL WHORES."
?
IT'S TERRIBLE, WHAT YOU'RE SAYING!
HOW HUMILIATING!
FARTS...
TO HAVE THE IRAQIS ATTACK, AND TO LOSE IN AN INSTANT, EVERYTHING YOU HAD BUILT OVER A LIFETIME, THAT'S ONE THING... BUT TO BE SPAT UPON BY YOUR OWN KIND, IT IS INTOLERABLE!
I FELT SO ASHAMED FOR MYSELF...
?
...AND FELT SO SORRY FOR HER.

THE KEY

list of dead is long, enraging at the wastefulness of all the innocent lives

THE IRAQI ARMY HAD CONQUERED THE CITY OF KHORRAMSHAHR. THEIR ARMS WERE MODERN, BUT WHERE IRAQ HAD QUALITY, WE HAD QUANTITY. COMPARED TO IRAQ, IRAN HAD A HUGE RESERVOIR OF POTENTIAL SOLDIERS. THE NUMBER OF WAR MARTYRS EMPHASIZED THAT DIFFERENCE.

CAN YOU HELP ME STYLE MY HAIR?

HAVE YOU SEEN ALL THESE CASUALTIES?

HOW CAN I NOT SEE? THEY'RE DOING ALL THEY CAN TO SHOW HOW MANY PEOPLE HAVE DIED. THE STREETS ARE PACKED WITH NUPTIAL CHAMBERS.

ACCORDING TO SHIITE TRADITION, WHEN AN UNMARRIED MAN DIES, A NUPTIAL CHAMBER IS BUILT FOR HIM. THAT WAY, THE DEAD MAN CAN SYMBOLICALLY ATTAIN CARNAL KNOWLEDGE.

IT WAS OBVIOUS THAT MANY OF THE FIGHTERS DIED VIRGINS.

VRUUUUUU

MOM, DON'T ALL THESE DEAD MEAN ANYTHING TO YOU?

OF COURSE THEY MEAN SOMETHING TO ME! BUT WE ARE STILL LIVING!

OUR COUNTRY HAS ALWAYS KNOWN WAR AND MARTYRS. SO, LIKE MY FATHER SAID: "WHEN A BIG WAVE COMES, LOWER YOUR HEAD AND LET IT PASS!"

THAT'S VERY PERSIAN. THE PHILOSOPHY OF RESIGNATION.

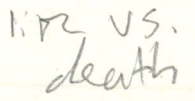

I AGREED WITH MY MOTHER. I TOO TRIED TO THINK ONLY OF LIFE. HOWEVER, IT WASN'T ALWAYS EASY: AT SCHOOL, THEY LINED US UP TWICE A DAY TO MOURN THE WAR DEAD. THEY PUT ON FUNERAL MARCHES, AND WE HAD TO BEAT OUR BREASTS.

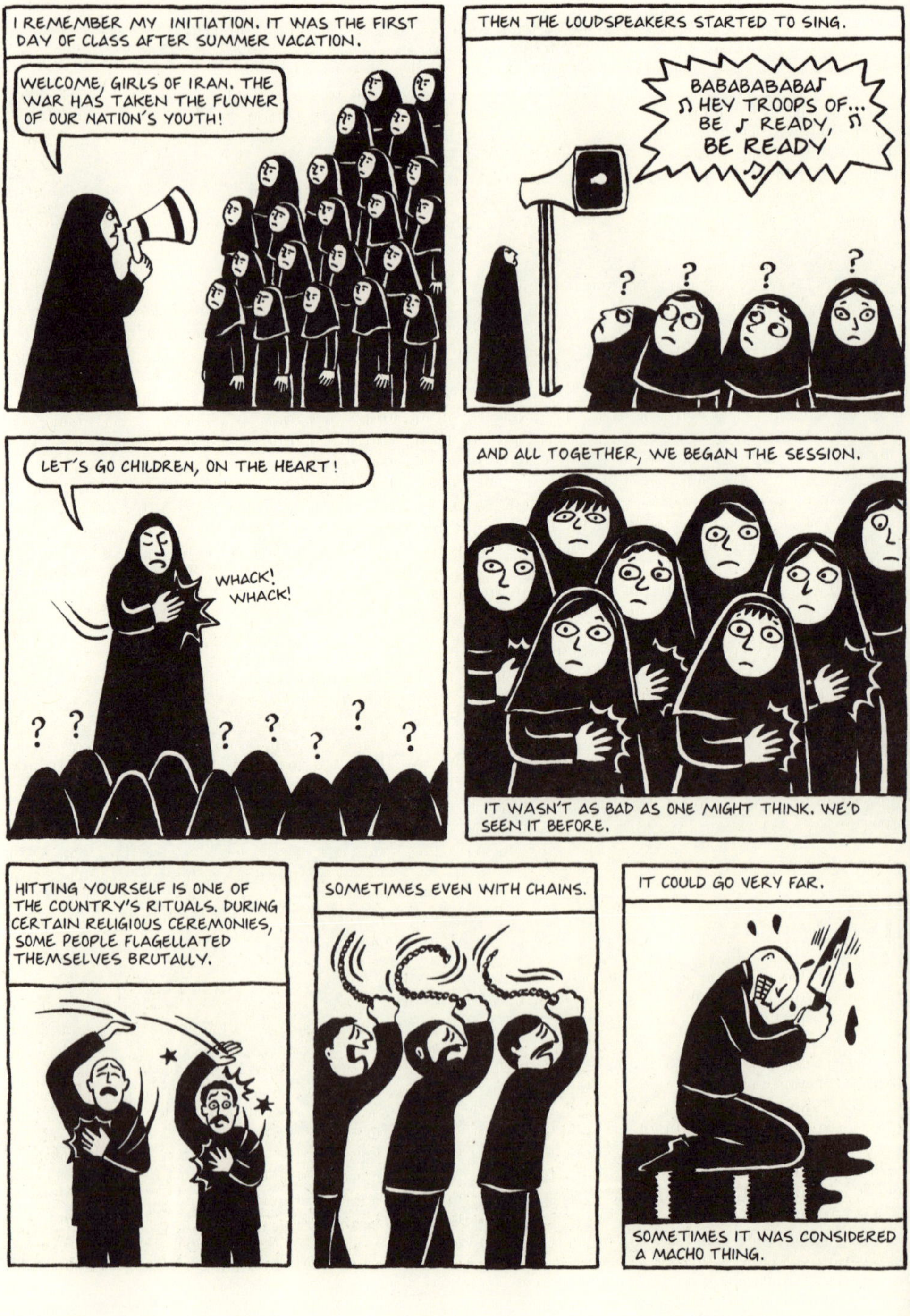
I REMEMBER MY INITIATION. IT WAS THE FIRST DAY OF CLASS AFTER SUMMER VACATION.
WELCOME, GIRLS OF IRAN. THE WAR HAS TAKEN THE FLOWER OF OUR NATION'S YOUTH!
THEN THE LOUDSPEAKERS STARTED TO SING.
BABABABABA HEY TROOPS OF... BE READY, BE READY
?
?
?
?
LET'S GO CHILDREN, ON THE HEART!
WHACK! WHACK!
? ? ? ? ? ? ?
AND ALL TOGETHER, WE BEGAN THE SESSION.
IT WASN'T AS BAD AS ONE MIGHT THINK. WE'D SEEN IT BEFORE.
HITTING YOURSELF IS ONE OF THE COUNTRY'S RITUALS. DURING CERTAIN RELIGIOUS CEREMONIES, SOME PEOPLE FLAGELLATED THEMSELVES BRUTALLY.
SOMETIMES EVEN WITH CHAINS.
IT COULD GO VERY FAR.
SOMETIMES IT WAS CONSIDERED A MACHO THING.

death is so normalized now

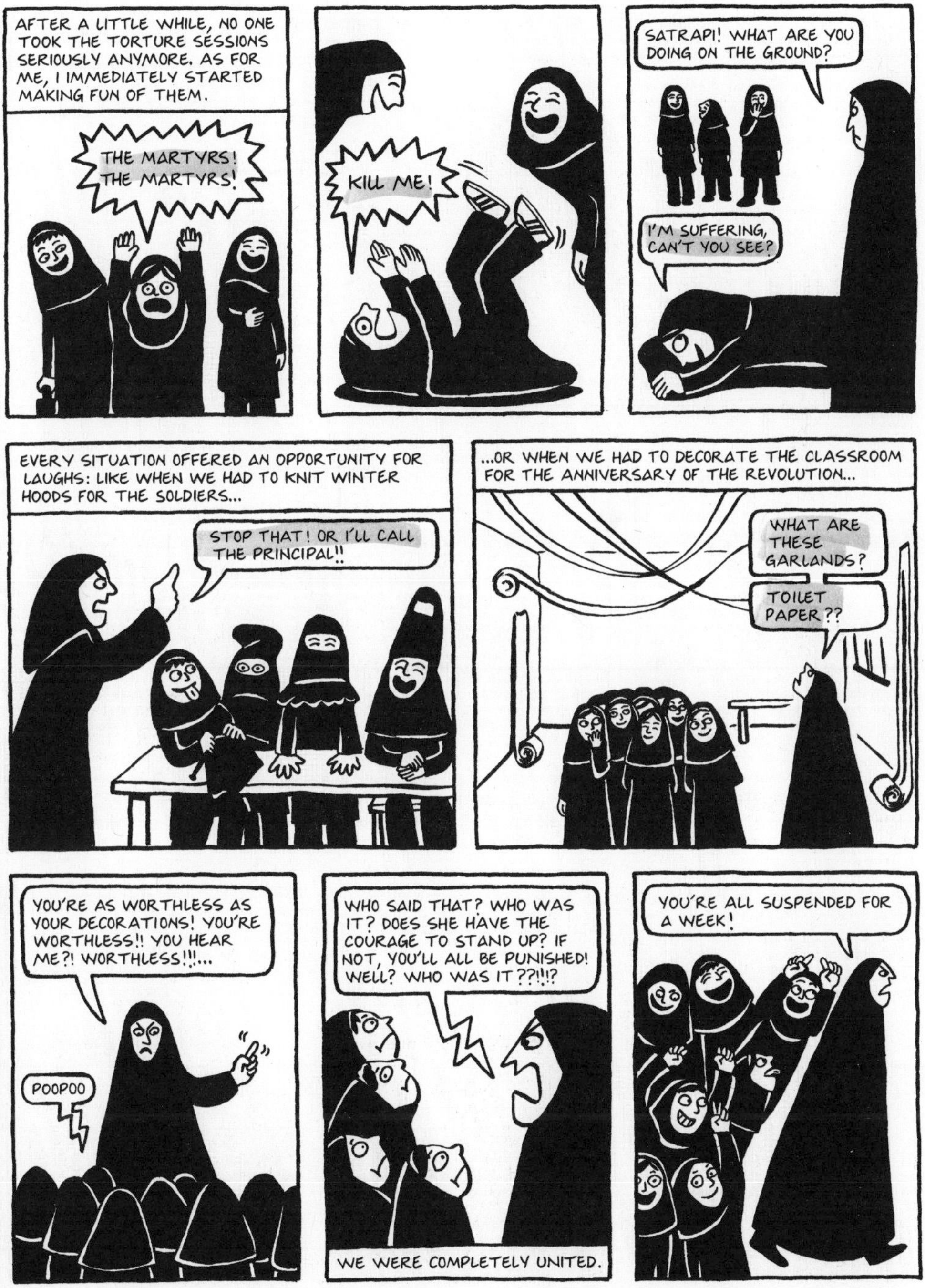

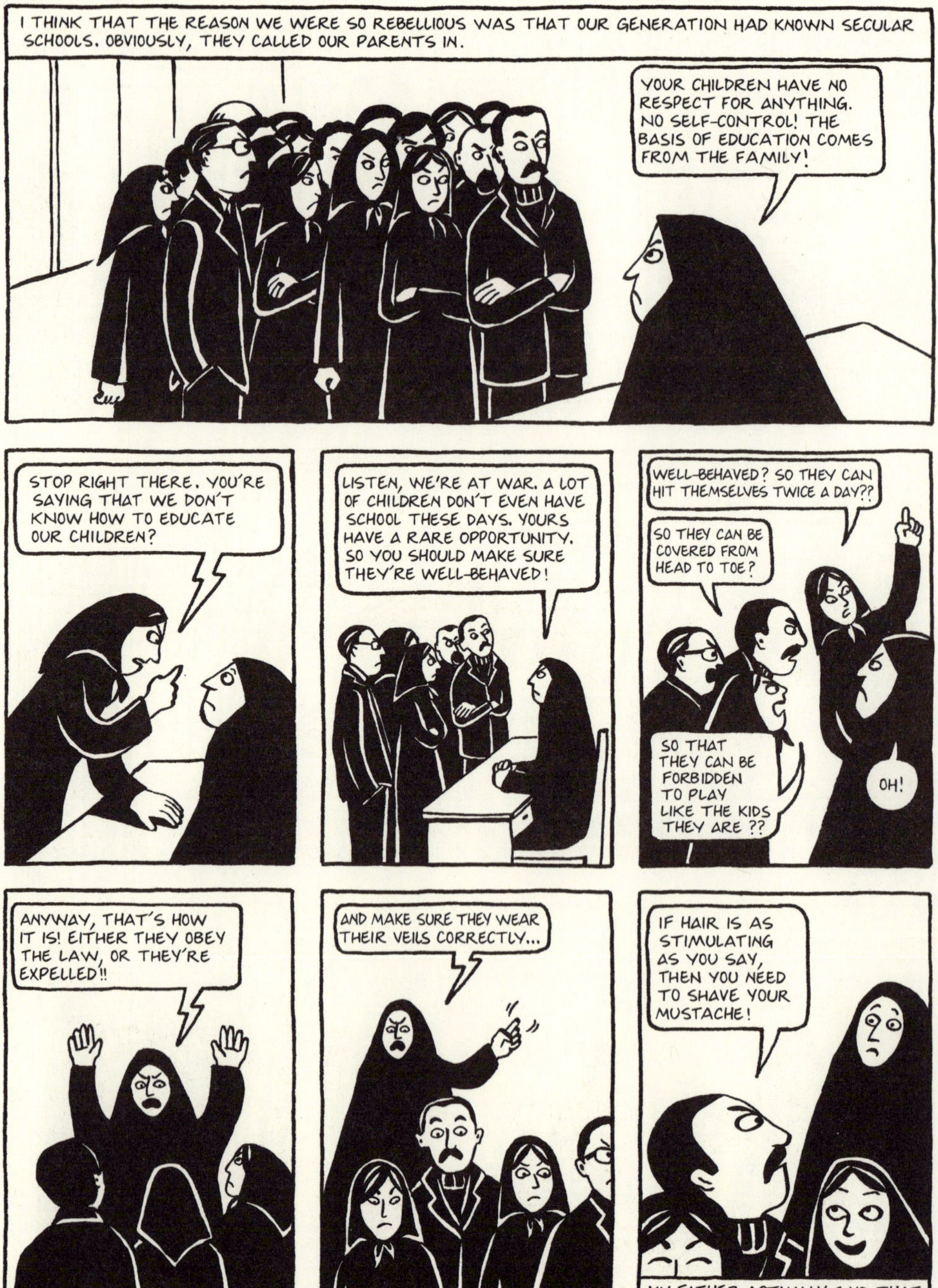
I THINK THAT THE REASON WE WERE SO REBELLIOUS WAS THAT OUR GENERATION HAD KNOWN SECULAR SCHOOLS. OBVIOUSLY, THEY CALLED OUR PARENTS IN.
YOUR CHILDREN HAVE NO RESPECT FOR ANYTHING. NO SELF-CONTROL! THE BASIS OF EDUCATION COMES FROM THE FAMILY!
STOP RIGHT THERE. YOU'RE SAYING THAT WE DON'T KNOW HOW TO EDUCATE OUR CHILDREN?
LISTEN, WE'RE AT WAR. A LOT OF CHILDREN DON'T EVEN HAVE SCHOOL THESE DAYS. YOURS HAVE A RARE OPPORTUNITY. SO YOU SHOULD MAKE SURE THEY'RE WELL-BEHAVED!
WELL-BEHAVED? SO THEY CAN HIT THEMSELVES TWICE A DAY??
SO THEY CAN BE COVERED FROM HEAD TO TOE?
SO THAT THEY CAN BE FORBIDDEN TO PLAY LIKE THE KIDS THEY ARE??
OH!
ANYWAY, THAT'S HOW IT IS! EITHER THEY OBEY THE LAW, OR THEY'RE EXPELLED!!
AND MAKE SURE THEY WEAR THEIR VEILS CORRECTLY...
IF HAIR IS AS STIMULATING AS YOU SAY, THEN YOU NEED TO SHAVE YOUR MUSTACHE!
MY FATHER ACTUALLY SAID THAT.

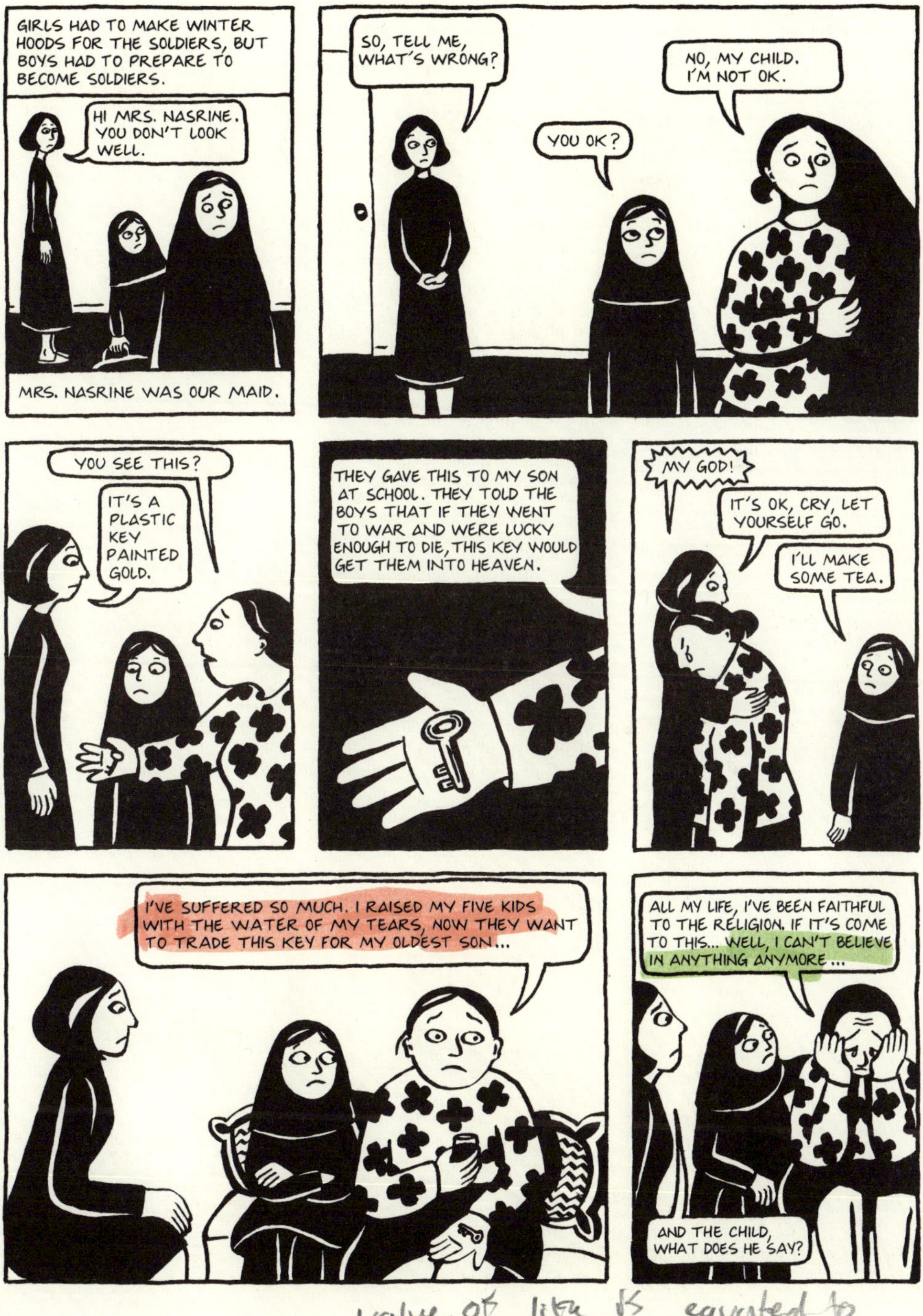

value of life is equated to an object

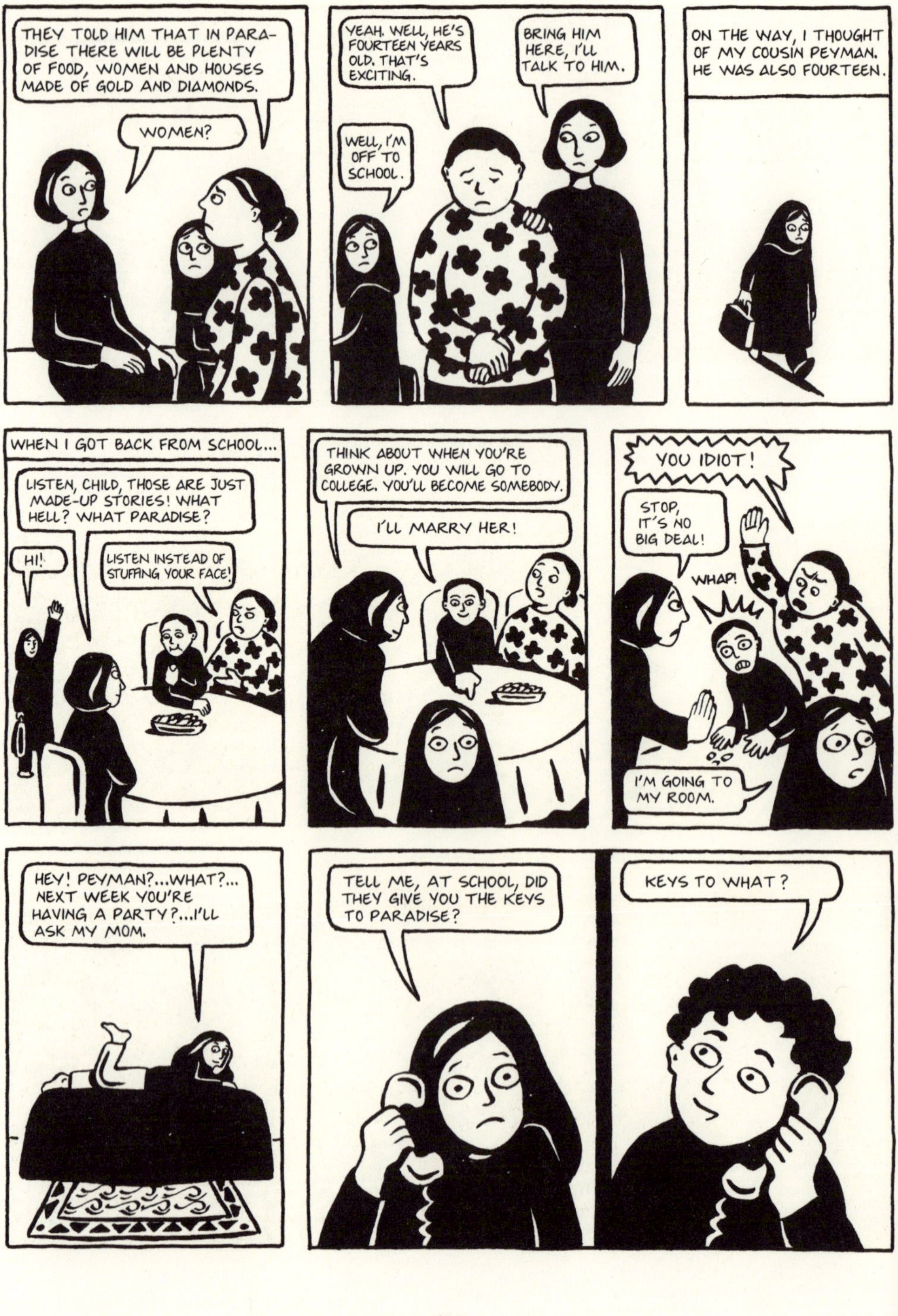
THEY TOLD HIM THAT IN PARADISE THERE WILL BE PLENTY OF FOOD, WOMEN AND HOUSES MADE OF GOLD AND DIAMONDS.
WOMEN?
YEAH. WELL, HE'S FOURTEEN YEARS OLD. THAT'S EXCITING.
BRING HIM HERE, I'LL TALK TO HIM.
WELL, I'M OFF TO SCHOOL.
ON THE WAY, I THOUGHT OF MY COUSIN PEYMAN. HE WAS ALSO FOURTEEN.
WHEN I GOT BACK FROM SCHOOL...
LISTEN, CHILD, THOSE ARE JUST MADE-UP STORIES! WHAT HELL? WHAT PARADISE?
HI!
LISTEN INSTEAD OF STUFFING YOUR FACE!
THINK ABOUT WHEN YOU'RE GROWN UP. YOU WILL GO TO COLLEGE. YOU'LL BECOME SOMEBODY.
I'LL MARRY HER!
YOU IDIOT!
STOP, IT'S NO BIG DEAL!
WHAP!
I'M GOING TO MY ROOM.
HEY! PEYMAN?...WHAT?... NEXT WEEK YOU'RE HAVING A PARTY?...I'LL ASK MY MOM.
TELL ME, AT SCHOOL, DID THEY GIVE YOU THE KEYS TO PARADISE?
KEYS TO WHAT?

gov will do anything to win

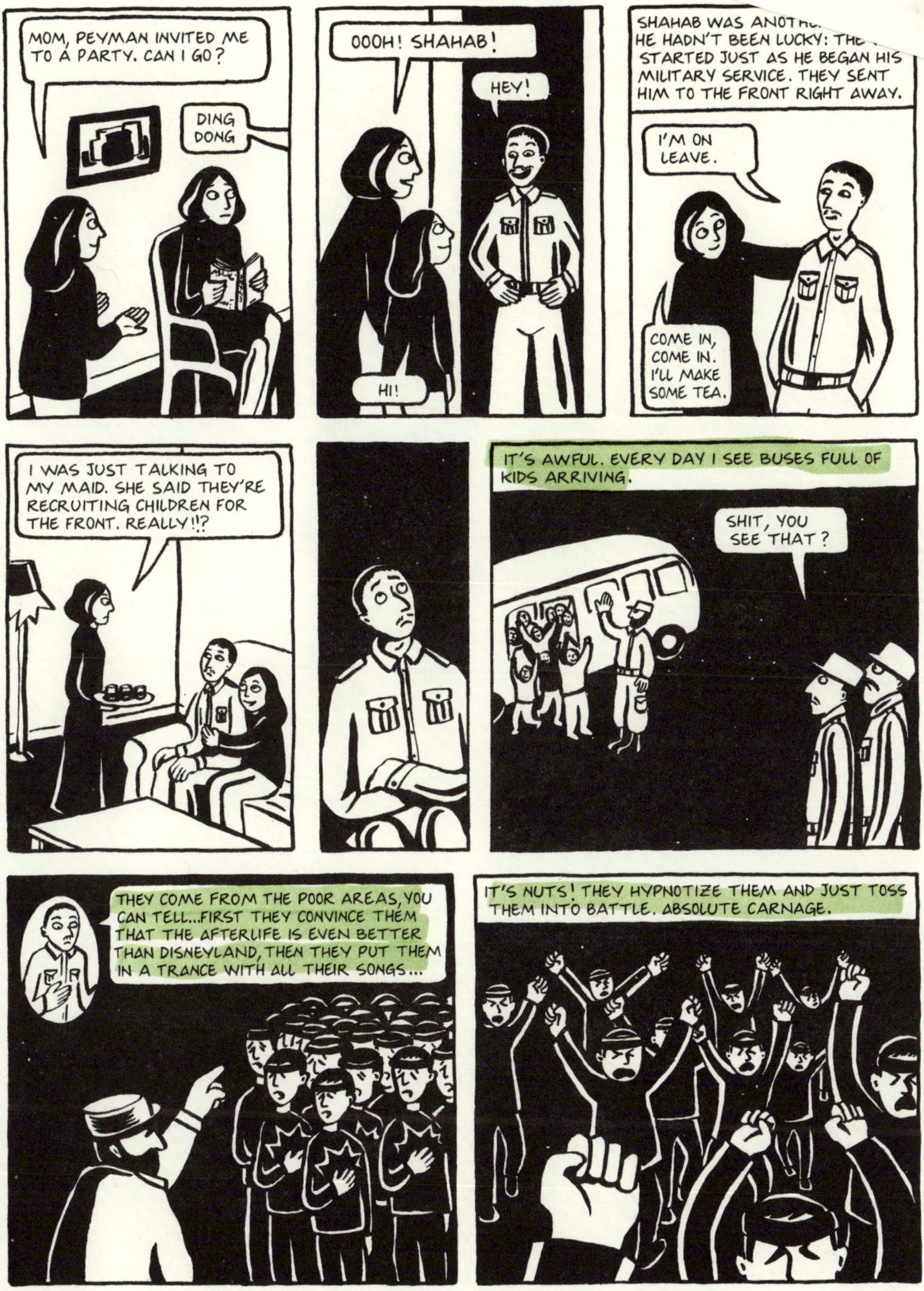

Contrast between the 2 pictures, Irony.

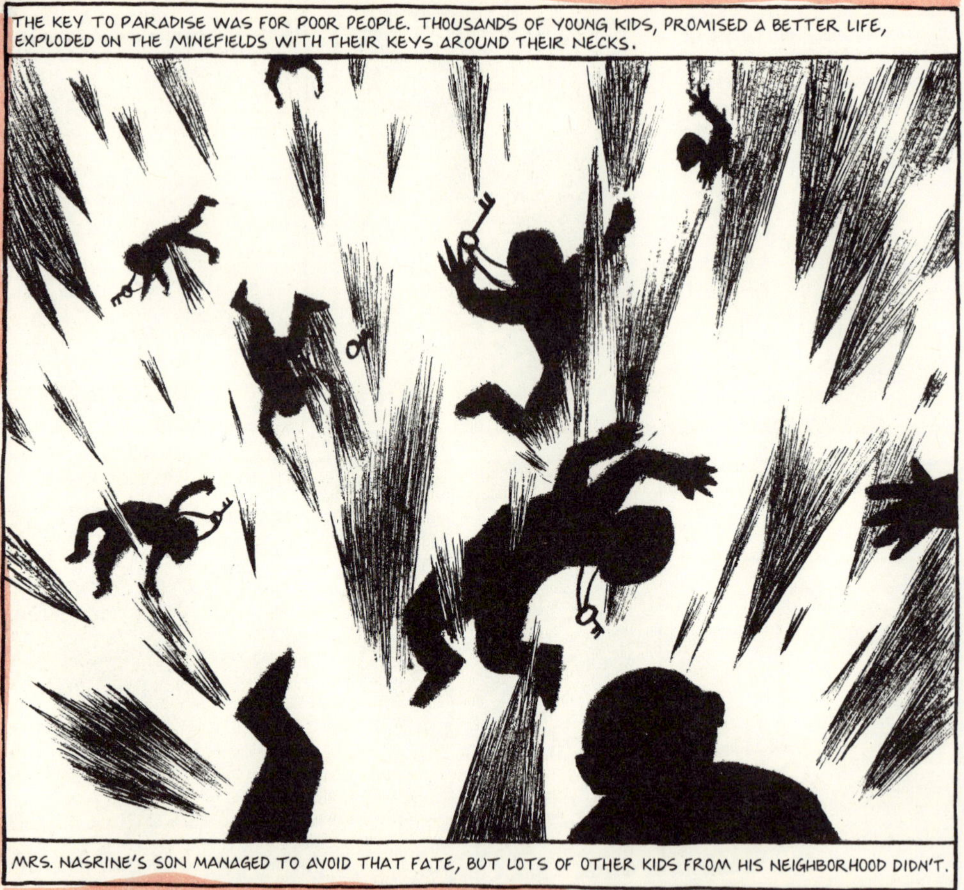
THE KEY TO PARADISE WAS FOR POOR PEOPLE. THOUSANDS OF YOUNG KIDS, PROMISED A BETTER LIFE, EXPLODED ON THE MINEFIELDS WITH THEIR KEYS AROUND THEIR NECKS.
MRS. NASRINE'S SON MANAGED TO AVOID THAT FATE, BUT LOTS OF OTHER KIDS FROM HIS NEIGHBORHOOD DIDN'T.

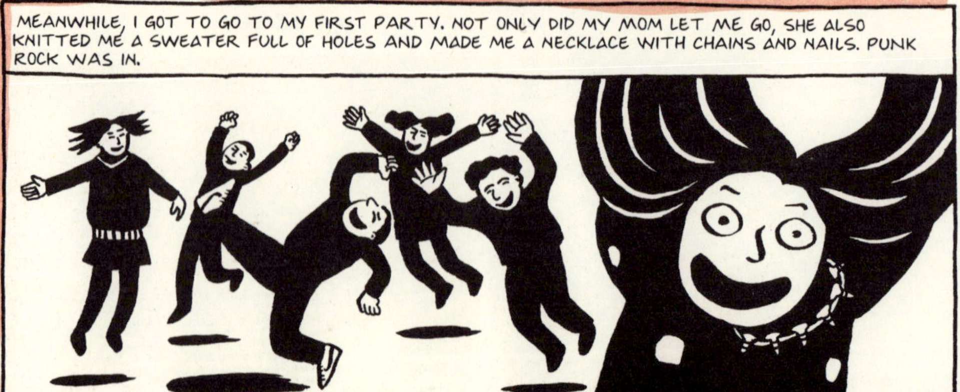
MEANWHILE, I GOT TO GO TO MY FIRST PARTY. NOT ONLY DID MY MOM LET ME GO, SHE ALSO KNITTED ME A SWEATER FULL OF HOLES AND MADE ME A NECKLACE WITH CHAINS AND NAILS. PUNK ROCK WAS IN.
I WAS LOOKING SHARP.

THE WINE

AFTER THE BORDER TOWNS, TEHRAN BECAME THE BOMBERS' MAIN TARGET. TOGETHER WITH THE OTHER PEOPLE IN OUR BUILDING, WE TURNED THE BASEMENT INTO A SHELTER. EVERY TIME THE SIREN RANG OUT, EVERYONE WOULD RUN DOWNSTAIRS...

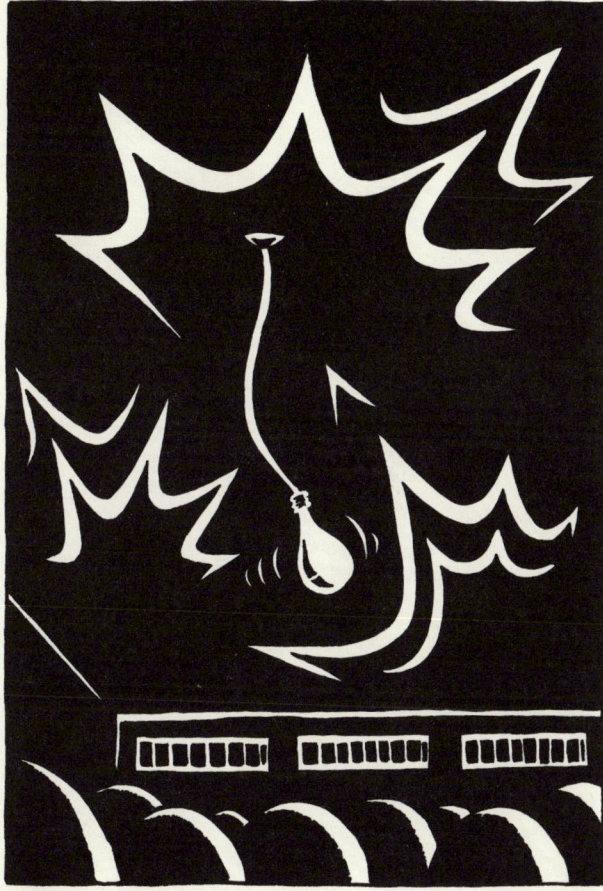

PUT YOUR CIGARETTE OUT. THEY SAY THAT THE GLOW OF A CIGARETTE IS THE EASIEST THING TO SEE FROM THE SKY.

BUT WE'RE IN THE BASEMENT HERE!

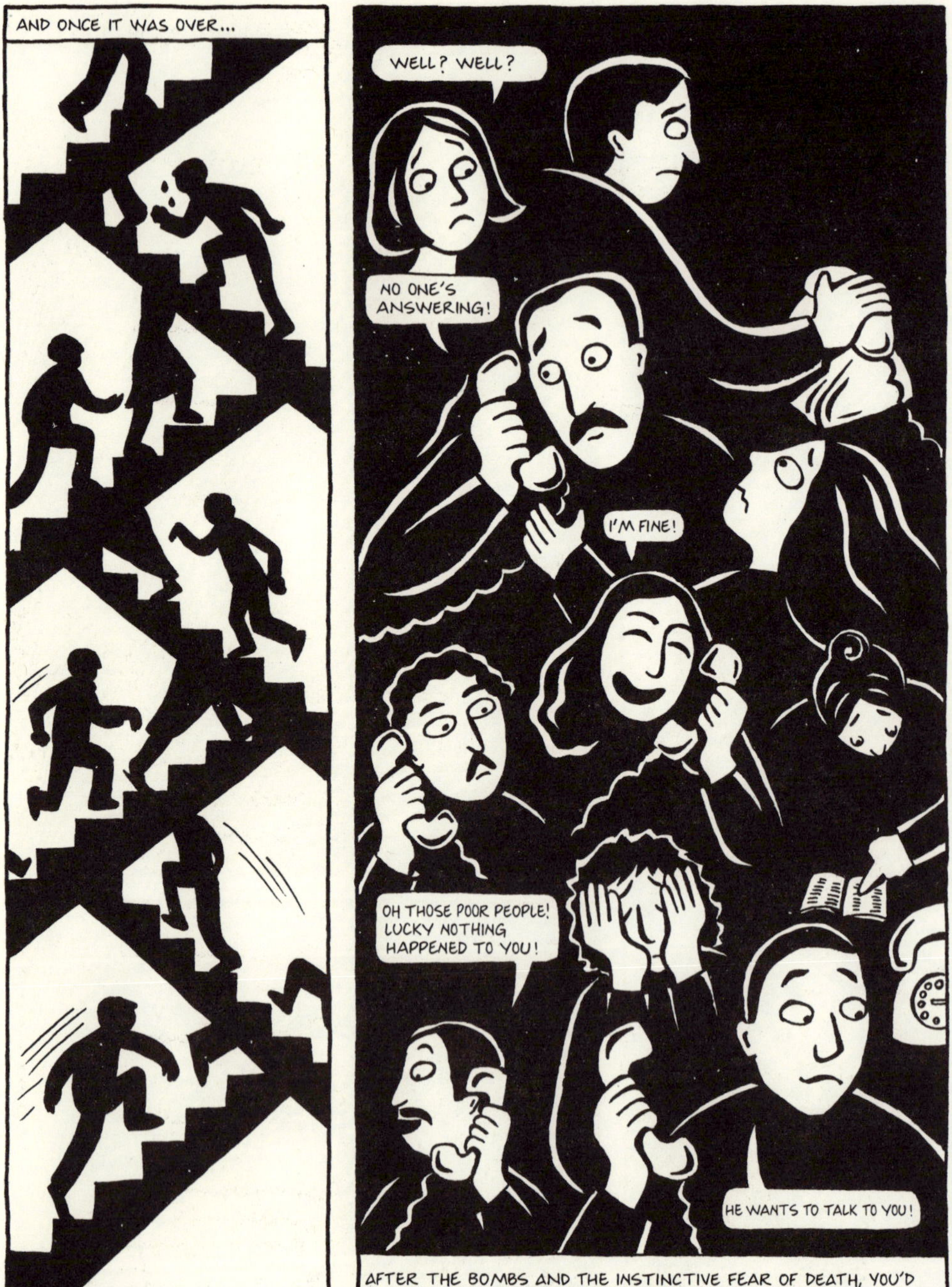
AND ONCE IT WAS OVER...
WELL? WELL?
NO ONE'S ANSWERING!
I'M FINE!
OH THOSE POOR PEOPLE! LUCKY NOTHING HAPPENED TO YOU!
HE WANTS TO TALK TO YOU!
AFTER THE BOMBS AND THE INSTINCTIVE FEAR OF DEATH, YOU'D THINK OF THE VICTIMS AND ANOTHER KIND OF ANXIETY SEIZED YOU.

restrictions on the people to "protect" them, however they treat their people unjustly

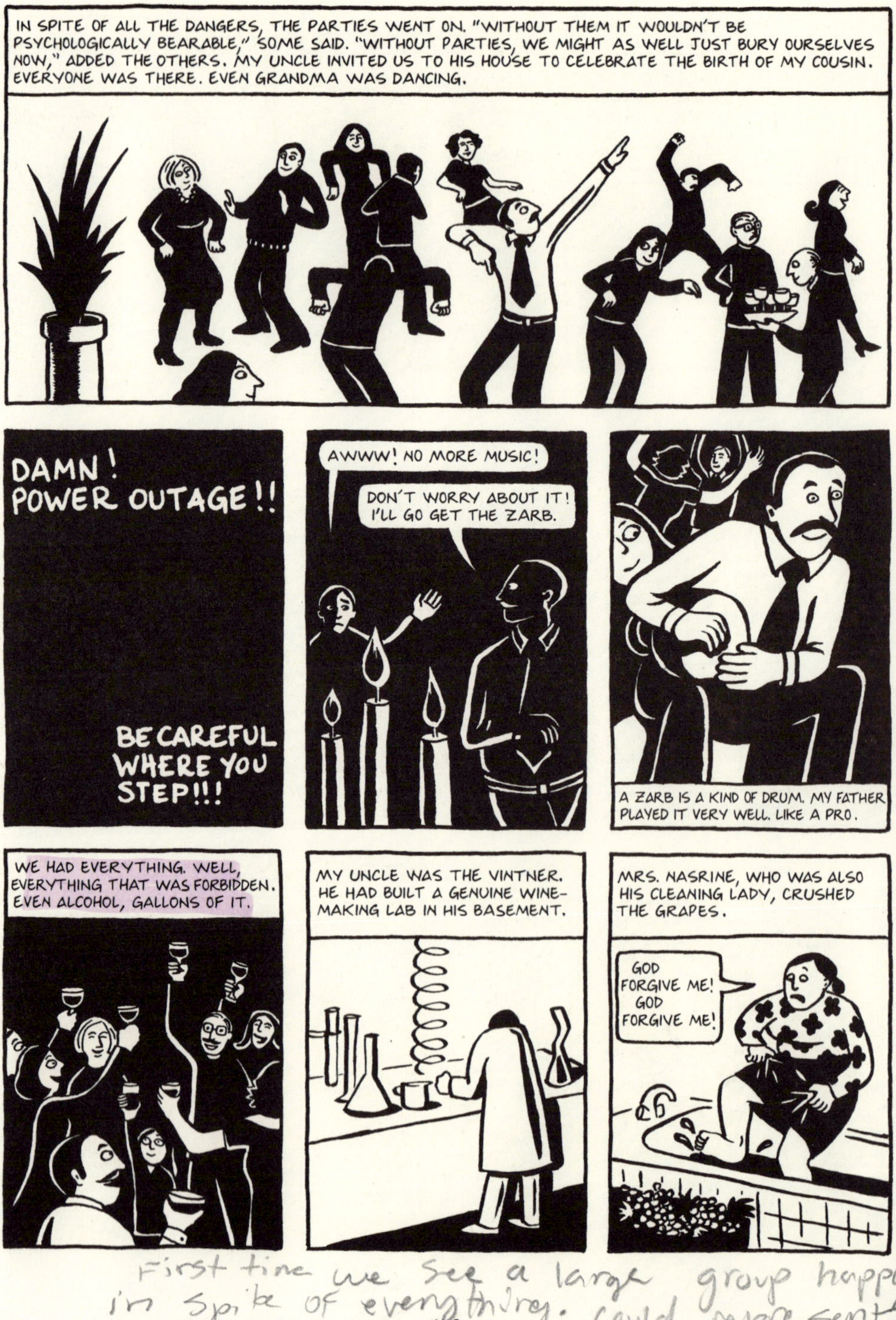

First time we see a large group happy in spite of everything. Could represent hope

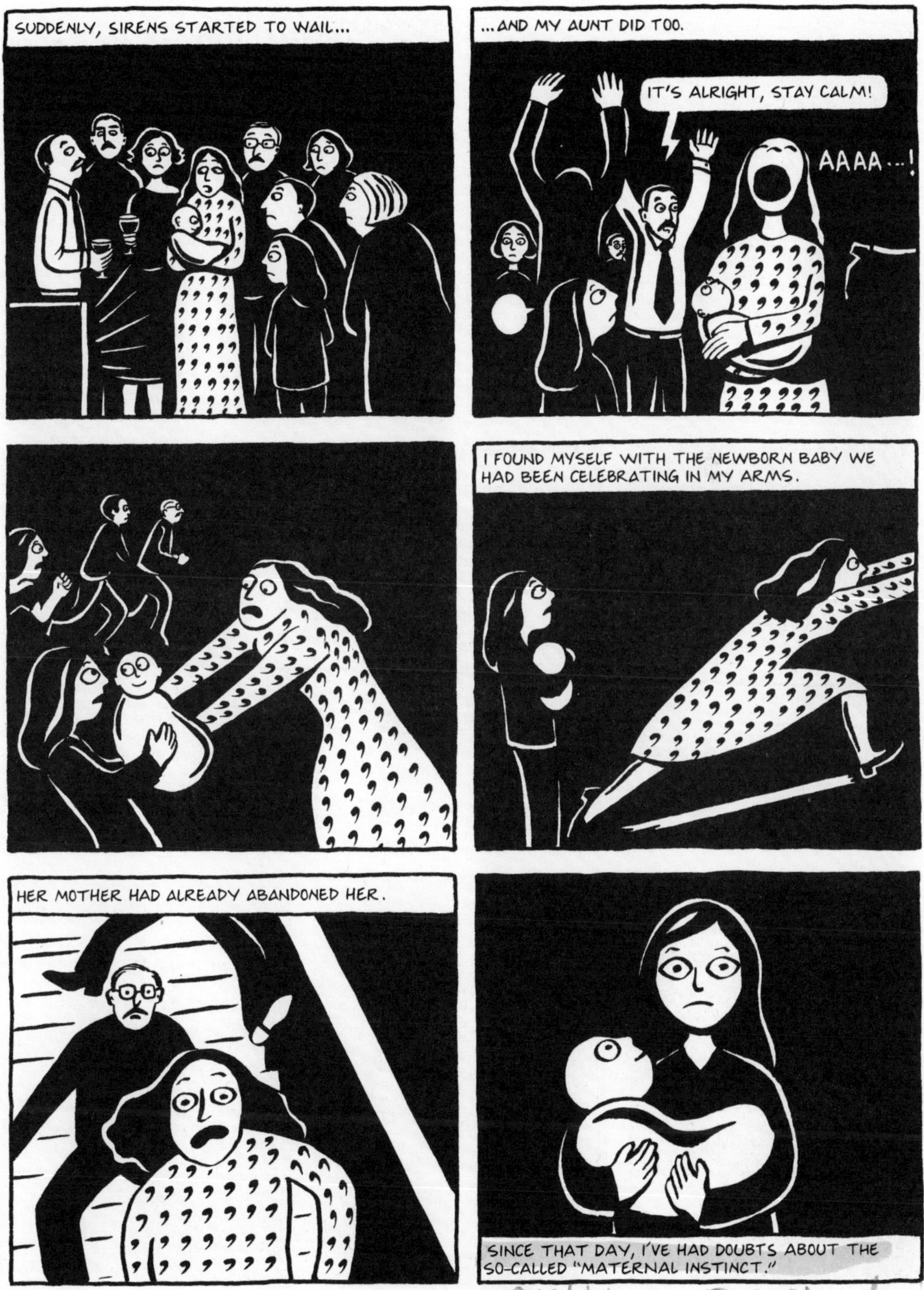

upsetting Foreshadowing on how her parents send her away

all normal interactions turn hostile.
war changes people

← humanity is replaced with rage, and theres little you can do in face of it

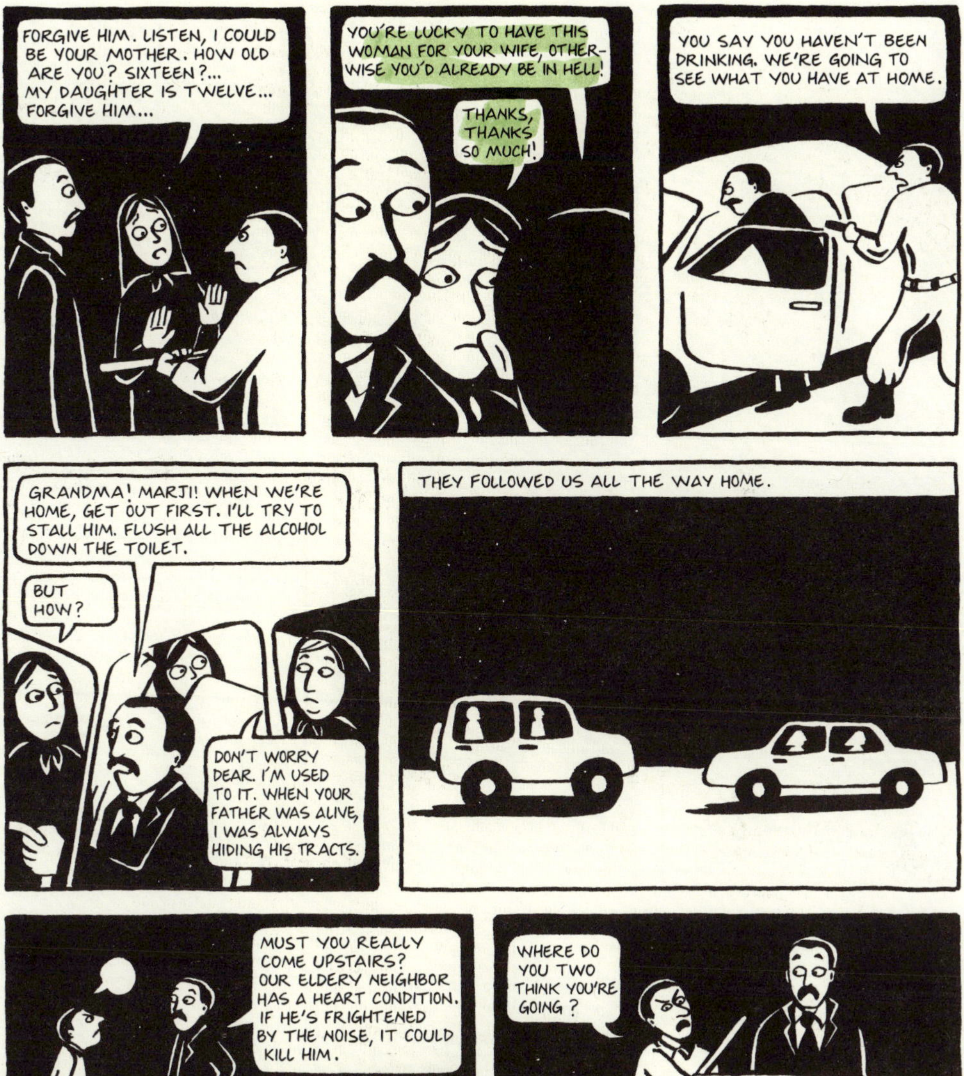
FORGIVE HIM. LISTEN, I COULD BE YOUR MOTHER. HOW OLD ARE YOU? SIXTEEN?... MY DAUGHTER IS TWELVE... FORGIVE HIM...
YOU'RE LUCKY TO HAVE THIS WOMAN FOR YOUR WIFE, OTHERWISE YOU'D ALREADY BE IN HELL!
THANKS, THANKS SO MUCH!
YOU SAY YOU HAVEN'T BEEN DRINKING. WE'RE GOING TO SEE WHAT YOU HAVE AT HOME.
GRANDMA! MARJI! WHEN WE'RE HOME, GET OUT FIRST. I'LL TRY TO STALL HIM. FLUSH ALL THE ALCOHOL DOWN THE TOILET.
BUT HOW?
DON'T WORRY DEAR. I'M USED TO IT. WHEN YOUR FATHER WAS ALIVE, I WAS ALWAYS HIDING HIS TRACTS.
THEY FOLLOWED US ALL THE WAY HOME.
MUST YOU REALLY COME UPSTAIRS? OUR ELDERY NEIGHBOR HAS A HEART CONDITION. IF HE'S FRIGHTENED BY THE NOISE, IT COULD KILL HIM.
HURRY UP!
WHERE DO YOU TWO THINK YOU'RE GOING?

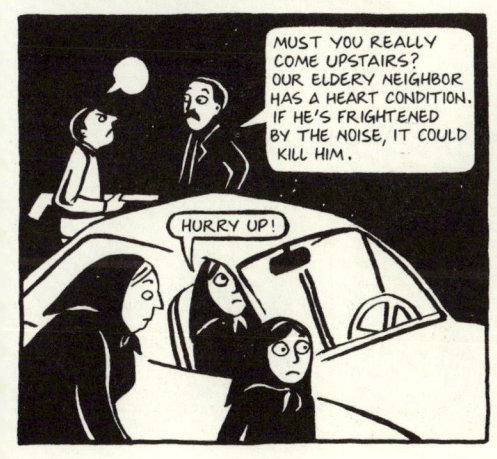

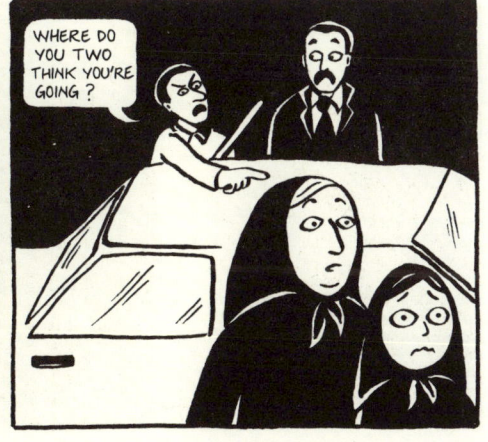

restrictions were never
about the people

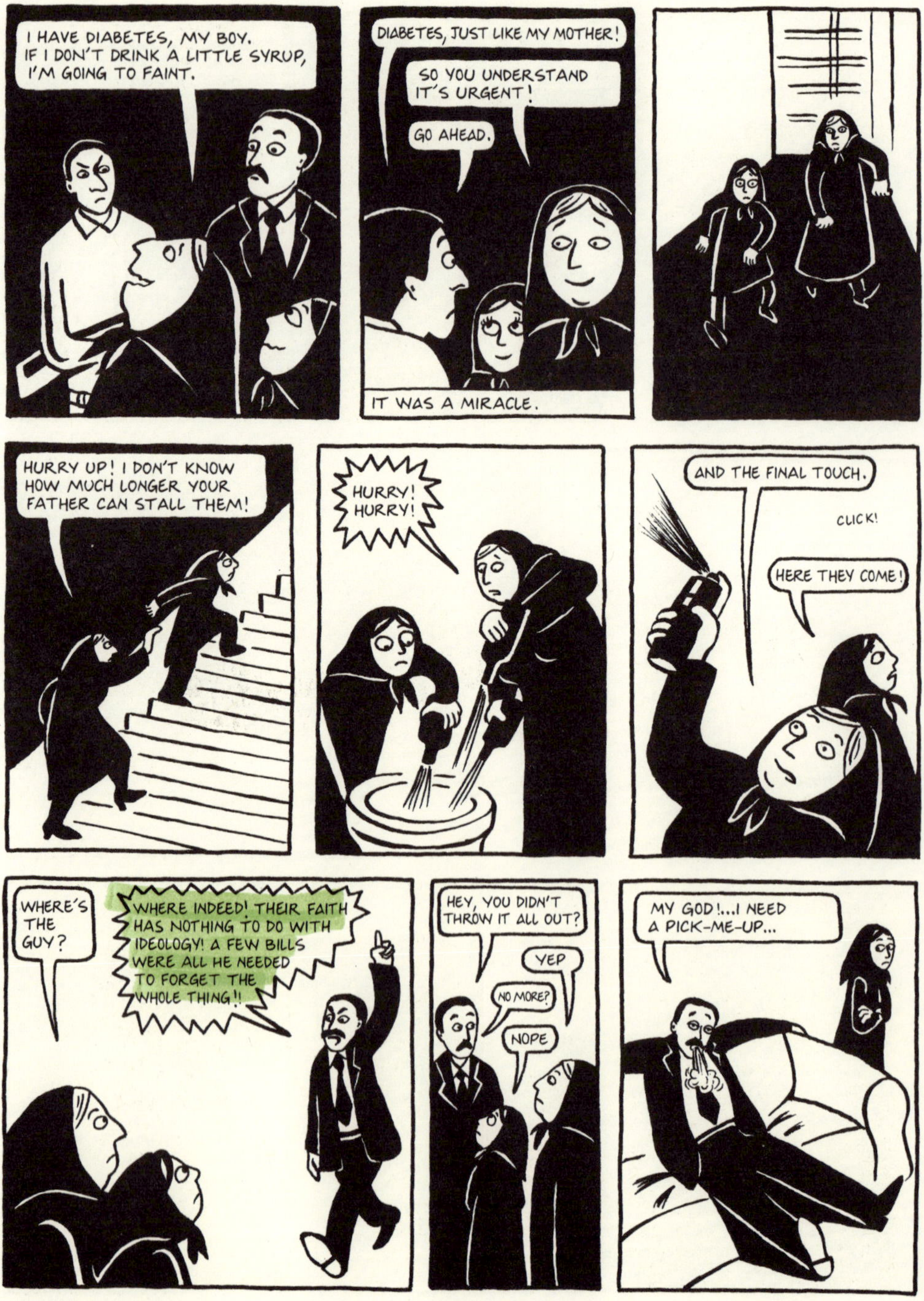

THE CIGARETTE

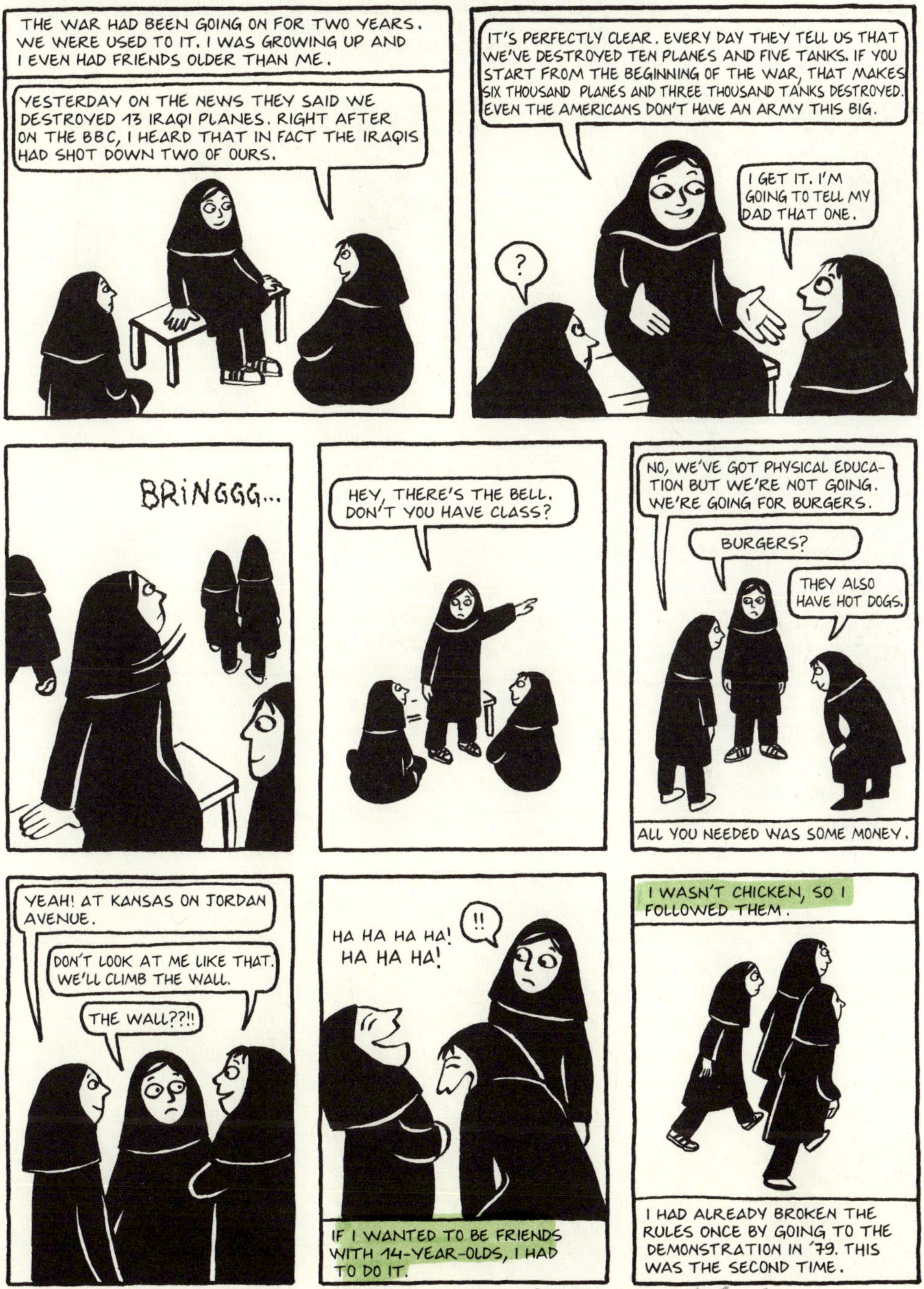

Peer pressure, works because she's already lost so much she craves familiarity

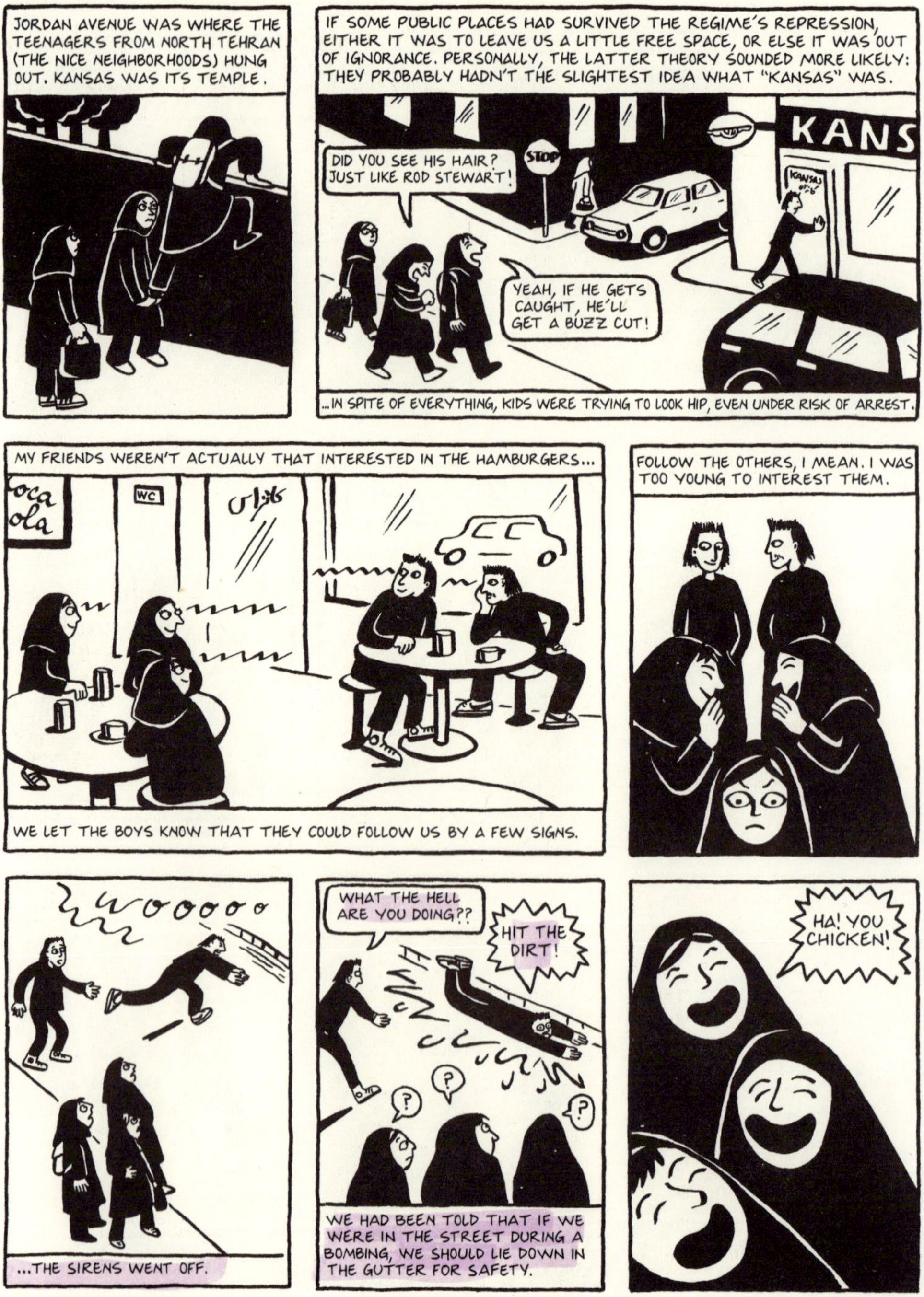
JORDAN AVENUE WAS WHERE THE TEENAGERS FROM NORTH TEHRAN (THE NICE NEIGHBORHOODS) HUNG OUT. KANSAS WAS ITS TEMPLE.
IF SOME PUBLIC PLACES HAD SURVIVED THE REGIME'S REPRESSION, EITHER IT WAS TO LEAVE US A LITTLE FREE SPACE, OR ELSE IT WAS OUT OF IGNORANCE. PERSONALLY, THE LATTER THEORY SOUNDED MORE LIKELY: THEY PROBABLY HADN'T THE SLIGHTEST IDEA WHAT "KANSAS" WAS.
STOP
KANS
DID YOU SEE HIS HAIR? JUST LIKE ROD STEWART!
YEAH, IF HE GETS CAUGHT, HE'LL GET A BUZZ CUT!
...IN SPITE OF EVERYTHING, KIDS WERE TRYING TO LOOK HIP, EVEN UNDER RISK OF ARREST.
MY FRIENDS WEREN'T ACTUALLY THAT INTERESTED IN THE HAMBURGERS...
WC
WE LET THE BOYS KNOW THAT THEY COULD FOLLOW US BY A FEW SIGNS.
FOLLOW THE OTHERS, I MEAN. I WAS TOO YOUNG TO INTEREST THEM.
WOOOOO
...THE SIRENS WENT OFF.
WHAT THE HELL ARE YOU DOING??
HIT THE DIRT!
?
?
?
WE HAD BEEN TOLD THAT IF WE WERE IN THE STREET DURING A BOMBING, WE SHOULD LIE DOWN IN THE GUTTER FOR SAFETY.
HA! YOU CHICKEN!

war has been so normalized that fear is not an immidiate reaction to danger anymore

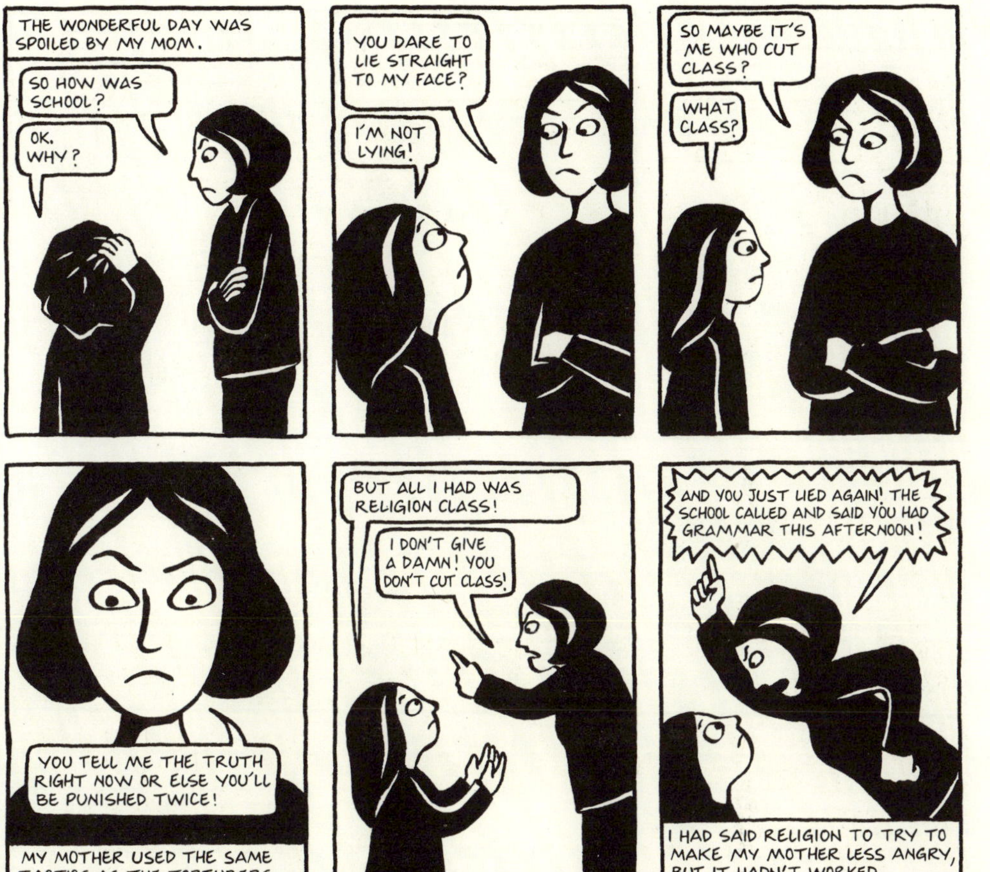

Symbolizes her becoming more independent and leaving her guidance behind, she's growing up.

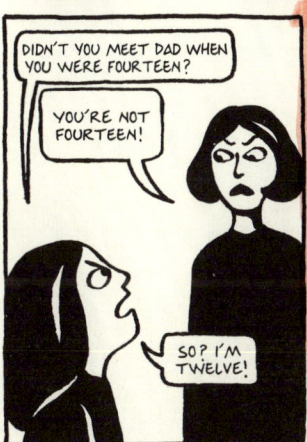

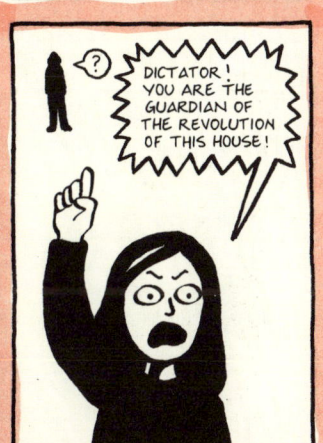

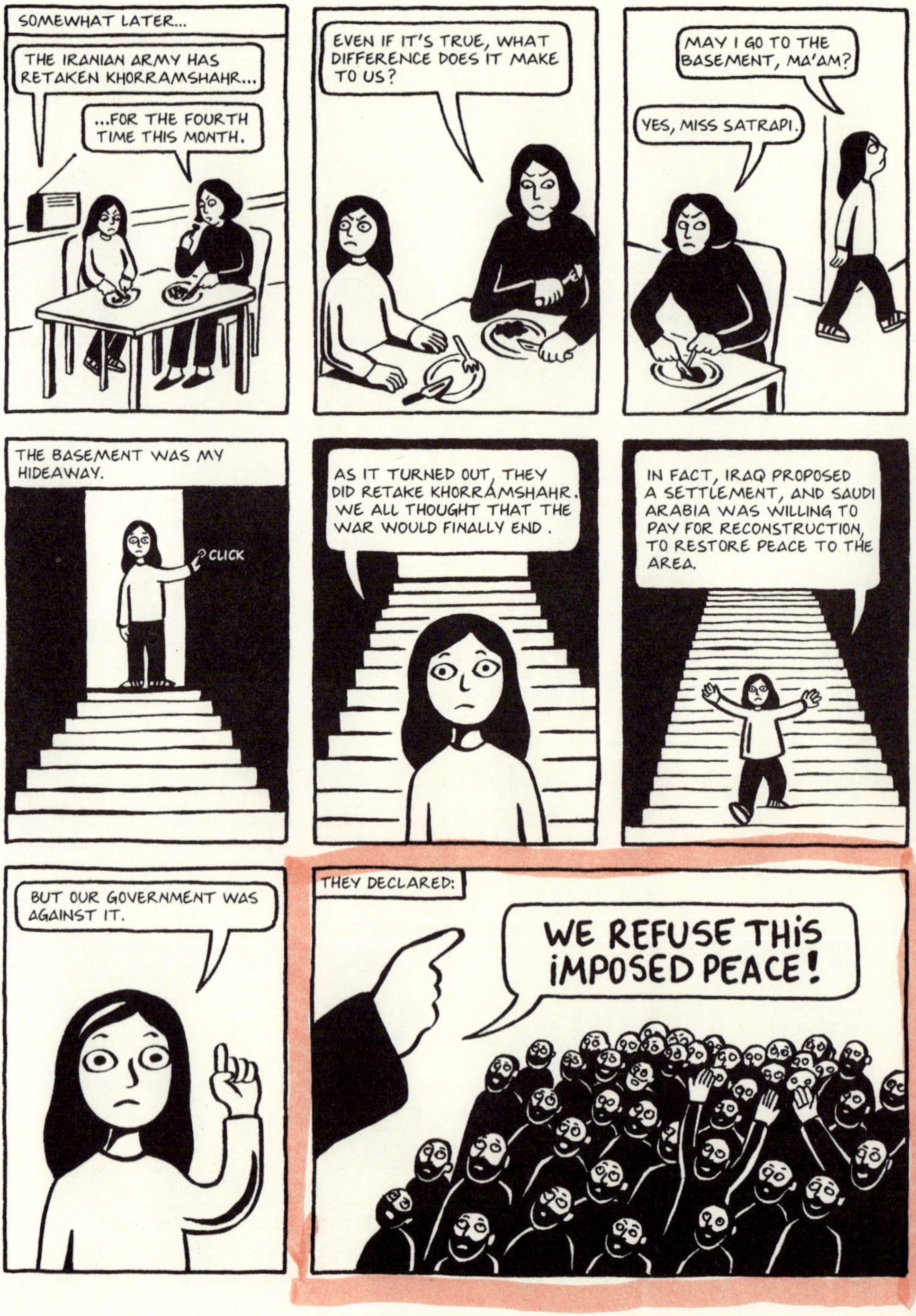

no one is happy, dread is created

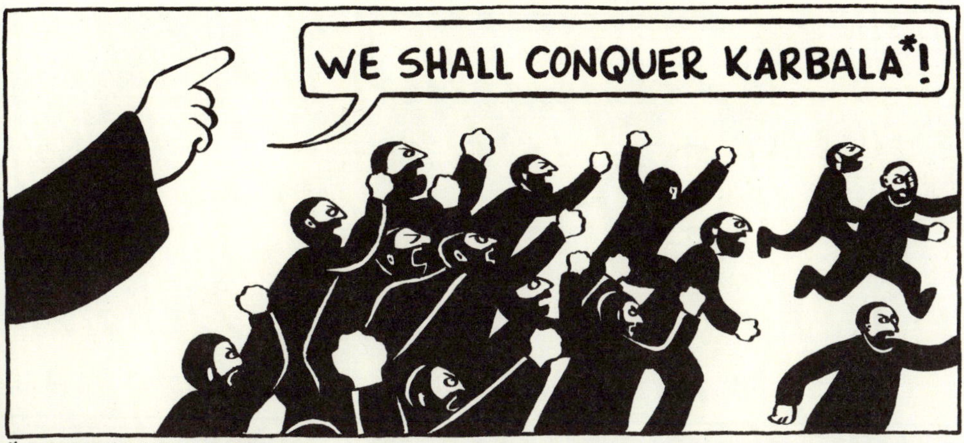
WE SHALL CONQUER KARBALA*!

* A SHIITE HOLY CITY IN IRAQ

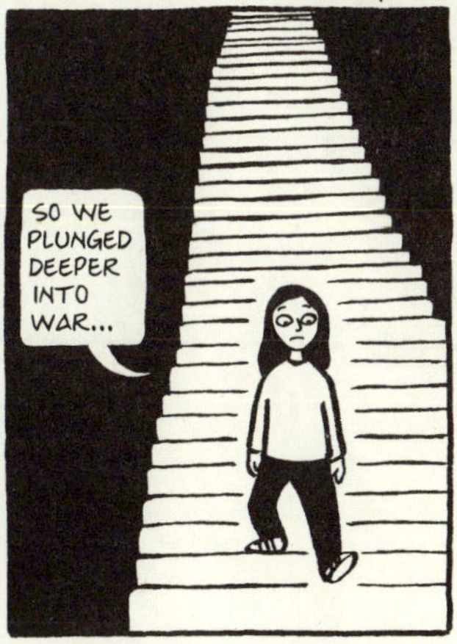
SO WE PLUNGED DEEPER INTO WAR...

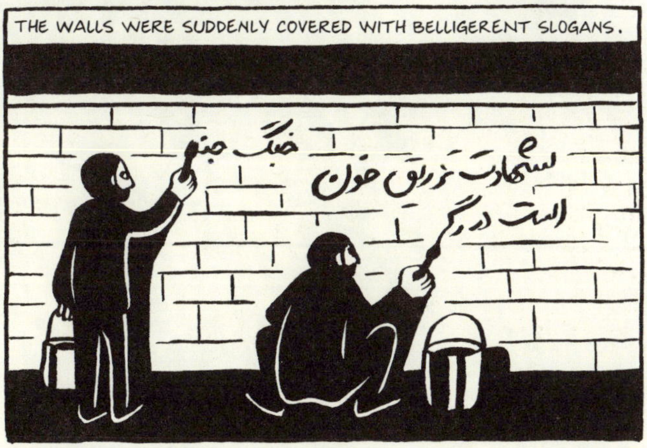
THE WALLS WERE SUDDENLY COVERED WITH BELLIGERENT SLOGANS.

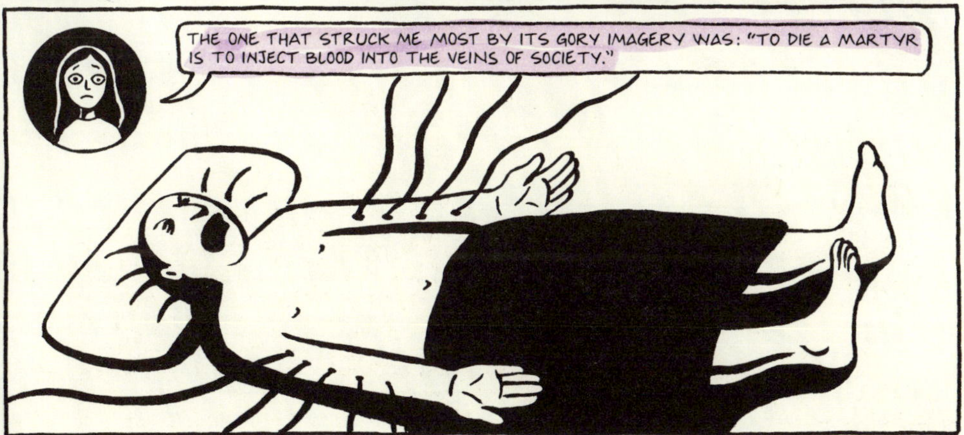
THE ONE THAT STRUCK ME MOST BY ITS GORY IMAGERY WAS: "TO DIE A MARTYR IS TO INJECT BLOOD INTO THE VEINS OF SOCIETY."

death is used as a political pawn

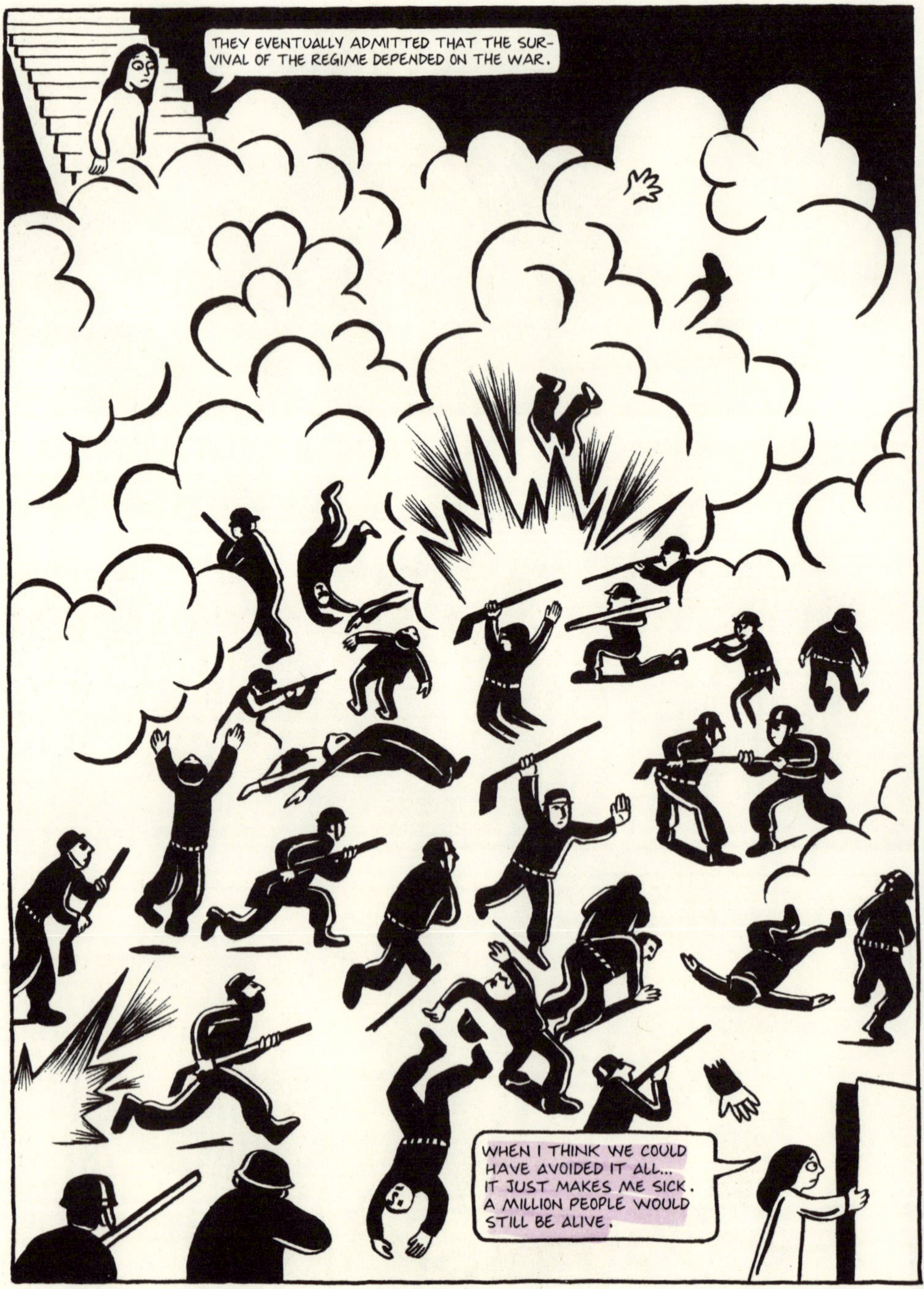
THEY EVENTUALLY ADMITTED THAT THE SURVIVAL OF THE REGIME DEPENDED ON THE WAR.
WHEN I THINK WE COULD HAVE AVOIDED IT ALL... IT JUST MAKES ME SICK. A MILLION PEOPLE WOULD STILL BE ALIVE.

makes the reader feel hopless at a seemingly impossible situation.

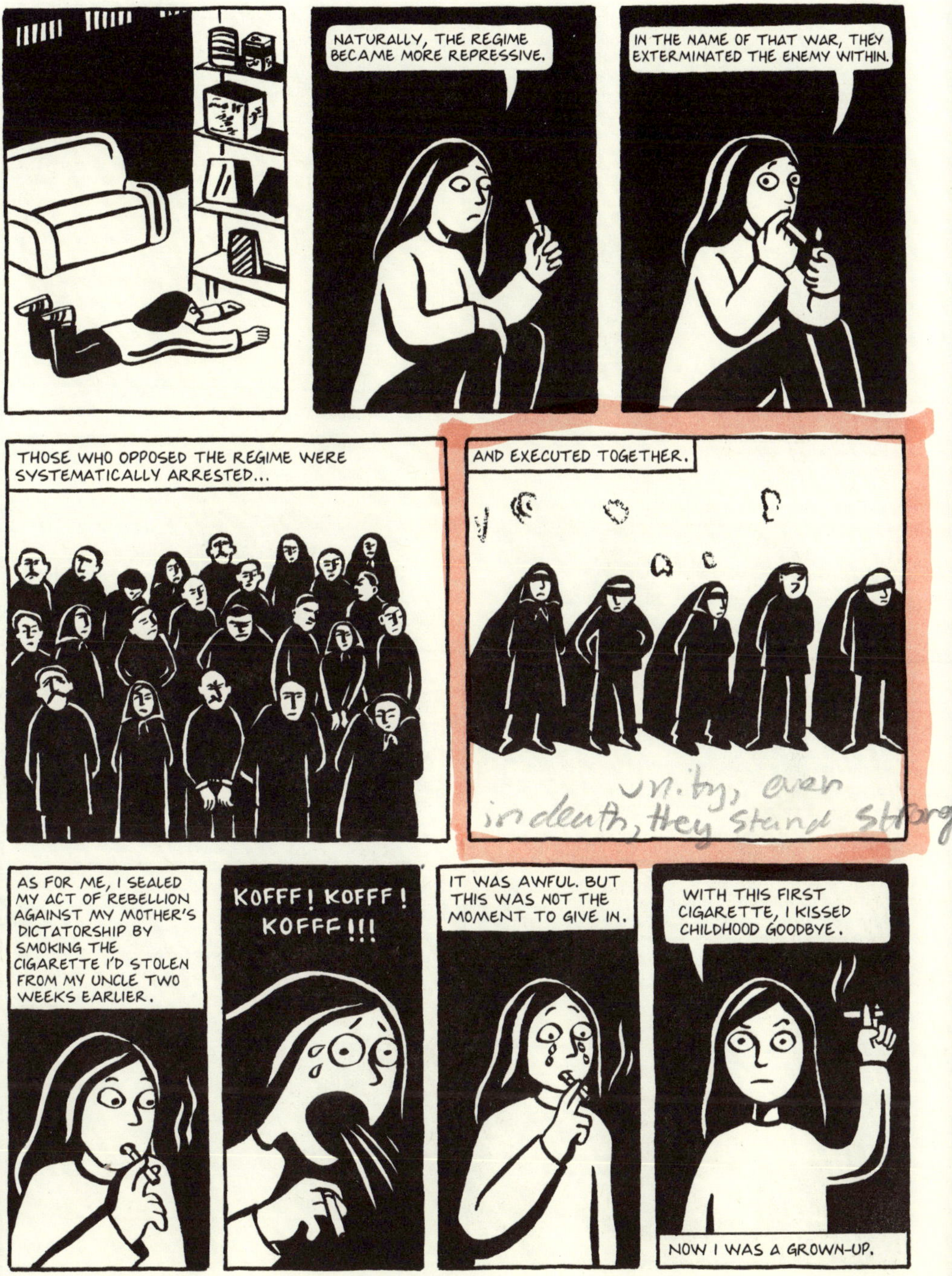
NATURALLY, THE REGIME BECAME MORE REPRESSIVE.
IN THE NAME OF THAT WAR, THEY EXTERMINATED THE ENEMY WITHIN.
THOSE WHO OPPOSED THE REGIME WERE SYSTEMATICALLY ARRESTED...
AND EXECUTED TOGETHER.
unity, even in death, they stand strong
AS FOR ME, I SEALED MY ACT OF REBELLION AGAINST MY MOTHER'S DICTATORSHIP BY SMOKING THE CIGARETTE I'D STOLEN FROM MY UNCLE TWO WEEKS EARLIER.
KOFFF! KOFFF! KOFFF!!!
IT WAS AWFUL. BUT THIS WAS NOT THE MOMENT TO GIVE IN.
WITH THIS FIRST CIGARETTE, I KISSED CHILDHOOD GOODBYE.
NOW I WAS A GROWN-UP.

THE PASSPORT

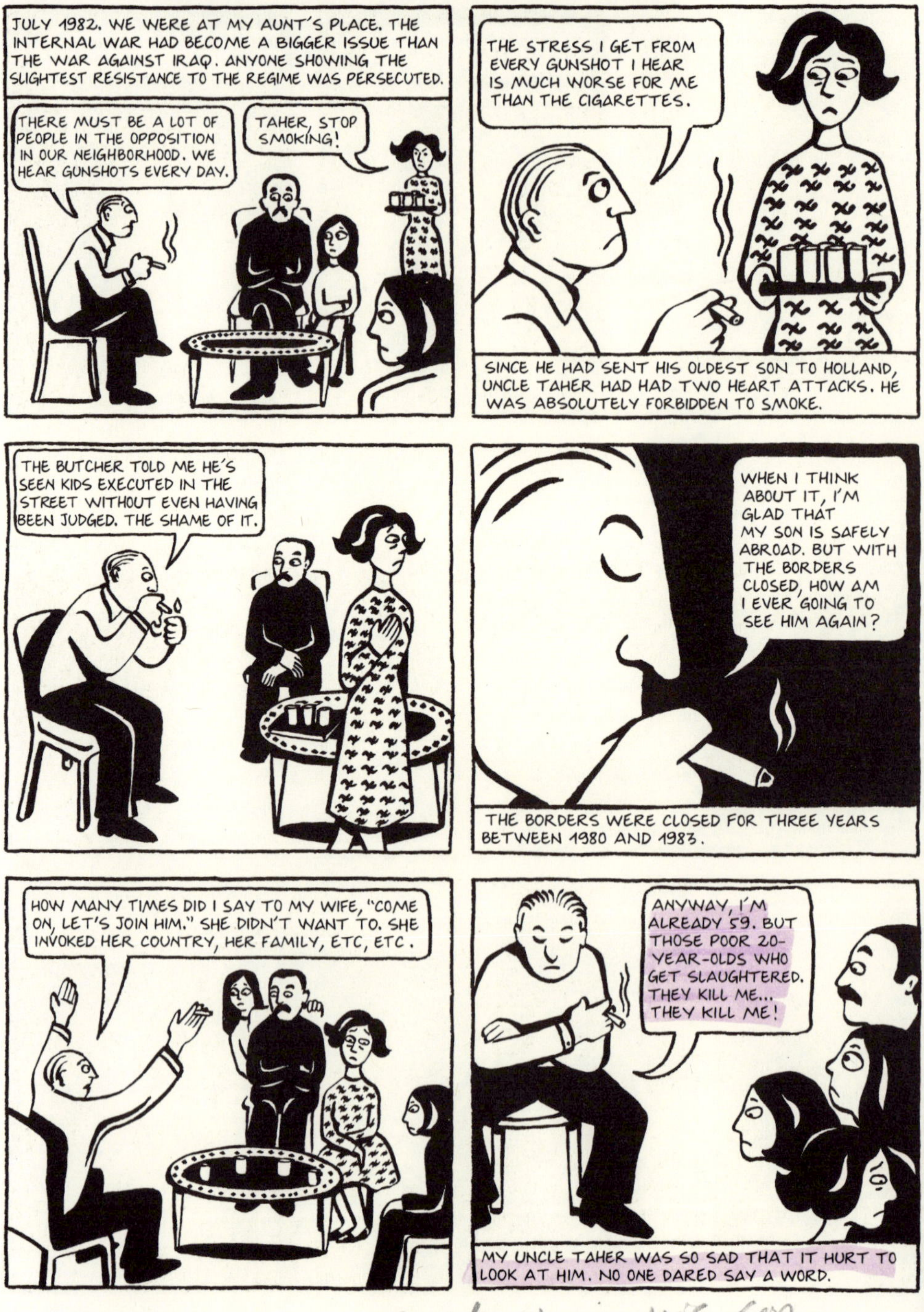

Couldhe been it's son

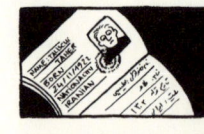

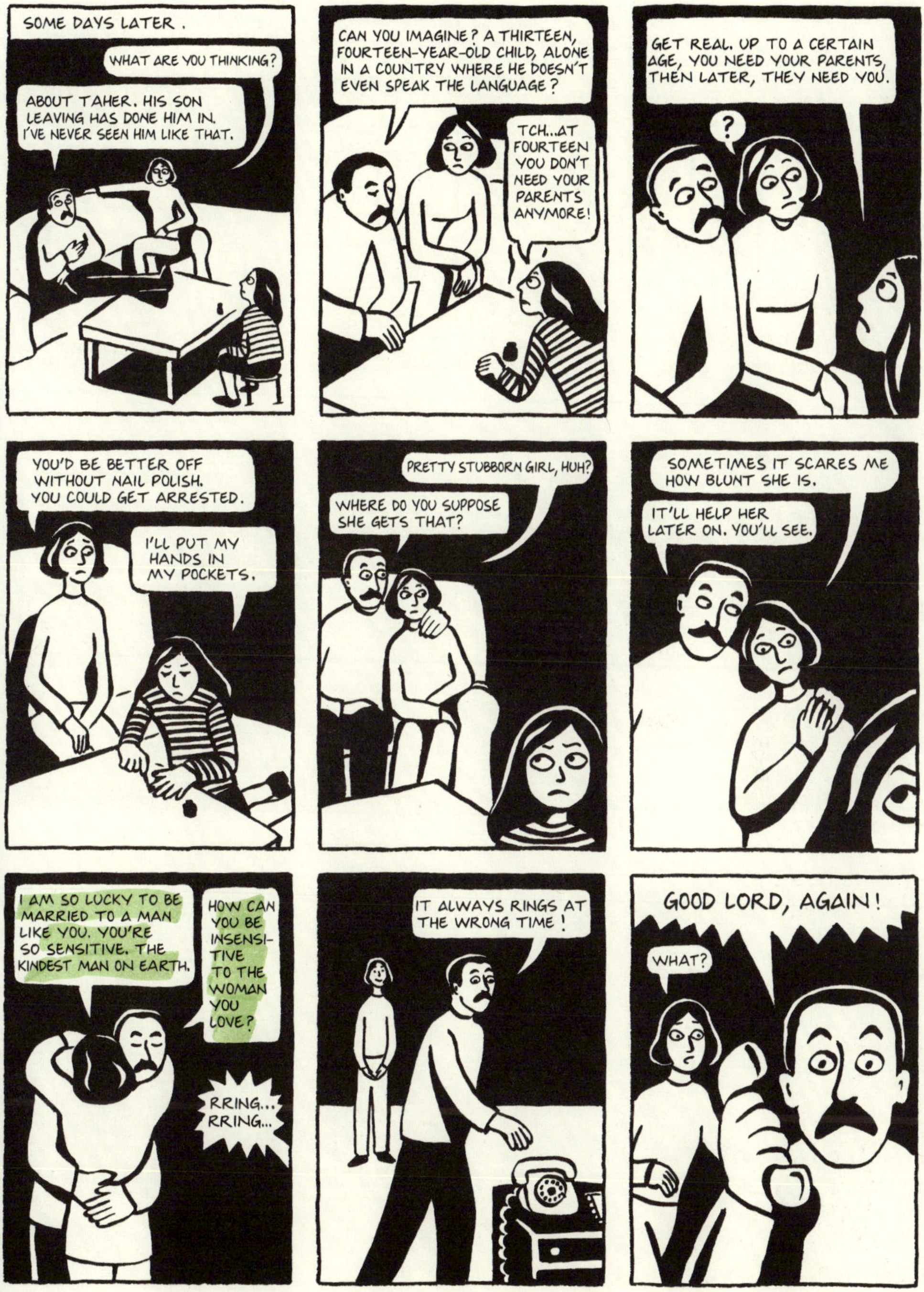

Find happiness in the face of war, it's what makes life worth living

visual imagery makes the reader see how everyone is affected, gives somewhat of a perspective

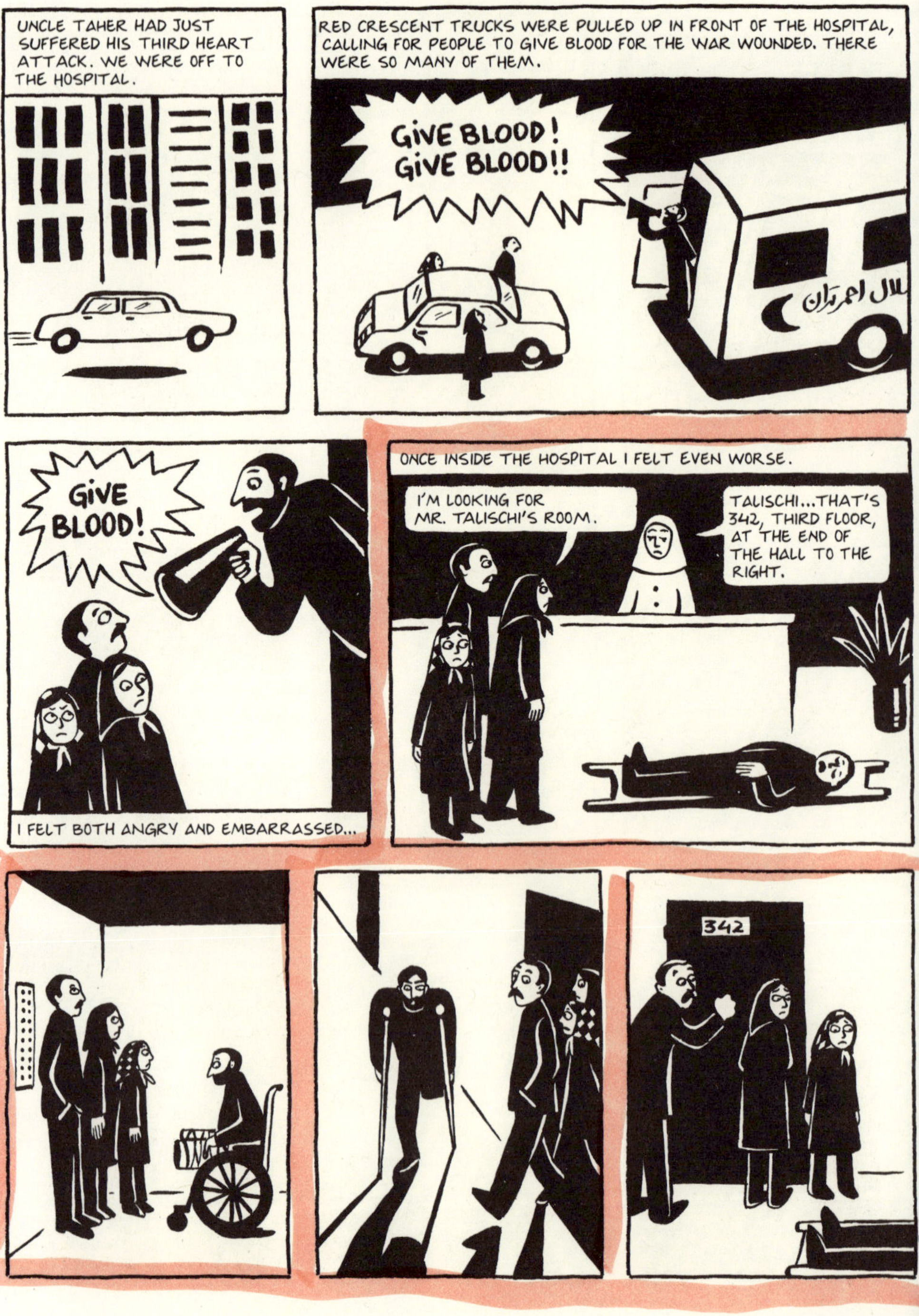

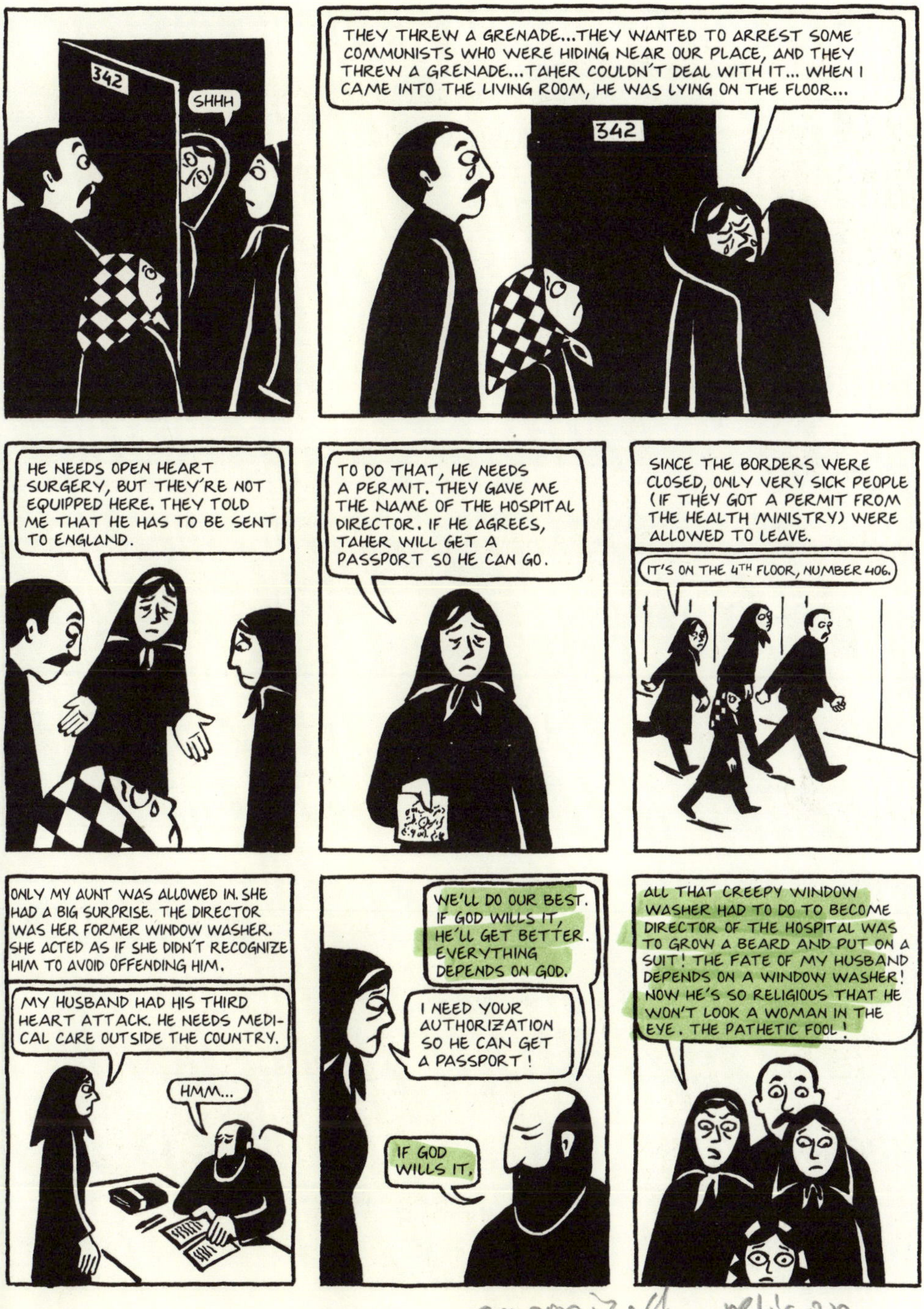

weaponized religon

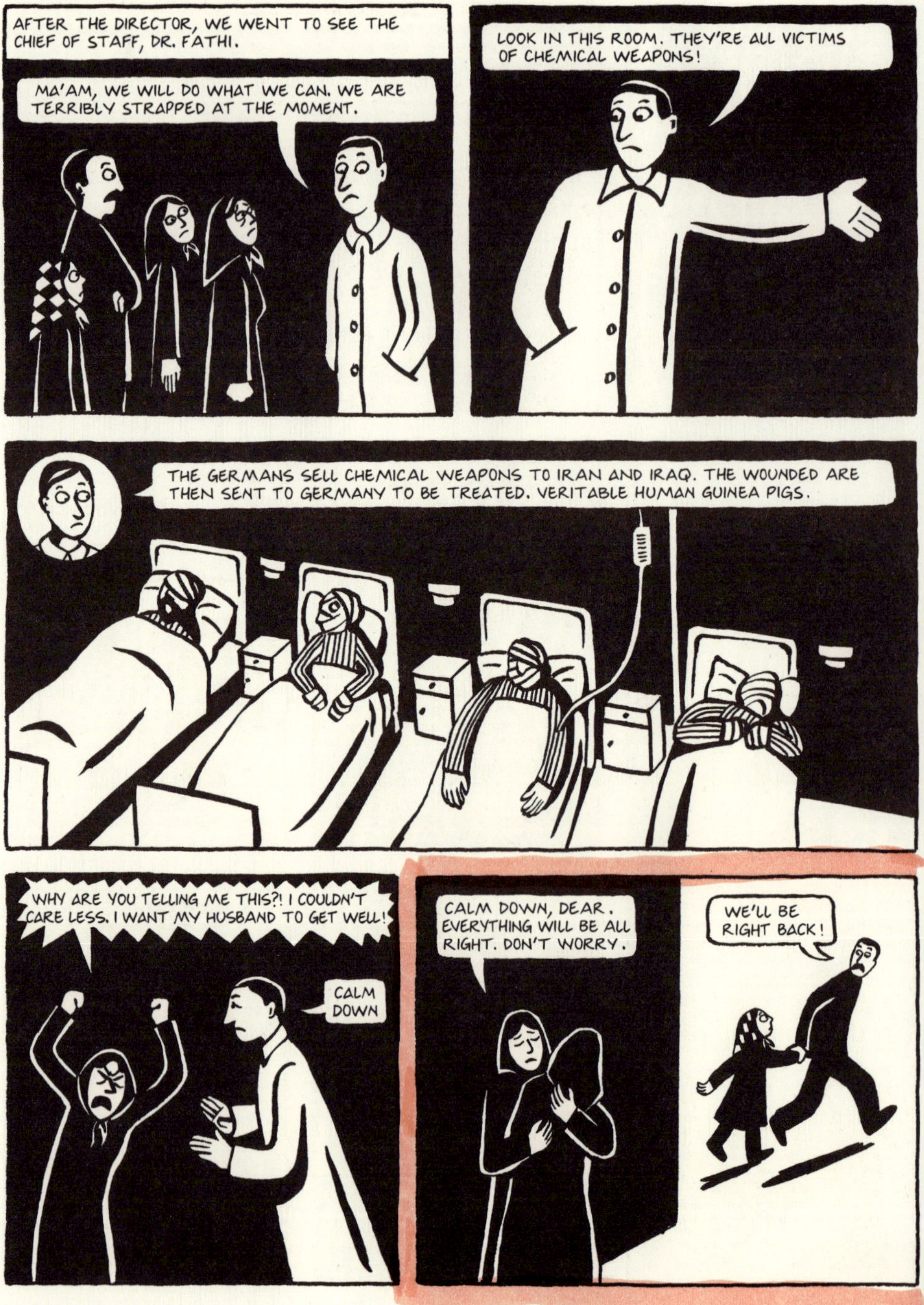

Color contrast shows how grim things seem to Marji's mom vs. her still somewhat innocent view of the wo

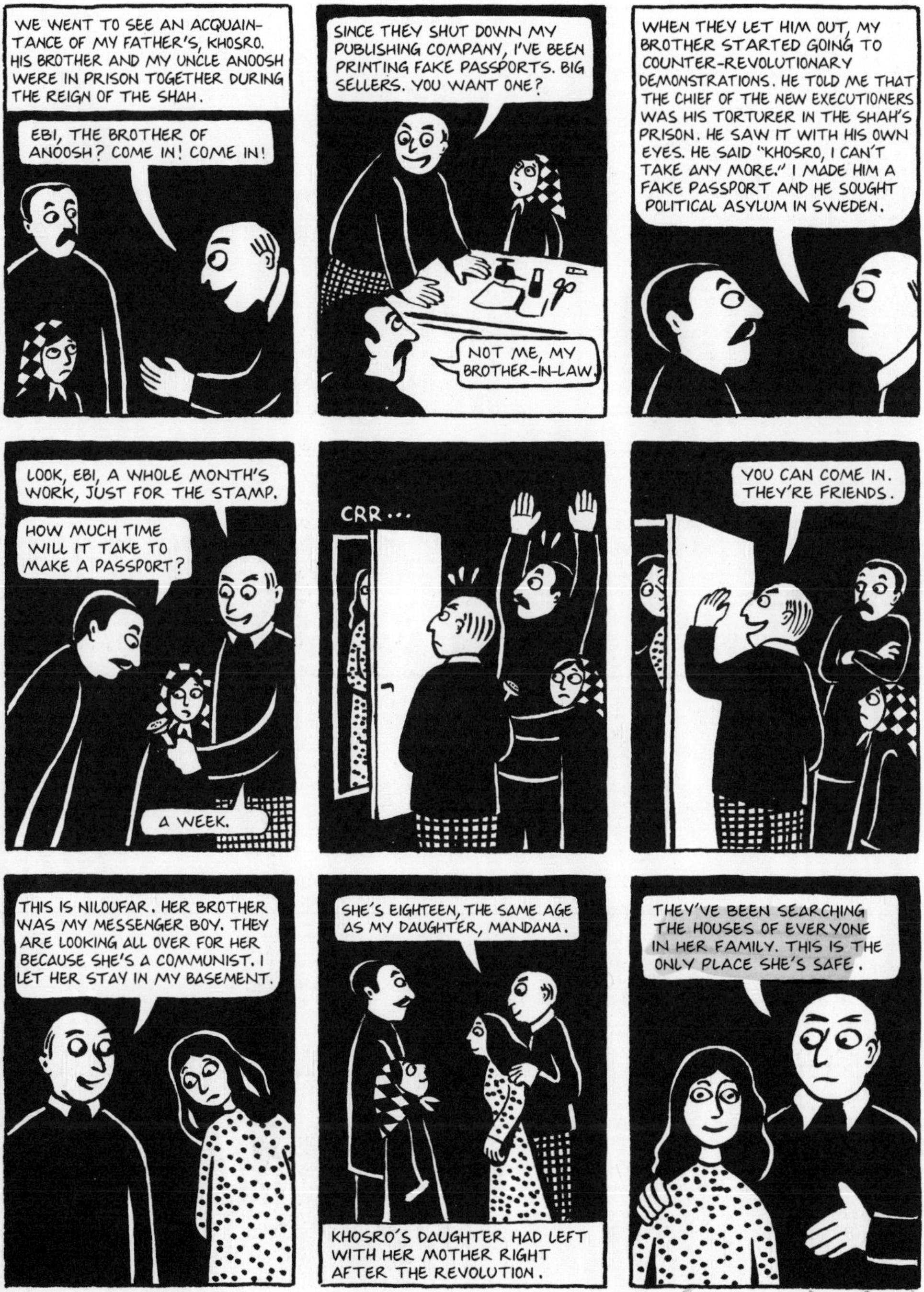

rare acts of kindness in the face of war, evokes hope in the situation

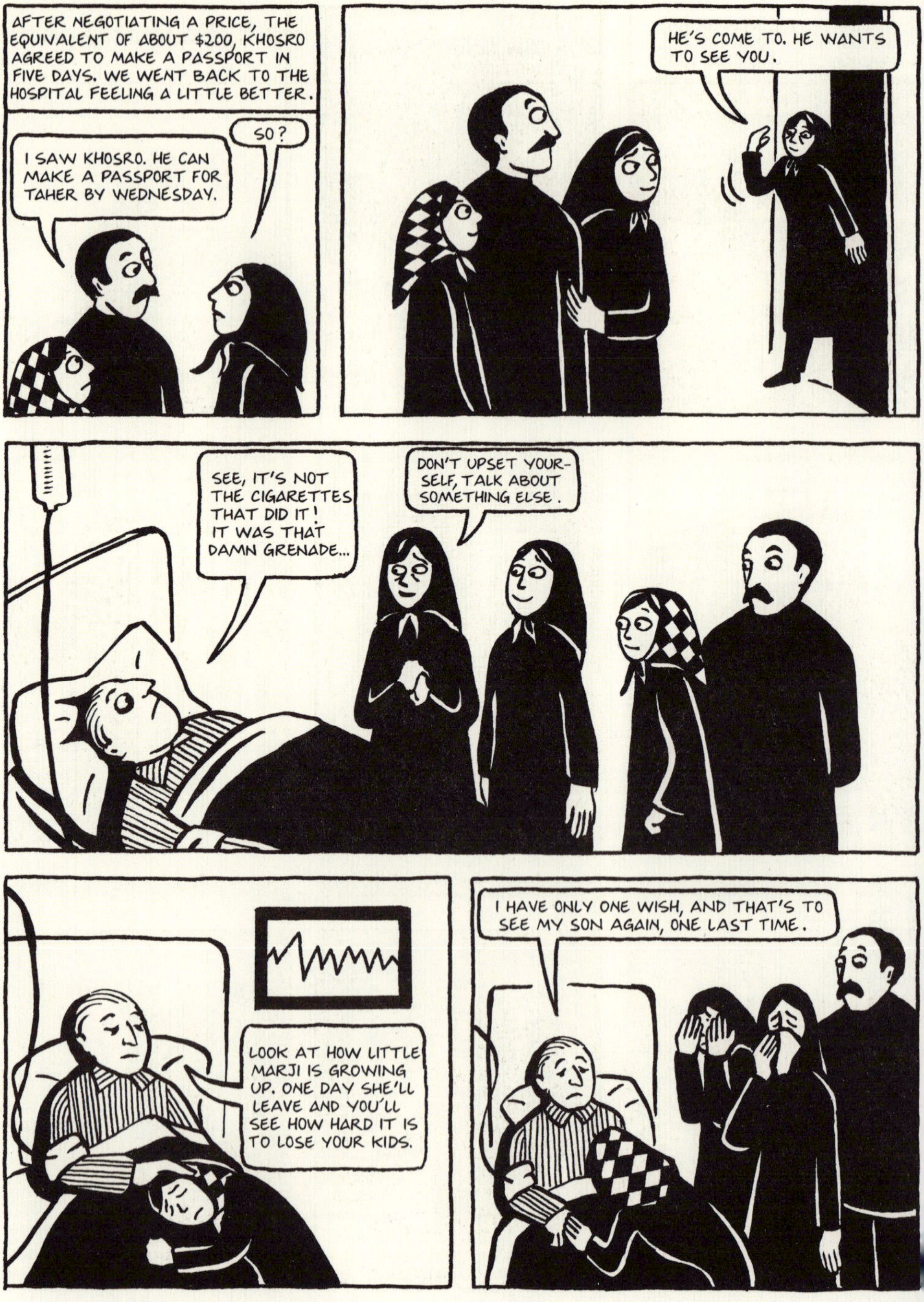
AFTER NEGOTIATING A PRICE, THE EQUIVALENT OF ABOUT $200, KHOSRO AGREED TO MAKE A PASSPORT IN FIVE DAYS. WE WENT BACK TO THE HOSPITAL FEELING A LITTLE BETTER.
I SAW KHOSRO. HE CAN MAKE A PASSPORT FOR TAHER BY WEDNESDAY.
SO?
HE'S COME TO. HE WANTS TO SEE YOU.
SEE, IT'S NOT THE CIGARETTES THAT DID IT! IT WAS THAT DAMN GRENADE...
DON'T UPSET YOURSELF, TALK ABOUT SOMETHING ELSE.
LOOK AT HOW LITTLE MARJI IS GROWING UP. ONE DAY SHE'LL LEAVE AND YOU'LL SEE HOW HARD IT IS TO LOSE YOUR KIDS.
I HAVE ONLY ONE WISH, AND THAT'S TO SEE MY SON AGAIN, ONE LAST TIME.

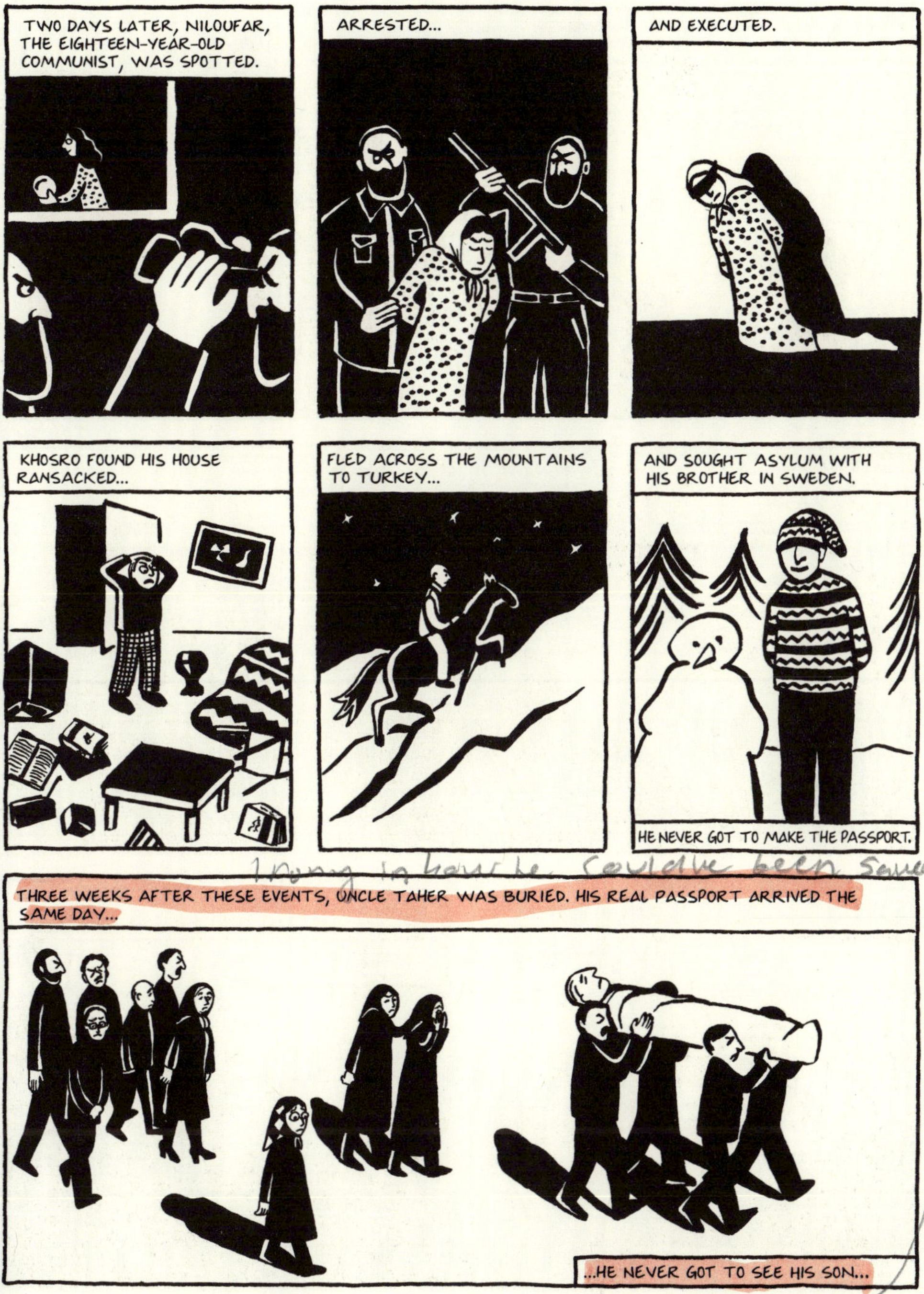

Irony in how he could've been saved

religon indirectly < ended up killing him

KIM WILDE

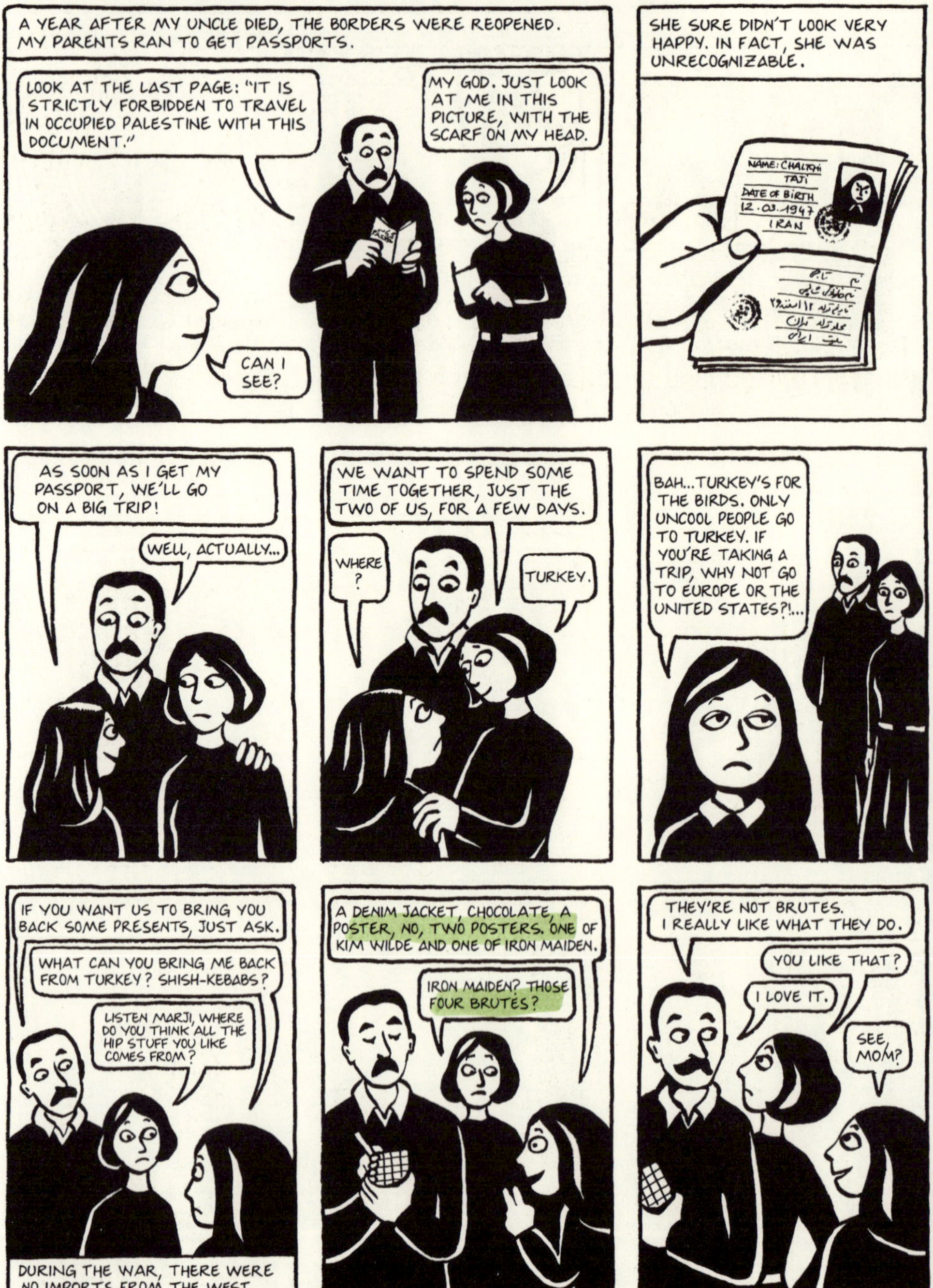

trying to maintain a sense of normalcy in her childhood, how she copes

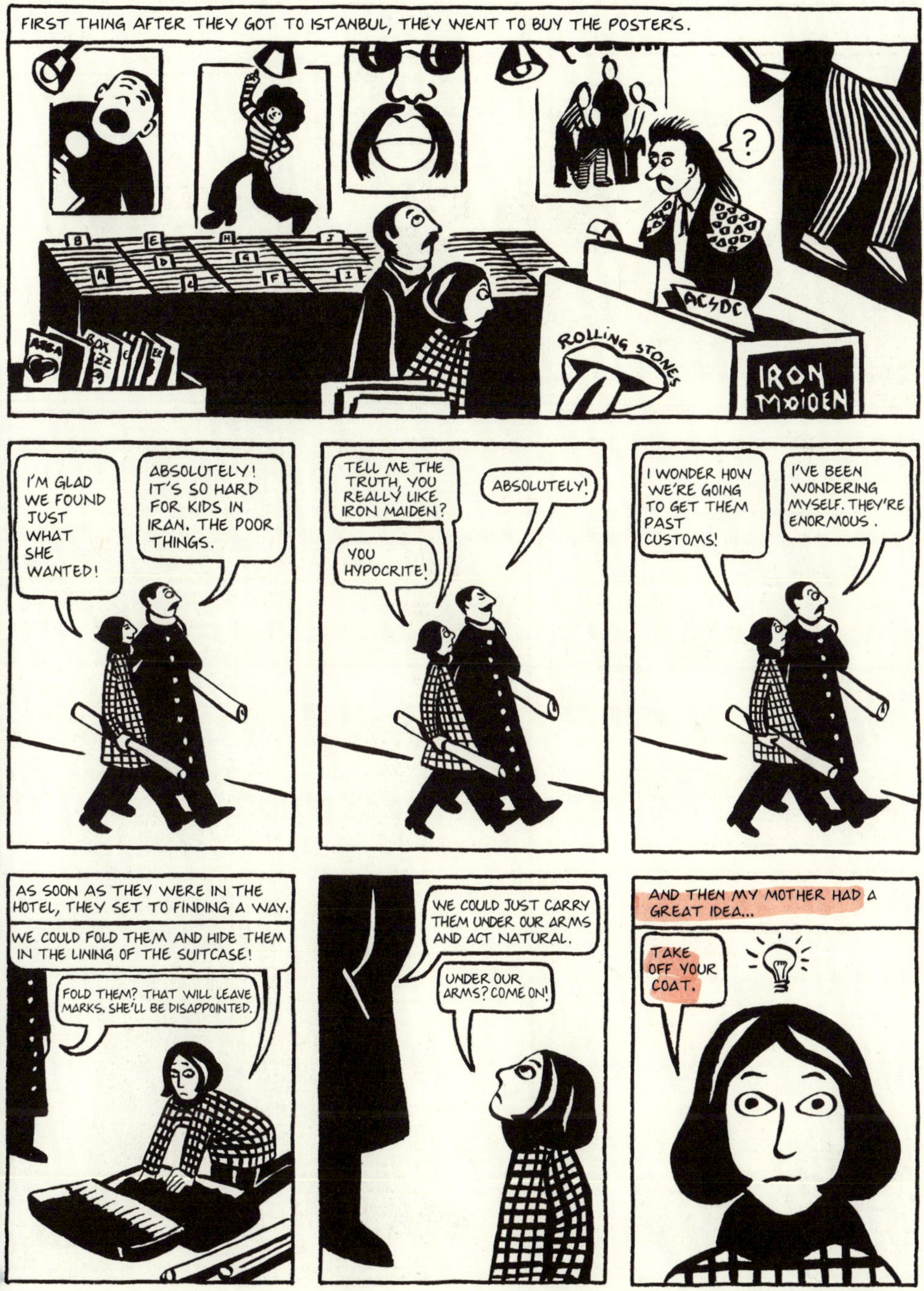

Irony in how they have to jump through so many hoops for a right that should be protected

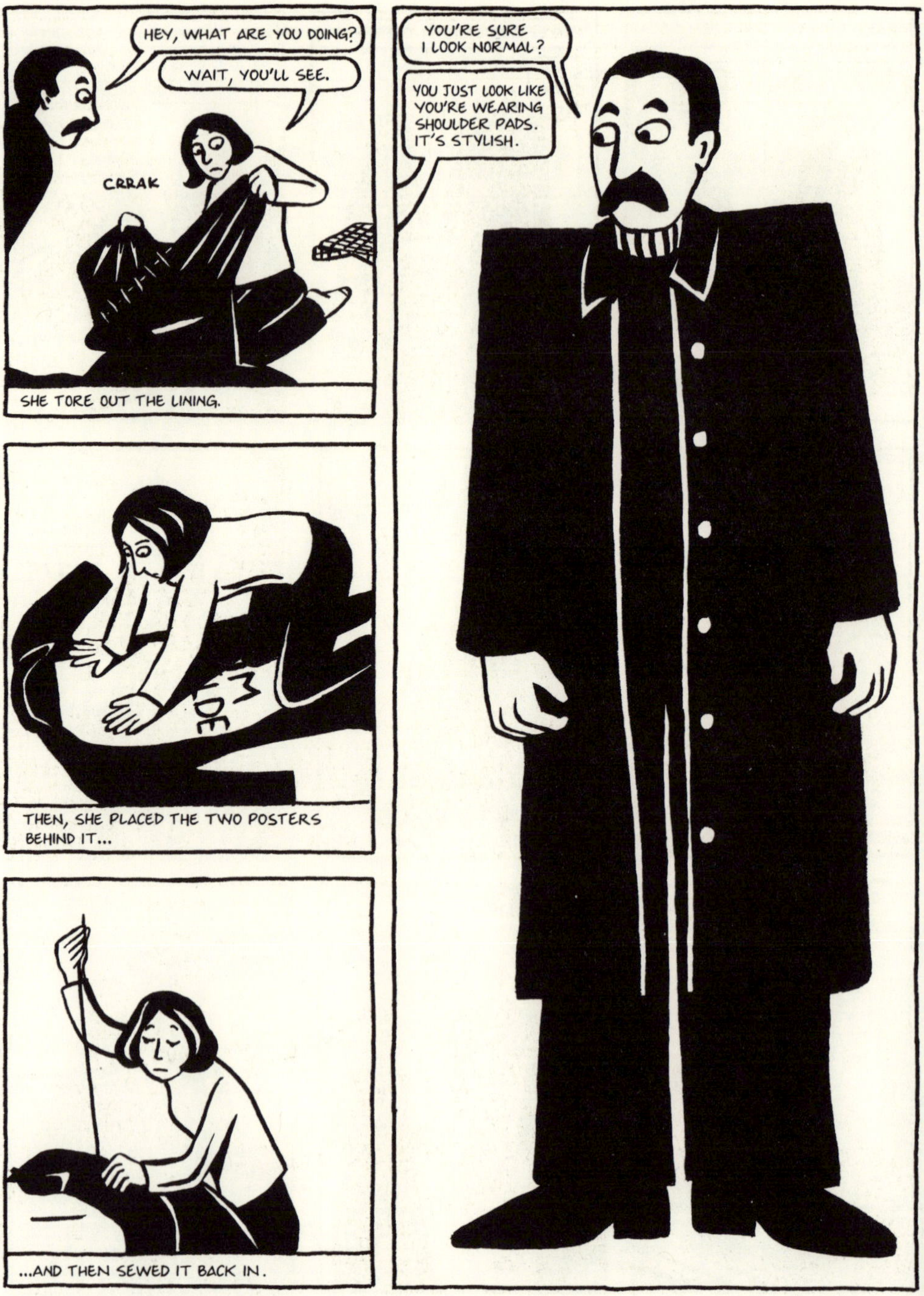
HEY, WHAT ARE YOU DOING?
WAIT, YOU'LL SEE.
CRRAK
SHE TORE OUT THE LINING.
THEN, SHE PLACED THE TWO POSTERS BEHIND IT...
...AND THEN SEWED IT BACK IN.
YOU'RE SURE I LOOK NORMAL?
YOU JUST LOOK LIKE YOU'RE WEARING SHOULDER PADS. IT'S STYLISH.

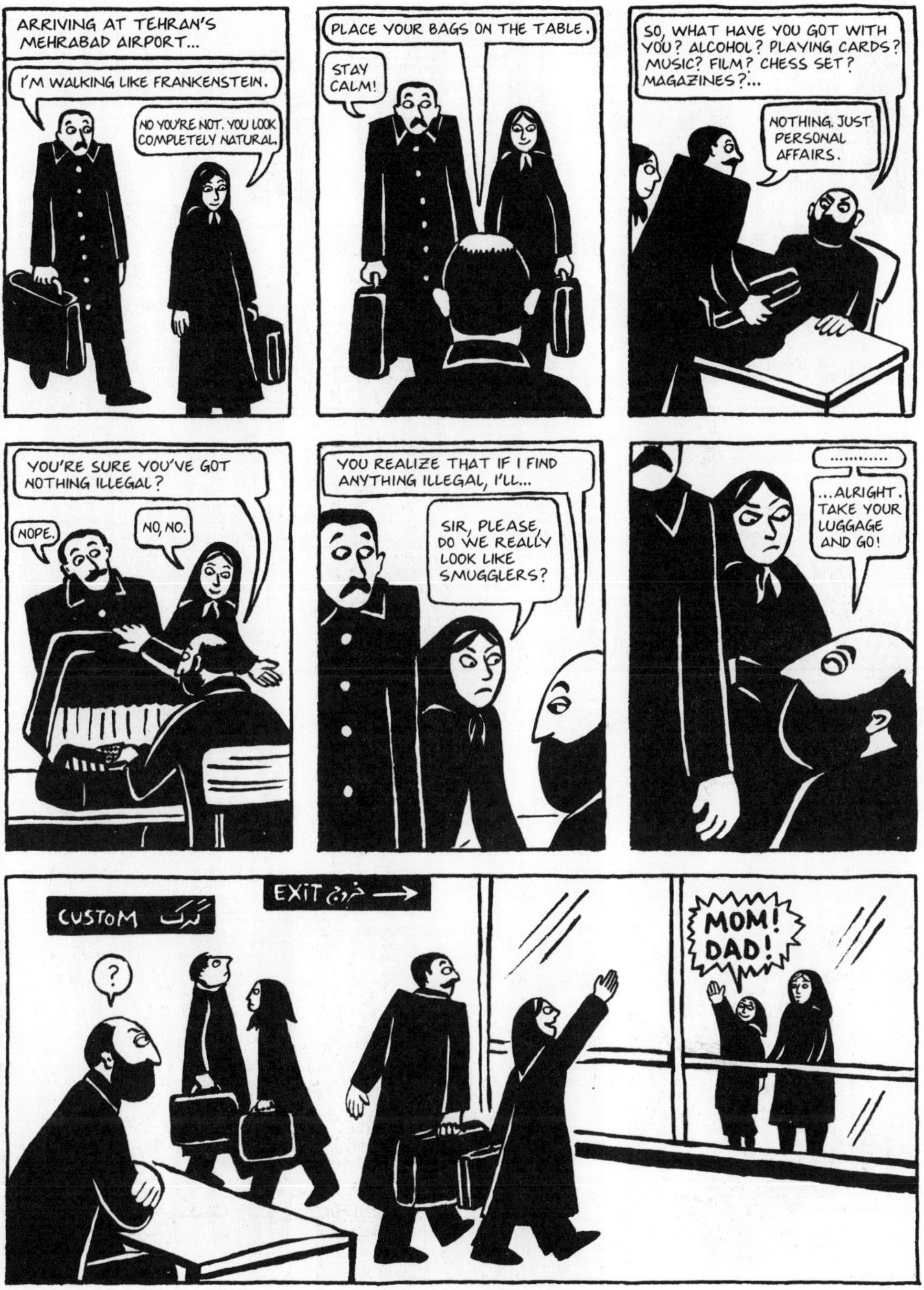
ARRIVING AT TEHRAN'S MEHRABAD AIRPORT...
I'M WALKING LIKE FRANKENSTEIN.
NO YOU'RE NOT. YOU LOOK COMPLETELY NATURAL.
PLACE YOUR BAGS ON THE TABLE.
STAY CALM!
SO, WHAT HAVE YOU GOT WITH YOU? ALCOHOL? PLAYING CARDS? MUSIC? FILM? CHESS SET? MAGAZINES?...
NOTHING. JUST PERSONAL AFFAIRS.
YOU'RE SURE YOU'VE GOT NOTHING ILLEGAL?
NOPE.
NO, NO.
YOU REALIZE THAT IF I FIND ANYTHING ILLEGAL, I'LL...
SIR, PLEASE, DO WE REALLY LOOK LIKE SMUGGLERS?
....
...ALRIGHT. TAKE YOUR LUGGAGE AND GO!
CUSTOM گمرک
EXIT خروج →
?
MOM! DAD!

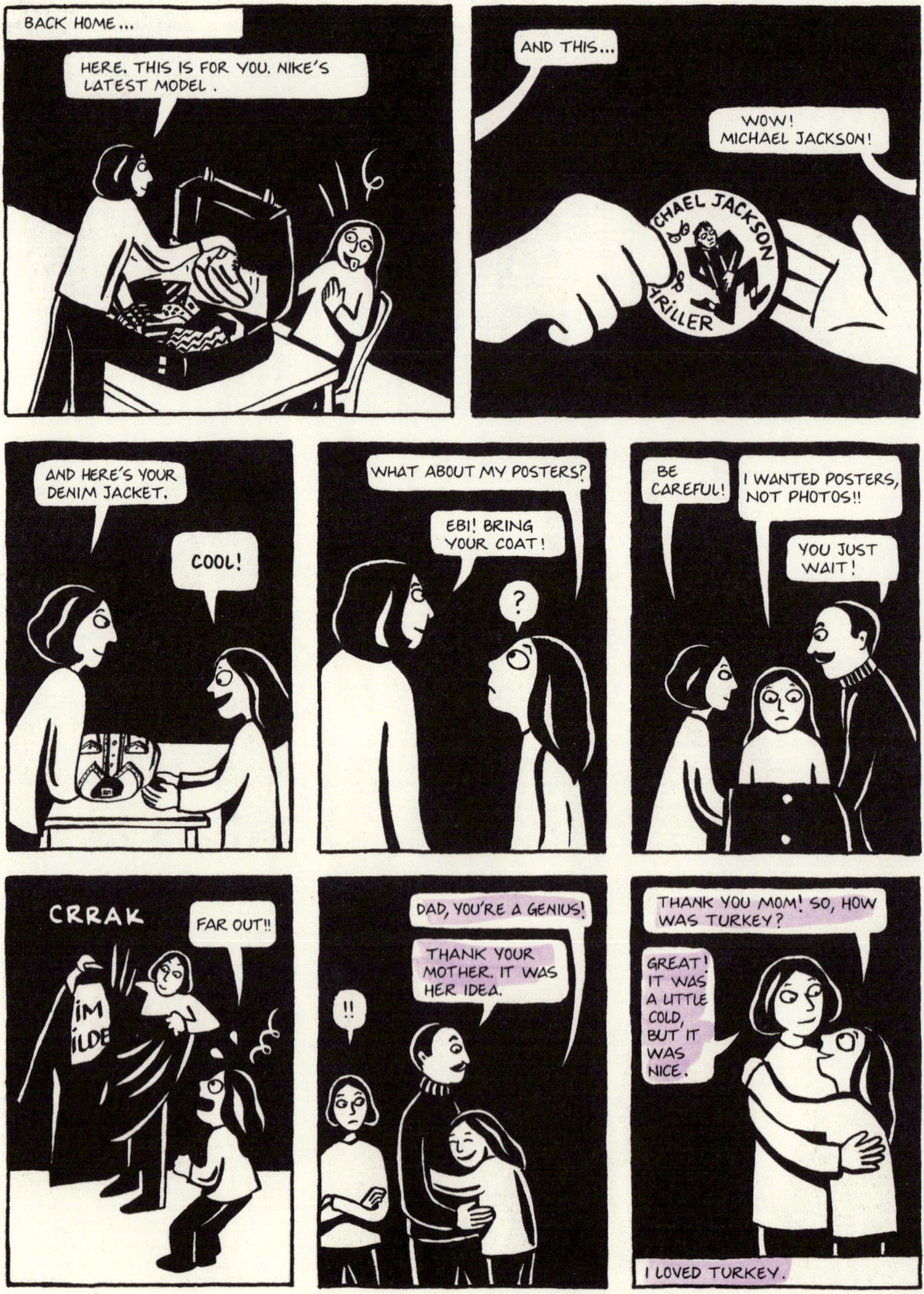

Family bonding despite their circumstances

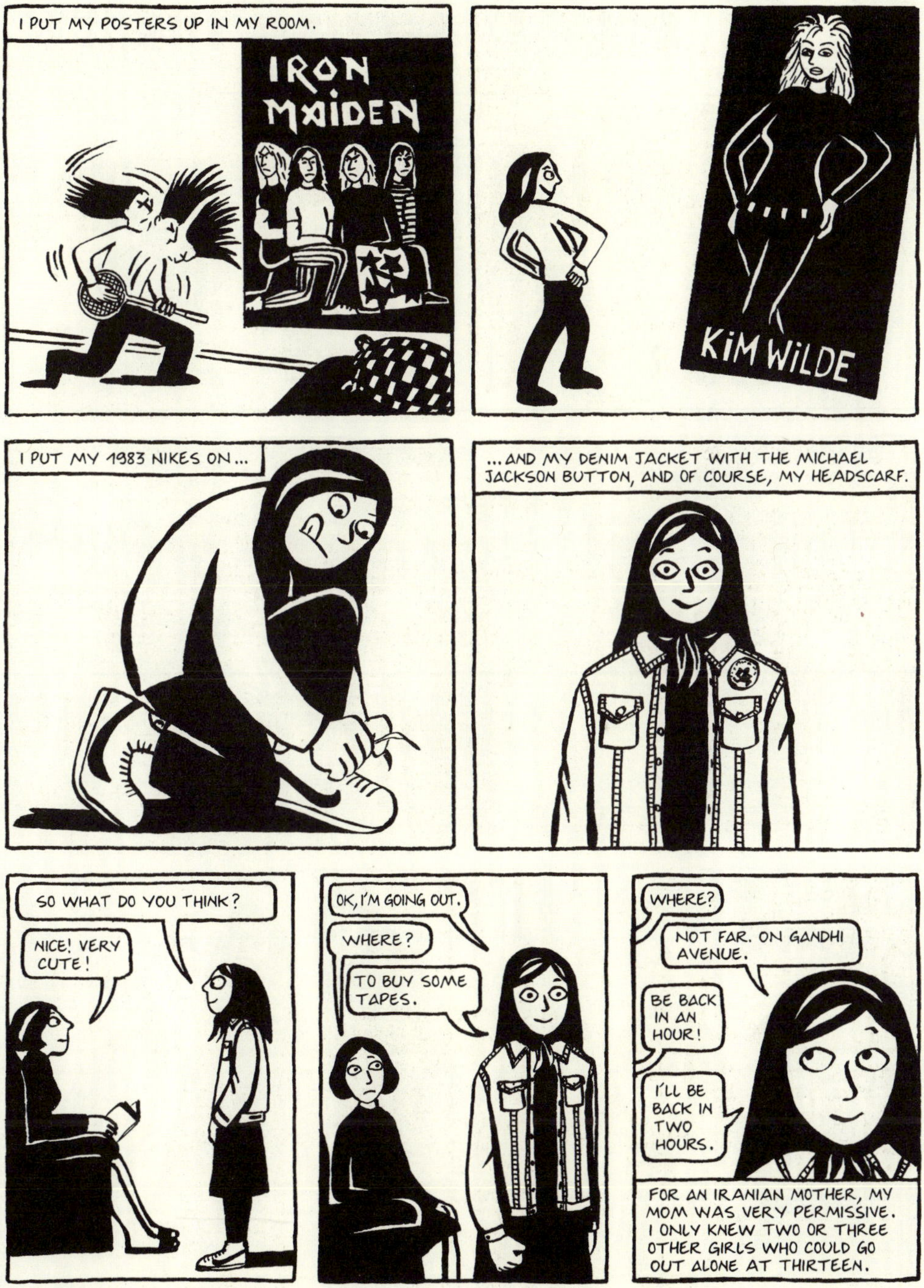
I PUT MY POSTERS UP IN MY ROOM.
IRON MAIDEN
KIM WILDE
I PUT MY 1983 NIKES ON...
...AND MY DENIM JACKET WITH THE MICHAEL JACKSON BUTTON, AND OF COURSE, MY HEADSCARF.
SO WHAT DO YOU THINK?
NICE! VERY CUTE!
OK, I'M GOING OUT.
WHERE?
TO BUY SOME TAPES.
WHERE?
NOT FAR. ON GANDHI AVENUE.
BE BACK IN AN HOUR!
I'LL BE BACK IN TWO HOURS.
FOR AN IRANIAN MOTHER, MY MOM WAS VERY PERMISSIVE. I ONLY KNEW TWO OR THREE OTHER GIRLS WHO COULD GO OUT ALONE AT THIRTEEN.

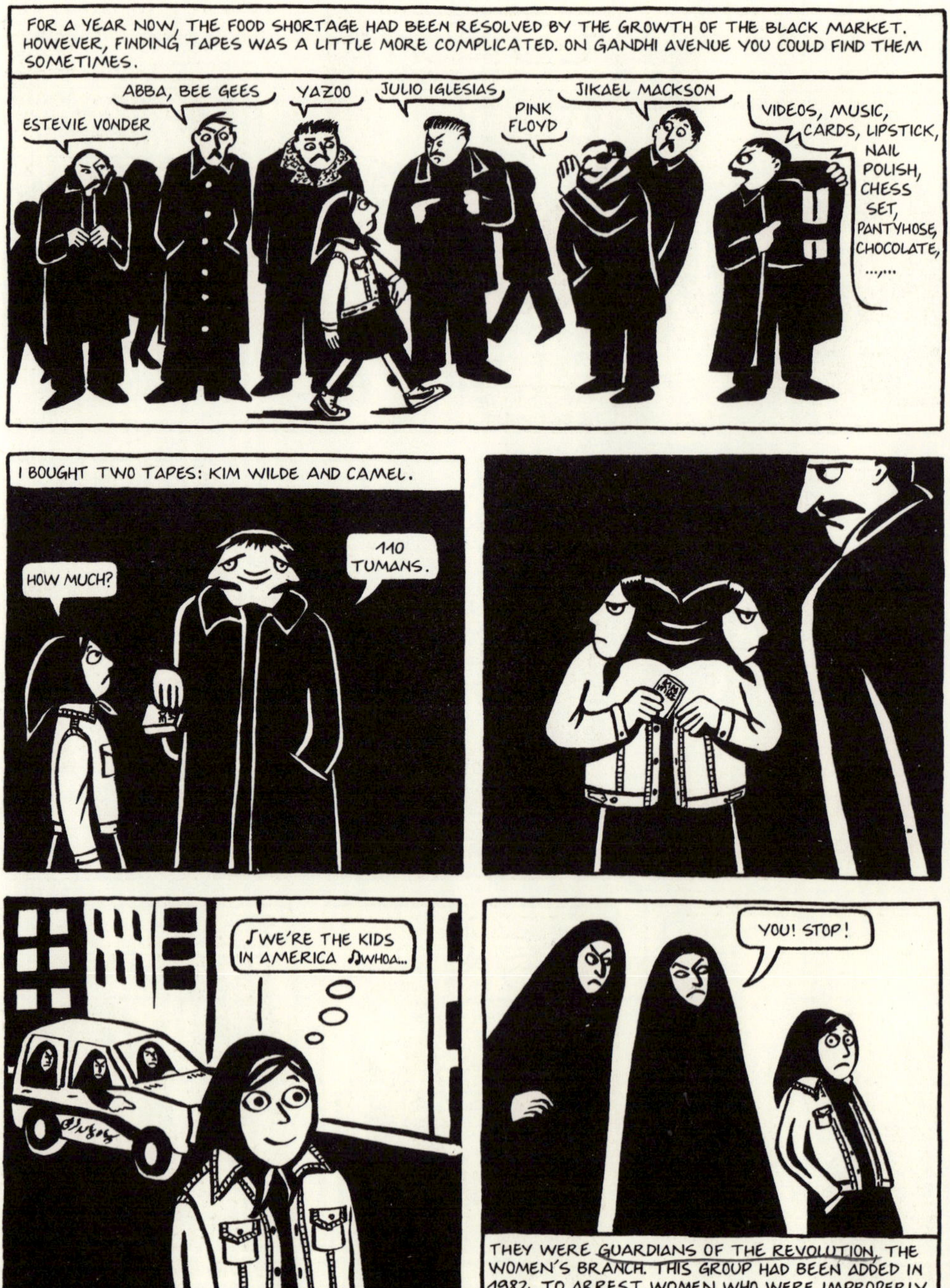
FOR A YEAR NOW, THE FOOD SHORTAGE HAD BEEN RESOLVED BY THE GROWTH OF THE BLACK MARKET. HOWEVER, FINDING TAPES WAS A LITTLE MORE COMPLICATED. ON GANDHI AVENUE YOU COULD FIND THEM SOMETIMES.
ESTEVIE VONDER
ABBA, BEE GEES
YAZOO
JULIO IGLESIAS
PINK FLOYD
JIKAEL MACKSON
VIDEOS, MUSIC, CARDS, LIPSTICK, NAIL POLISH, CHESS SET, PANTYHOSE, CHOCOLATE, ...,...
I BOUGHT TWO TAPES: KIM WILDE AND CAMEL.
HOW MUCH?
110 TUMANS.
♪WE'RE THE KIDS IN AMERICA ♫WHOA...
YOU! STOP!
THEY WERE GUARDIANS OF THE REVOLUTION, THE WOMEN'S BRANCH. THIS GROUP HAD BEEN ADDED IN 1982, TO ARREST WOMEN WHO WERE IMPROPERLY VEILED. (LIKE ME, FOR EXAMPLE.)

Shadow shows how she is evil

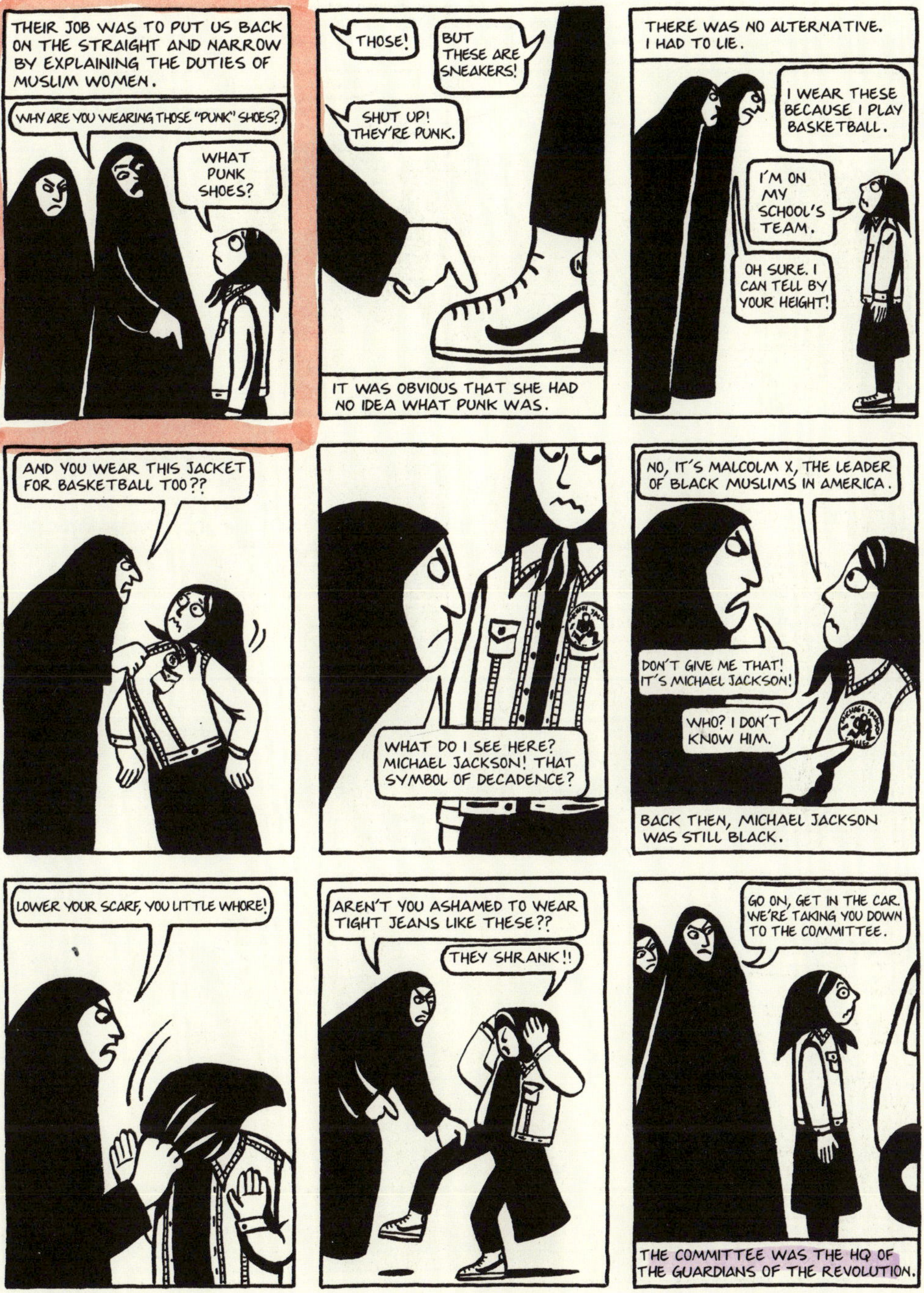

Sense of fear created, imposing figures trying to take Marji

unfair detainment, the people feel trapped

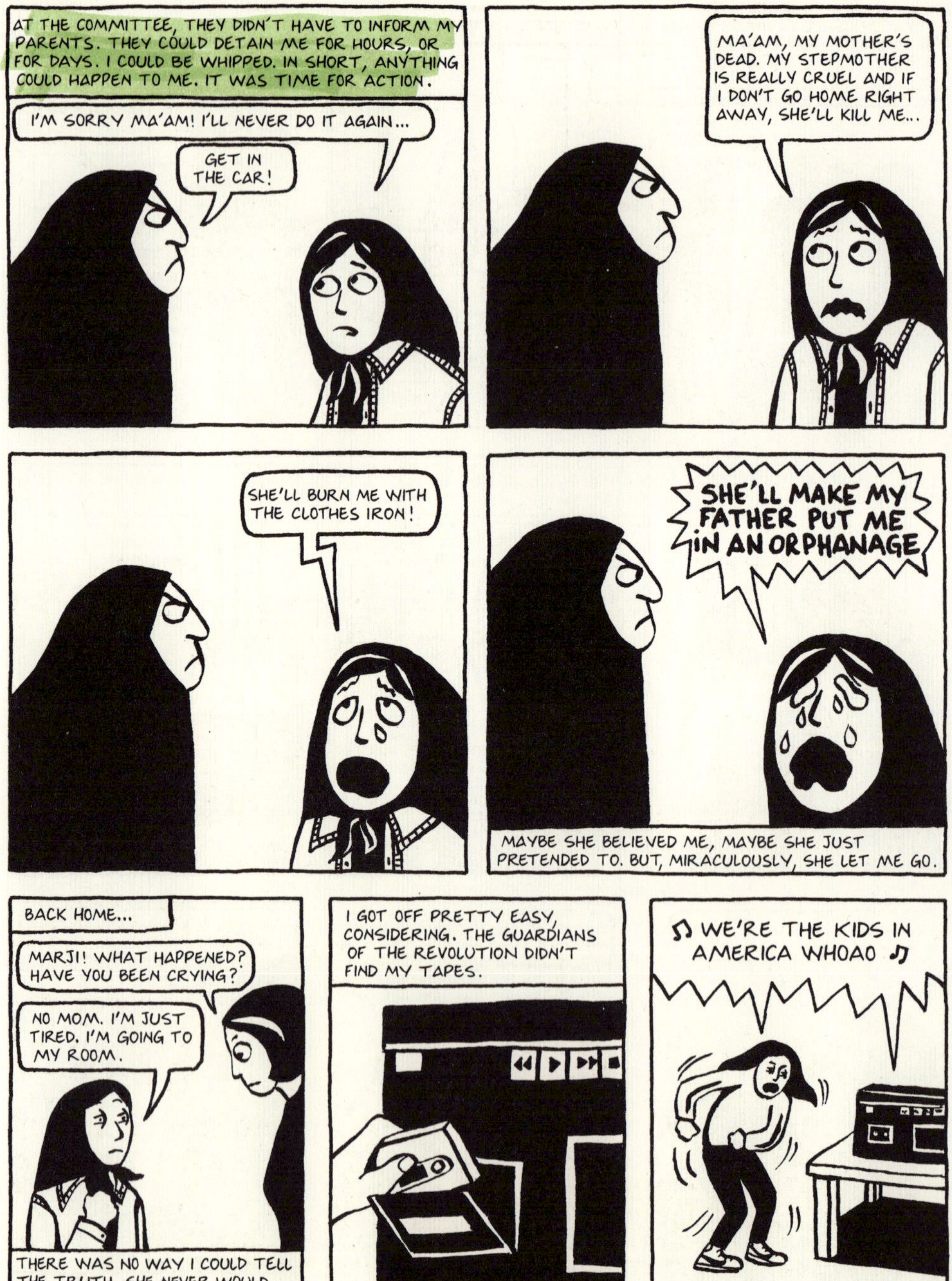

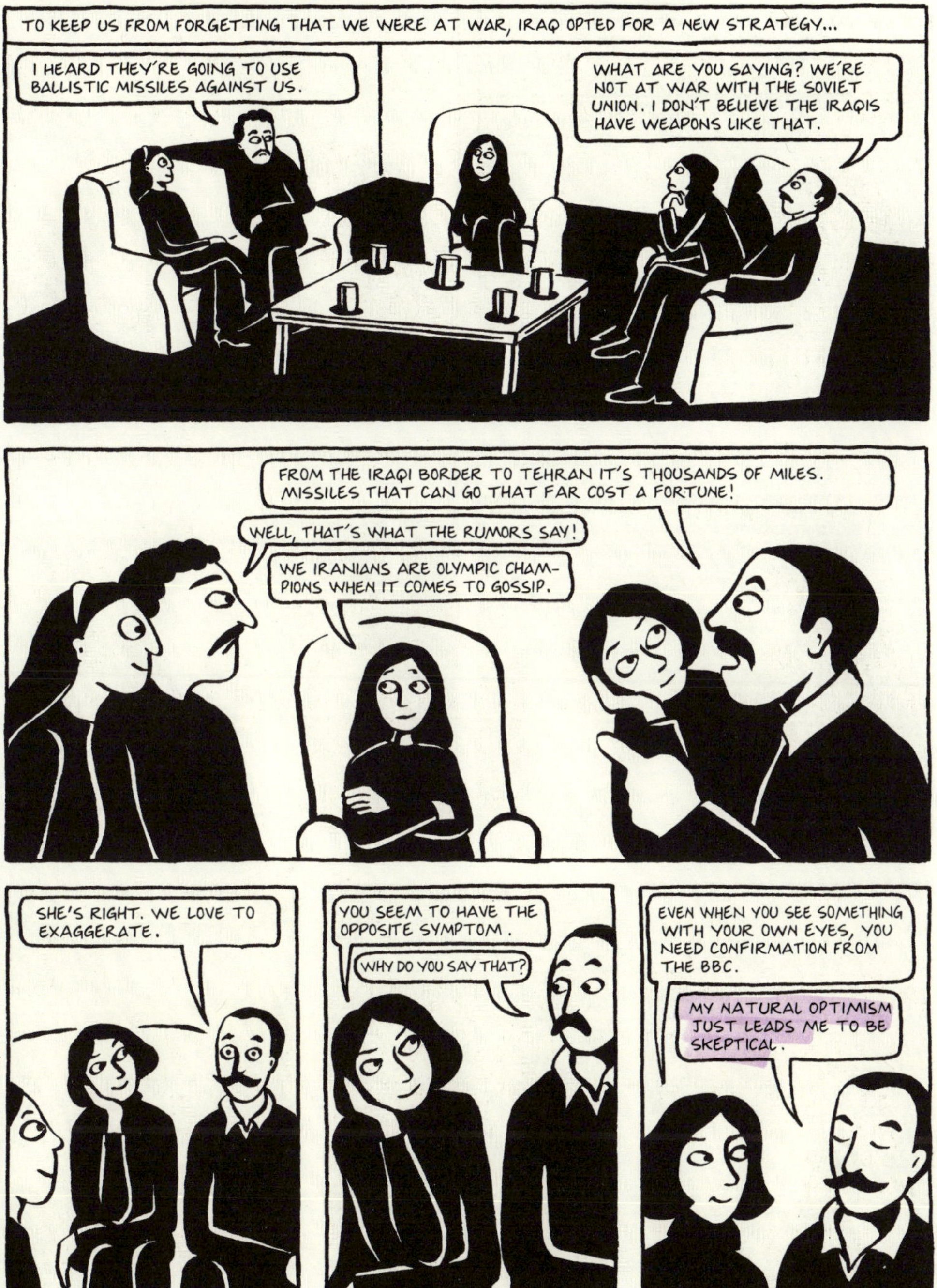

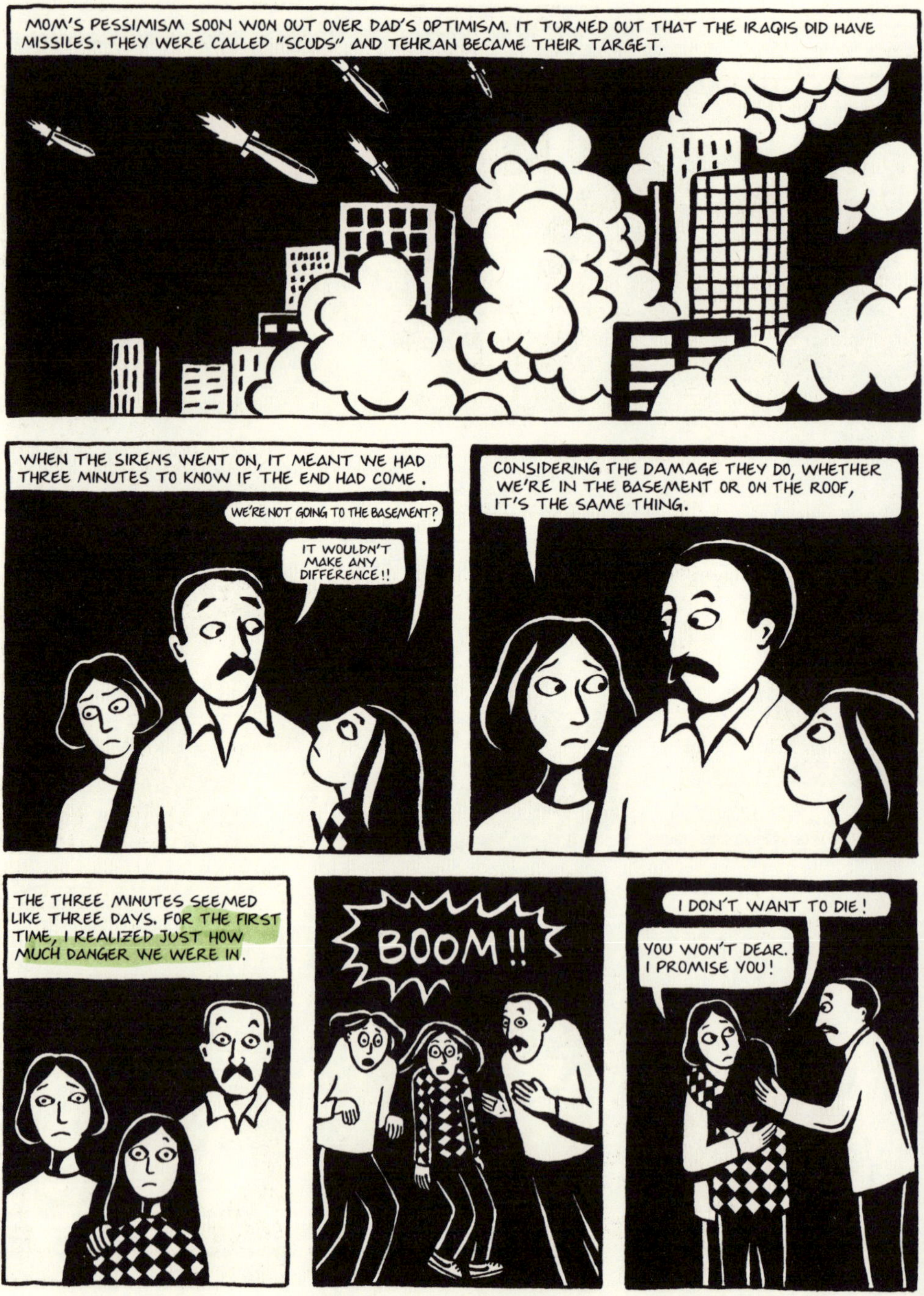

she truly understands her situation now, she rarely smiles the rest of the book

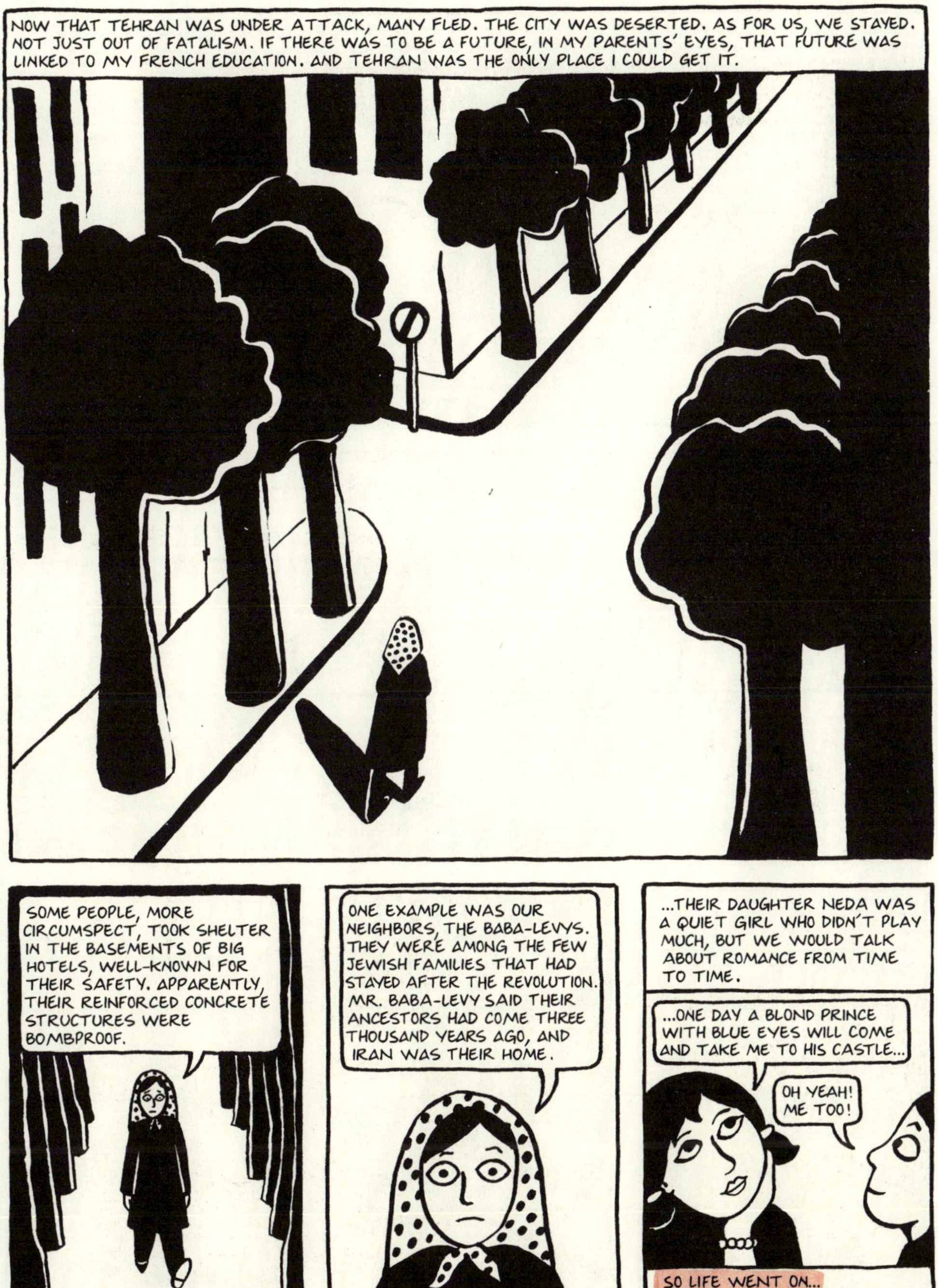

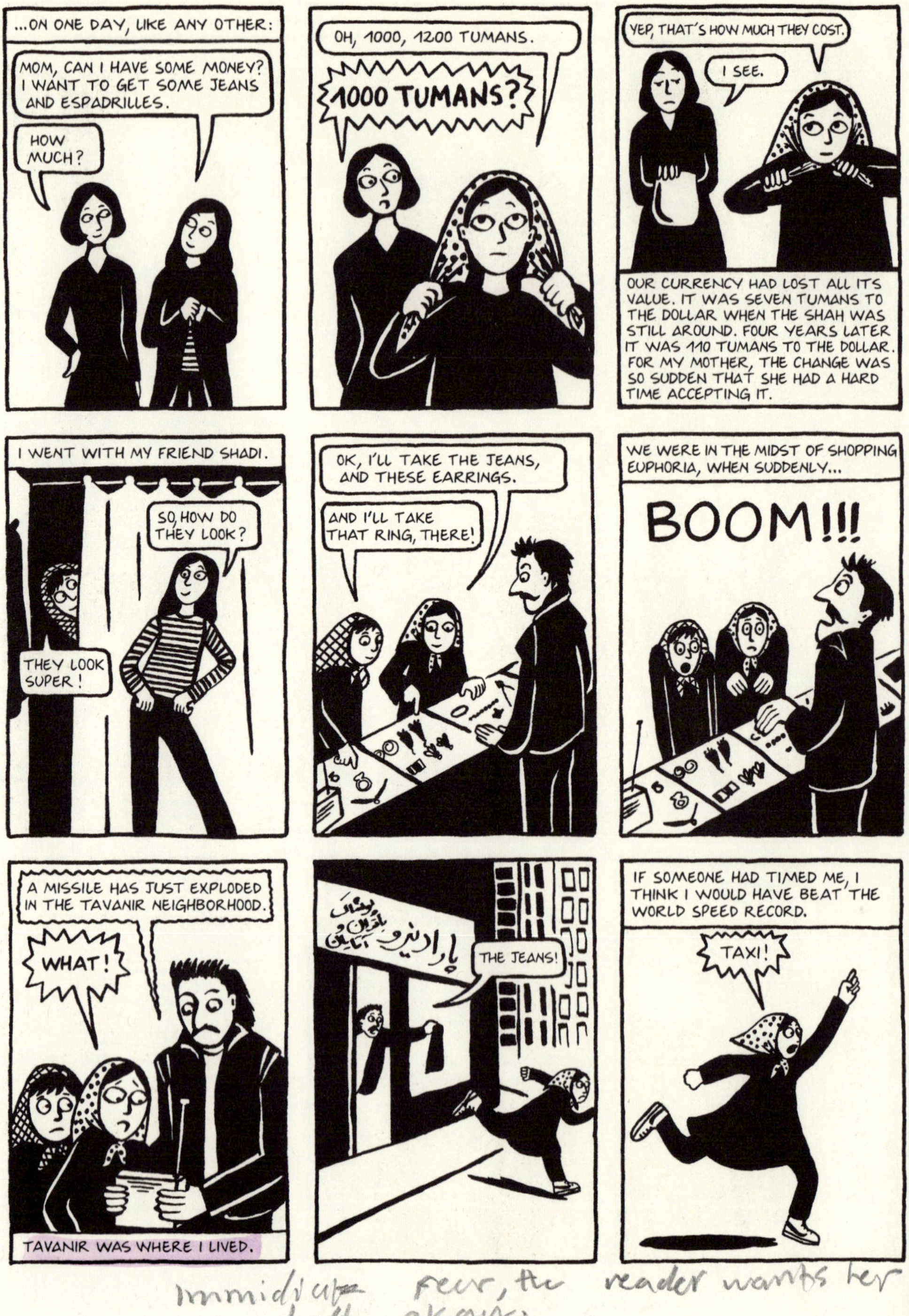

Immidiate fear, the reader wants her to be okay.

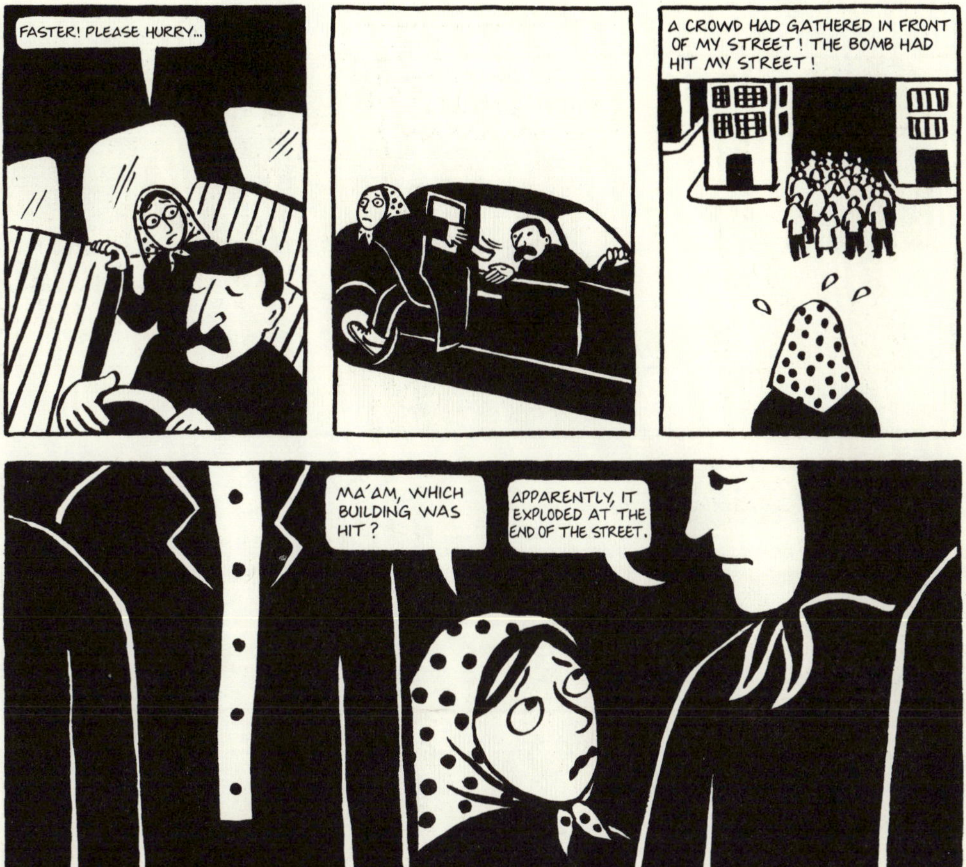

only one looking directly forwards

communicating her fear & anxiety

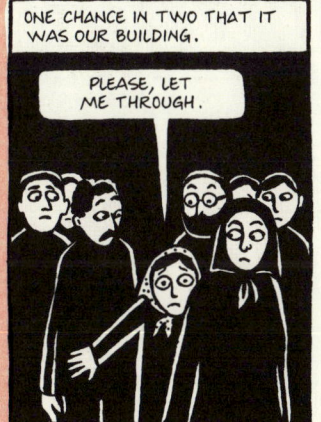

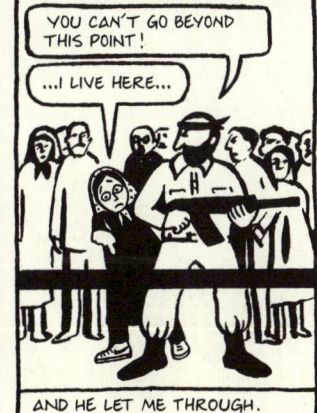

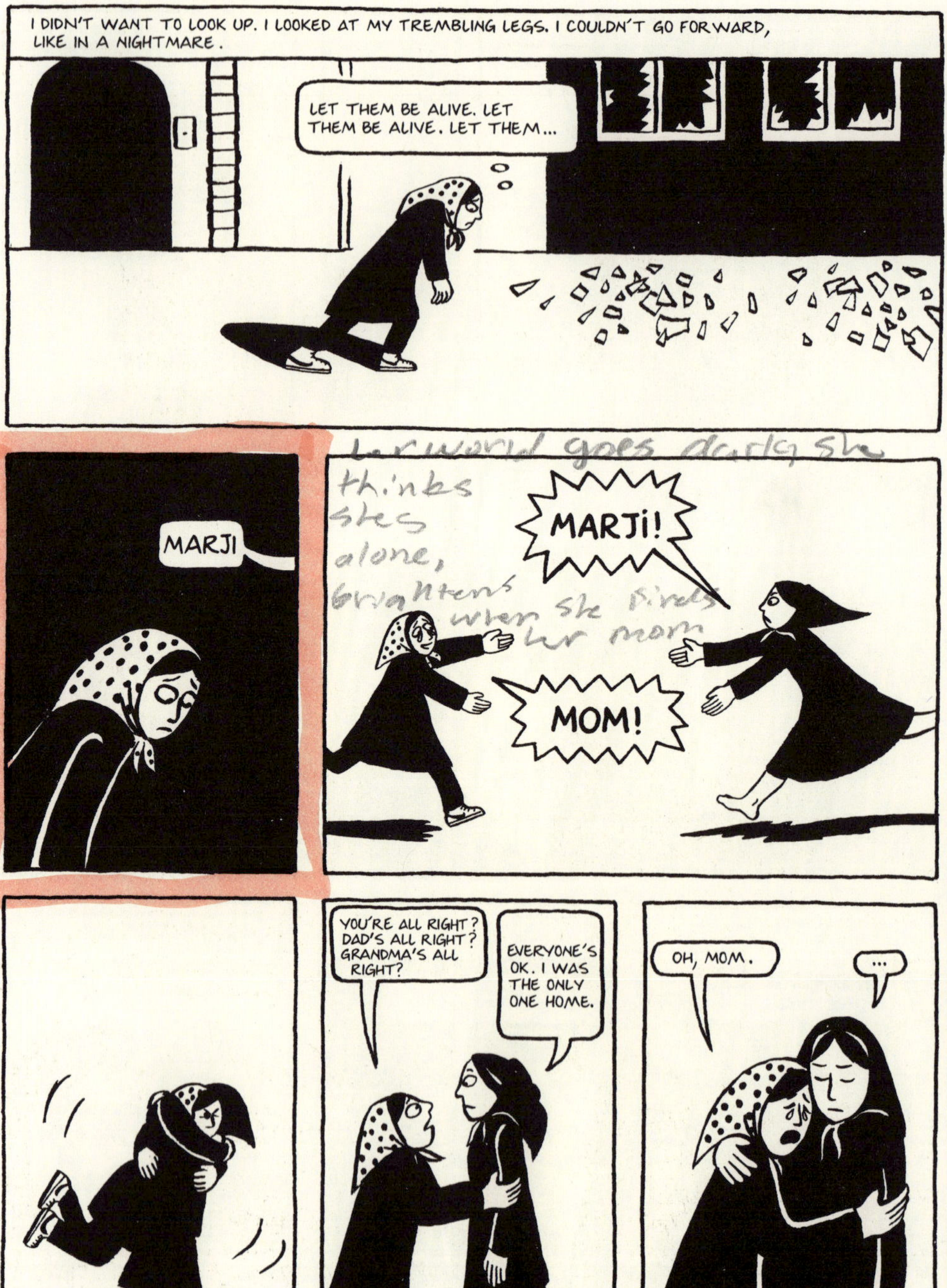

world goes dark she thinks she's alone, brightens when she finds her mom

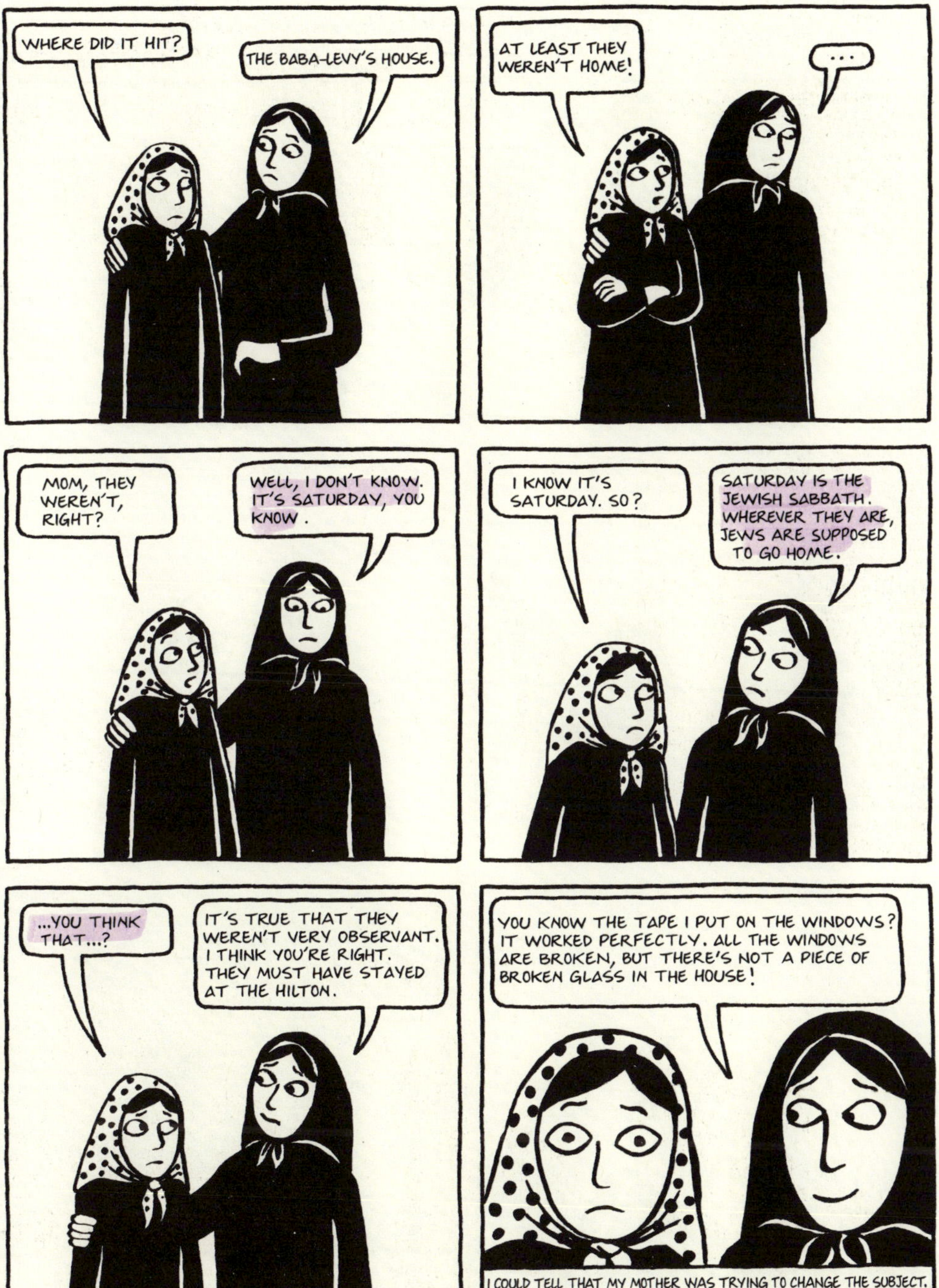

First time since she truly lost her innocence she experiences others death, changes her permanently

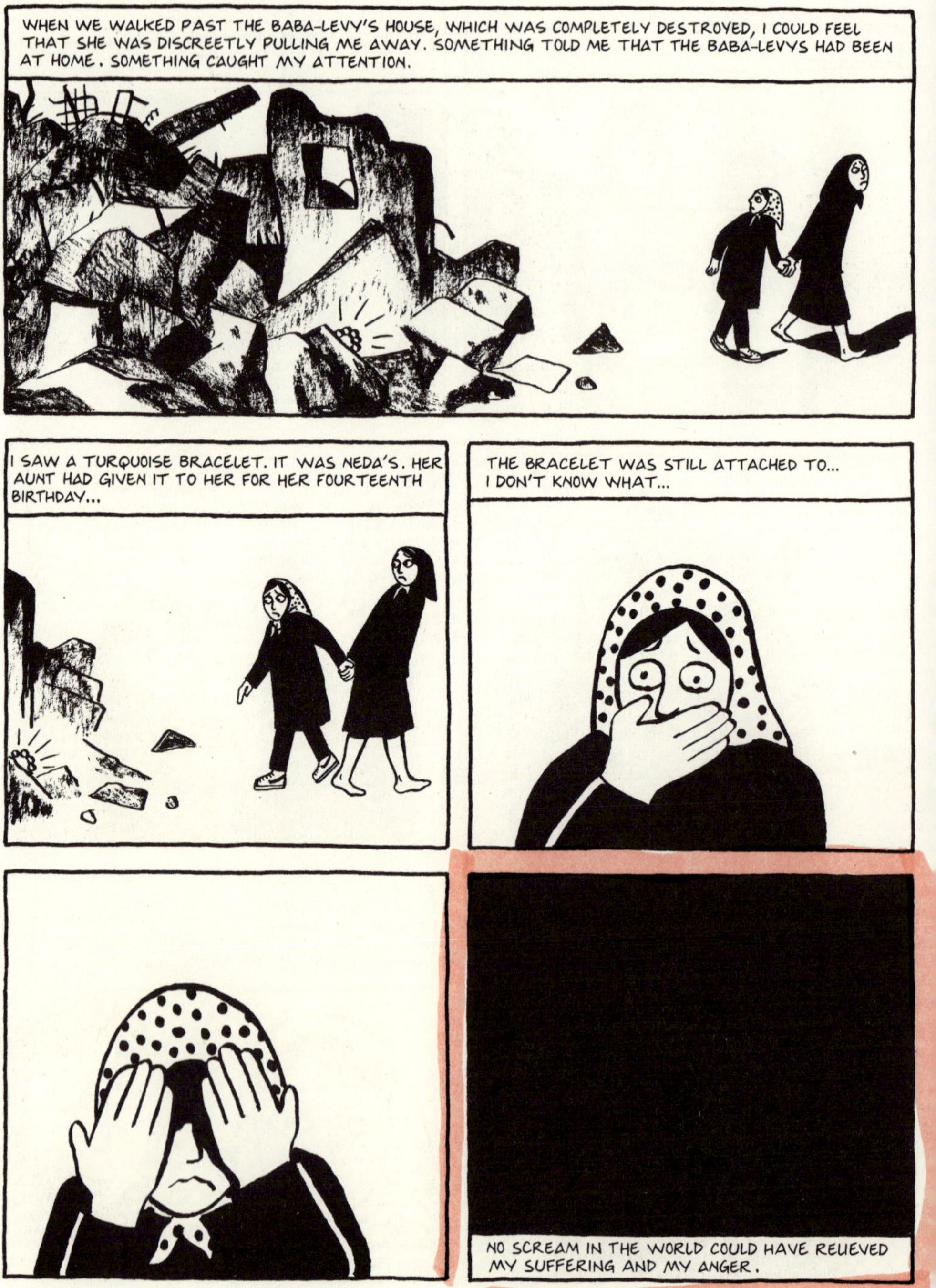

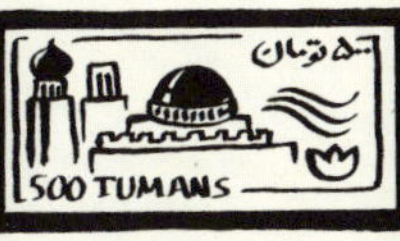
500 TUMANS

THE DOWRY

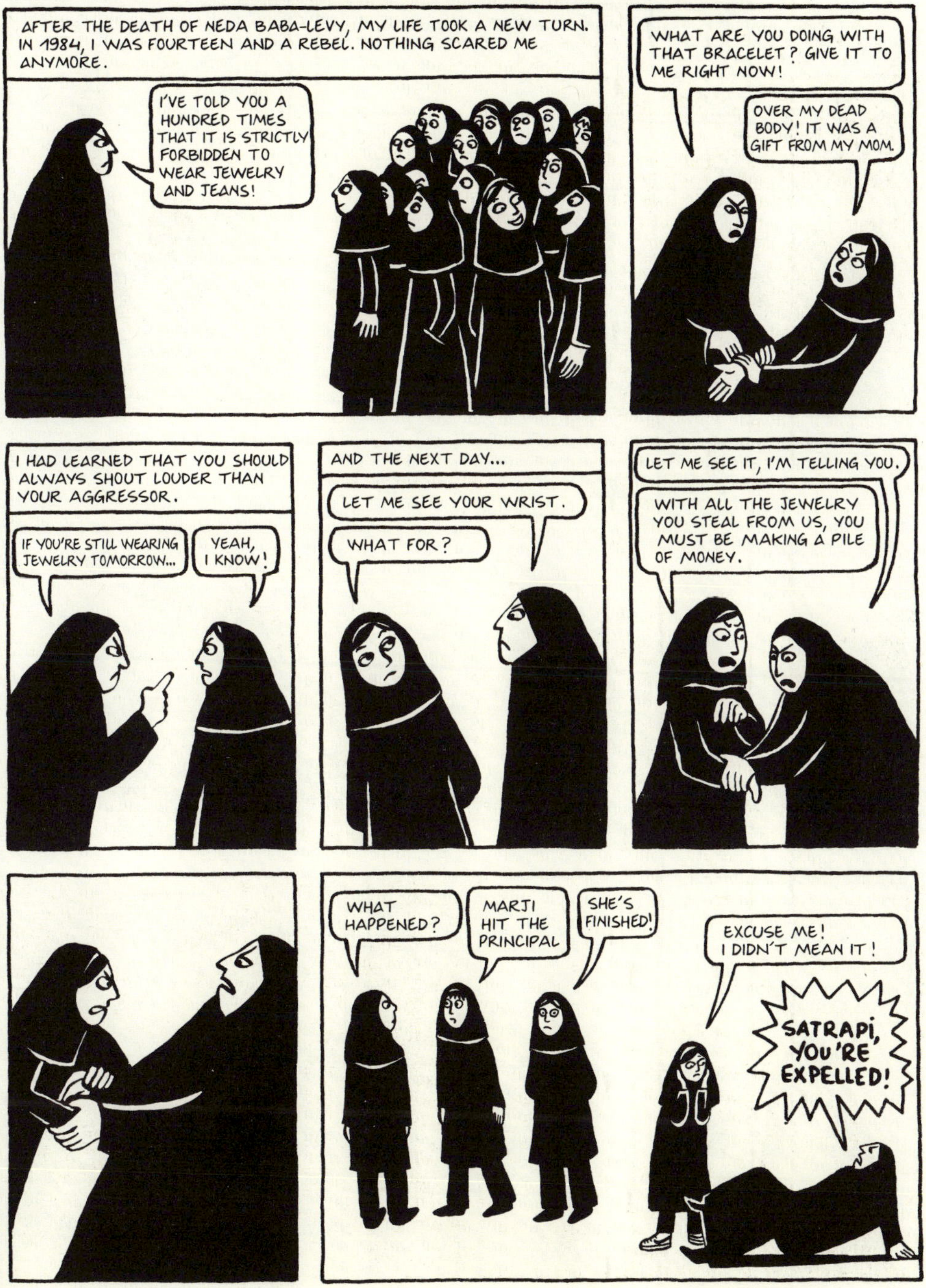
AFTER THE DEATH OF NEDA BABA-LEVY, MY LIFE TOOK A NEW TURN. IN 1984, I WAS FOURTEEN AND A REBEL. NOTHING SCARED ME ANYMORE.
I'VE TOLD YOU A HUNDRED TIMES THAT IT IS STRICTLY FORBIDDEN TO WEAR JEWELRY AND JEANS!
WHAT ARE YOU DOING WITH THAT BRACELET? GIVE IT TO ME RIGHT NOW!
OVER MY DEAD BODY! IT WAS A GIFT FROM MY MOM.
I HAD LEARNED THAT YOU SHOULD ALWAYS SHOUT LOUDER THAN YOUR AGGRESSOR.
IF YOU'RE STILL WEARING JEWELRY TOMORROW...
YEAH, I KNOW!
AND THE NEXT DAY...
LET ME SEE YOUR WRIST.
WHAT FOR?
LET ME SEE IT, I'M TELLING YOU.
WITH ALL THE JEWELRY YOU STEAL FROM US, YOU MUST BE MAKING A PILE OF MONEY.
WHAT HAPPENED?
MARJI HIT THE PRINCIPAL
SHE'S FINISHED!
EXCUSE ME! I DIDN'T MEAN IT!
SATRAPI, YOU'RE EXPELLED!

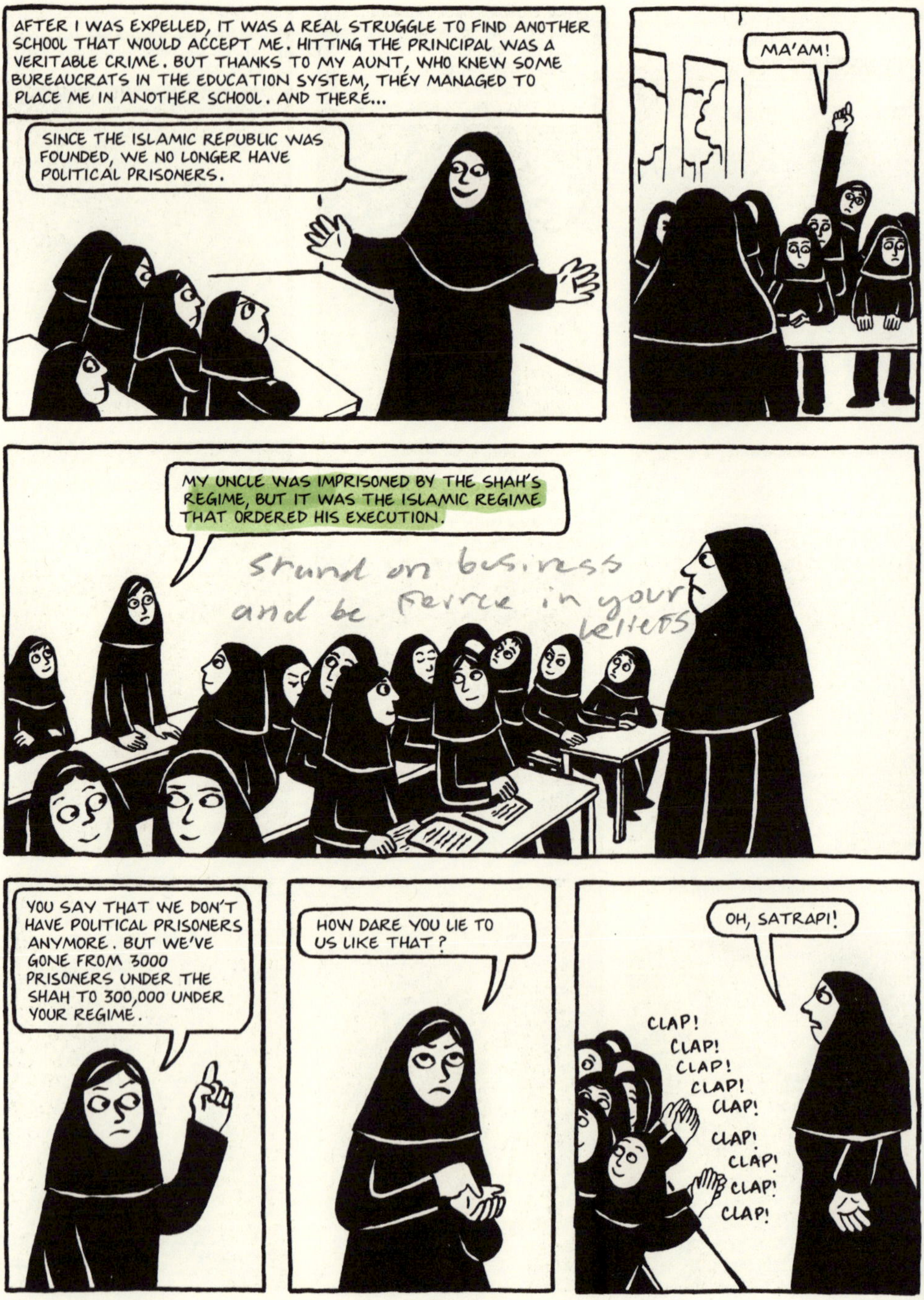
AFTER I WAS EXPELLED, IT WAS A REAL STRUGGLE TO FIND ANOTHER SCHOOL THAT WOULD ACCEPT ME. HITTING THE PRINCIPAL WAS A VERITABLE CRIME. BUT THANKS TO MY AUNT, WHO KNEW SOME BUREAUCRATS IN THE EDUCATION SYSTEM, THEY MANAGED TO PLACE ME IN ANOTHER SCHOOL. AND THERE...
SINCE THE ISLAMIC REPUBLIC WAS FOUNDED, WE NO LONGER HAVE POLITICAL PRISONERS.
MA'AM!
MY UNCLE WAS IMPRISONED BY THE SHAH'S REGIME, BUT IT WAS THE ISLAMIC REGIME THAT ORDERED HIS EXECUTION.
YOU SAY THAT WE DON'T HAVE POLITICAL PRISONERS ANYMORE. BUT WE'VE GONE FROM 3000 PRISONERS UNDER THE SHAH TO 300,000 UNDER YOUR REGIME.
HOW DARE YOU LIE TO US LIKE THAT?
OH, SATRAPI!
CLAP! CLAP! CLAP! CLAP! CLAP! CLAP! CLAP! CLAP! CLAP!

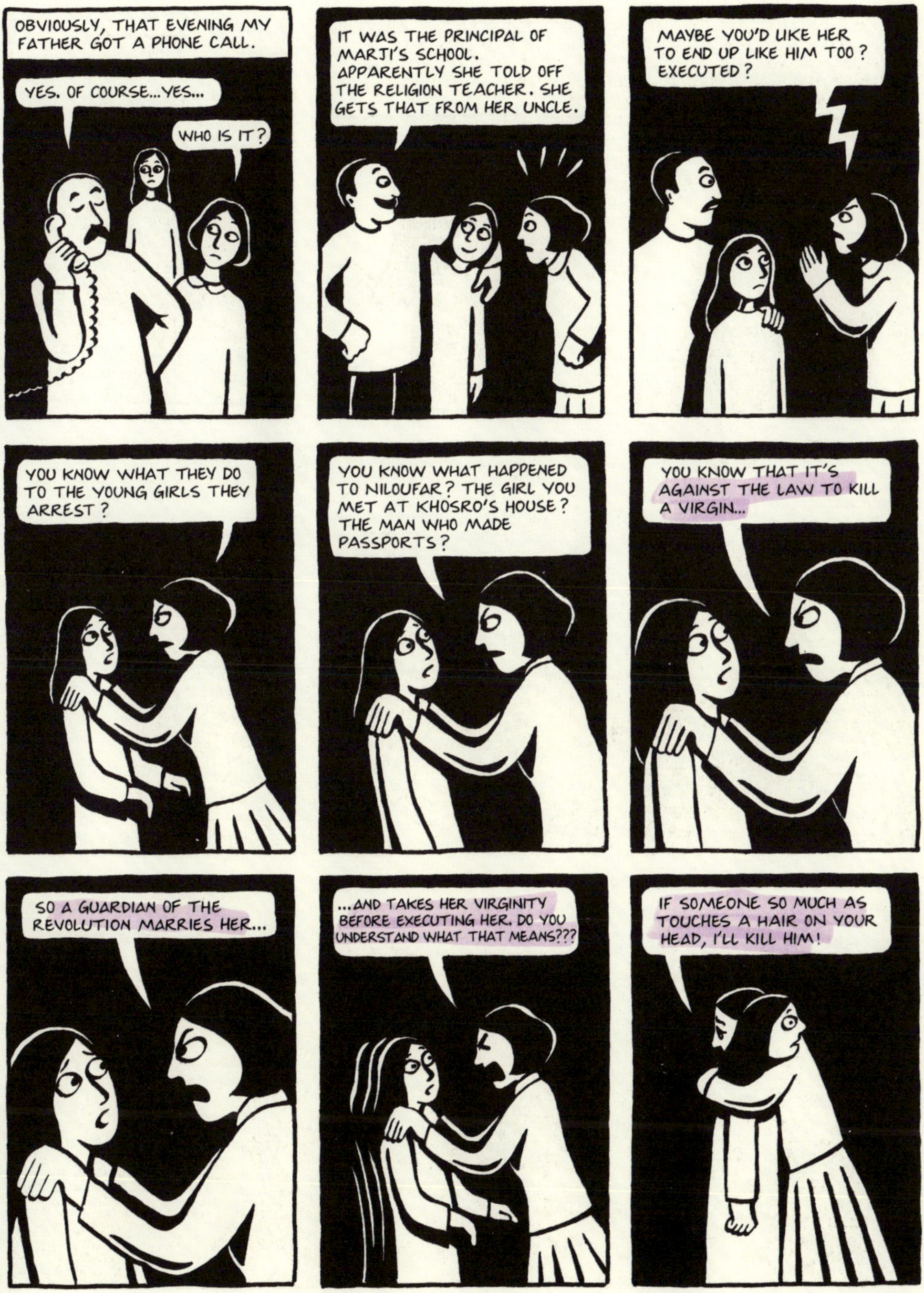
OBVIOUSLY, THAT EVENING MY FATHER GOT A PHONE CALL.
YES. OF COURSE...YES...
WHO IS IT?
IT WAS THE PRINCIPAL OF MARJI'S SCHOOL. APPARENTLY SHE TOLD OFF THE RELIGION TEACHER. SHE GETS THAT FROM HER UNCLE.
MAYBE YOU'D LIKE HER TO END UP LIKE HIM TOO? EXECUTED?
YOU KNOW WHAT THEY DO TO THE YOUNG GIRLS THEY ARREST?
YOU KNOW WHAT HAPPENED TO NILOUFAR? THE GIRL YOU MET AT KHOSRO'S HOUSE? THE MAN WHO MADE PASSPORTS?
YOU KNOW THAT IT'S AGAINST THE LAW TO KILL A VIRGIN...
SO A GUARDIAN OF THE REVOLUTION MARRIES HER...
...AND TAKES HER VIRGINITY BEFORE EXECUTING HER. DO YOU UNDERSTAND WHAT THAT MEANS???
IF SOMEONE SO MUCH AS TOUCHES A HAIR ON YOUR HEAD, I'LL KILL HIM!

evokes sadness in the reader as
it is entirely possible this could happen
as its happened to others before

the government and society never truly cared

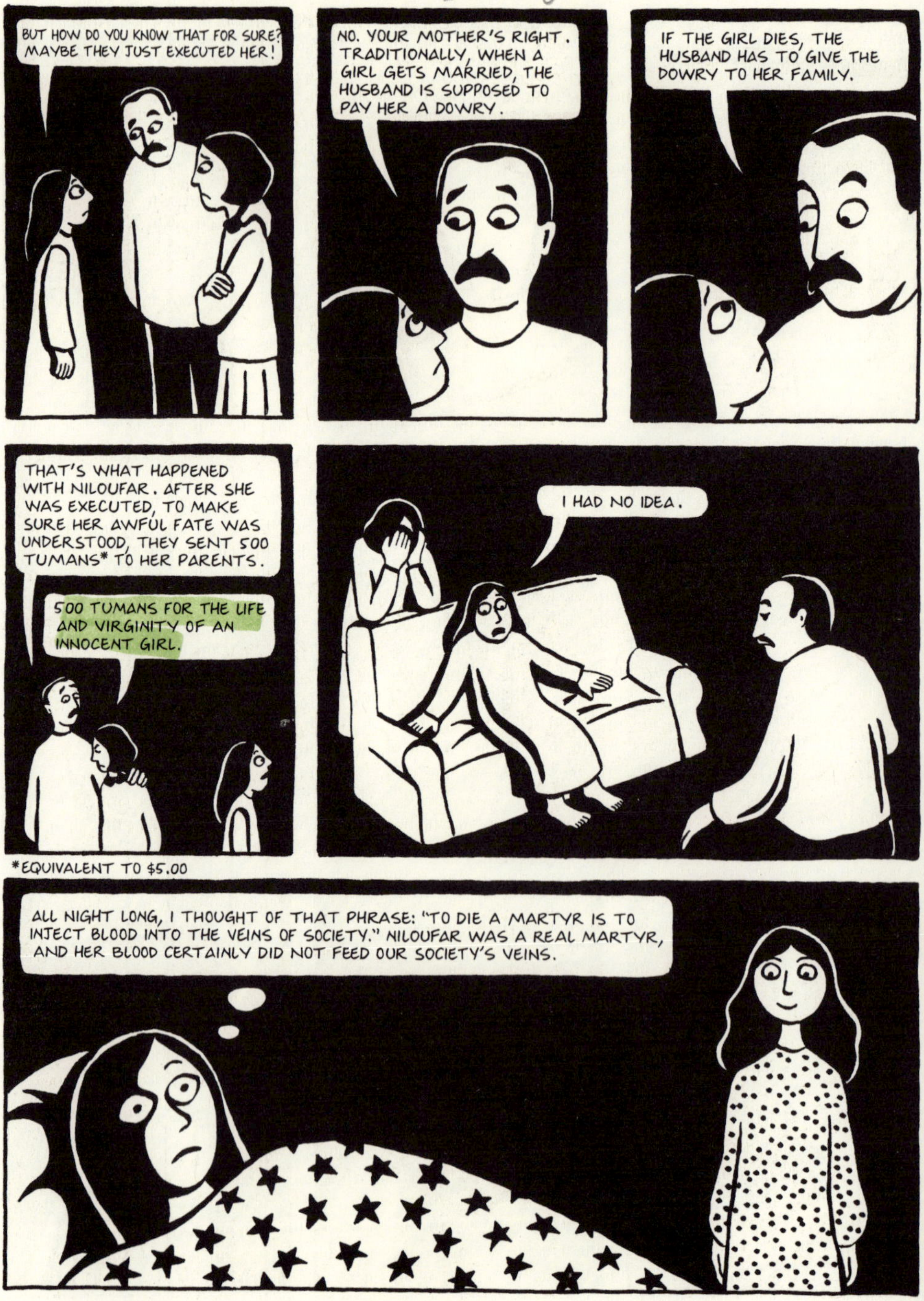

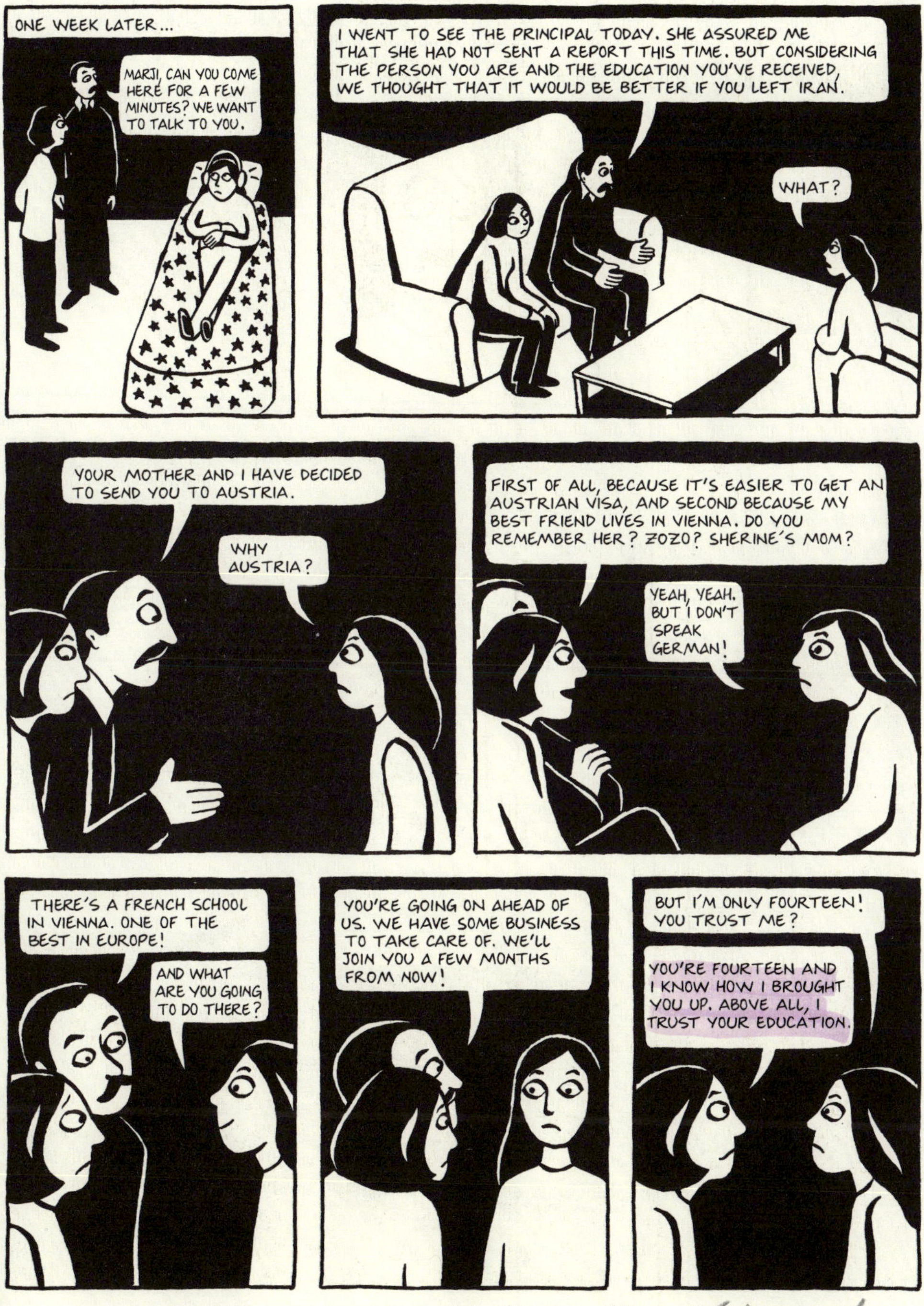

what they struggled for, if she can't get a good education everything would be for nothing

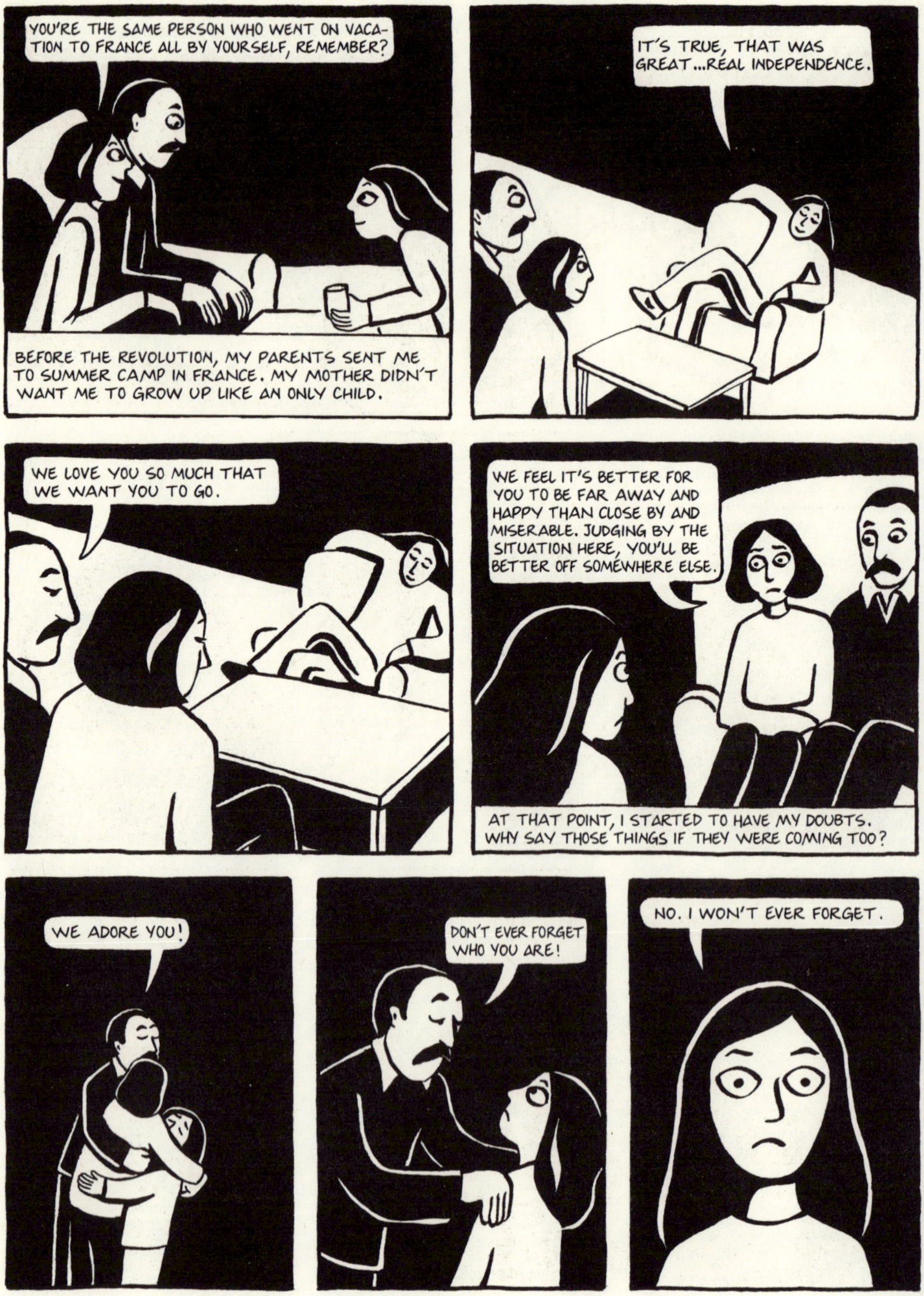
YOU'RE THE SAME PERSON WHO WENT ON VACATION TO FRANCE ALL BY YOURSELF, REMEMBER?
BEFORE THE REVOLUTION, MY PARENTS SENT ME TO SUMMER CAMP IN FRANCE. MY MOTHER DIDN'T WANT ME TO GROW UP LIKE AN ONLY CHILD.
IT'S TRUE, THAT WAS GREAT...REAL INDEPENDENCE.
WE LOVE YOU SO MUCH THAT WE WANT YOU TO GO.
WE FEEL IT'S BETTER FOR YOU TO BE FAR AWAY AND HAPPY THAN CLOSE BY AND MISERABLE. JUDGING BY THE SITUATION HERE, YOU'LL BE BETTER OFF SOMEWHERE ELSE.
AT THAT POINT, I STARTED TO HAVE MY DOUBTS. WHY SAY THOSE THINGS IF THEY WERE COMING TOO?
WE ADORE YOU!
DON'T EVER FORGET WHO YOU ARE!
NO. I WON'T EVER FORGET.

shes continually lost more and more people throughout her life, shes about to lose her last 3 peoples and she will be alone

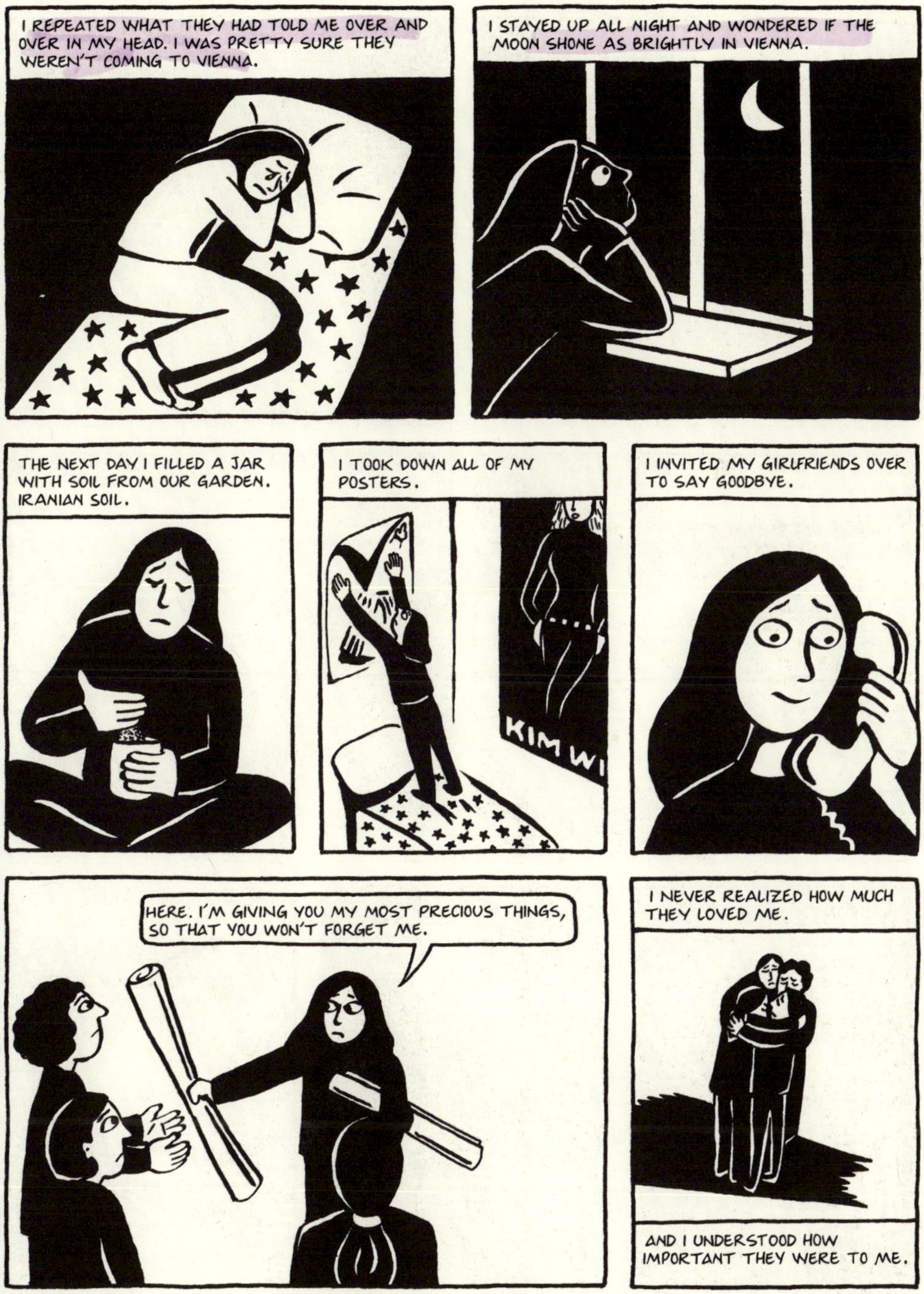

she only has the memori left, the last thing she has

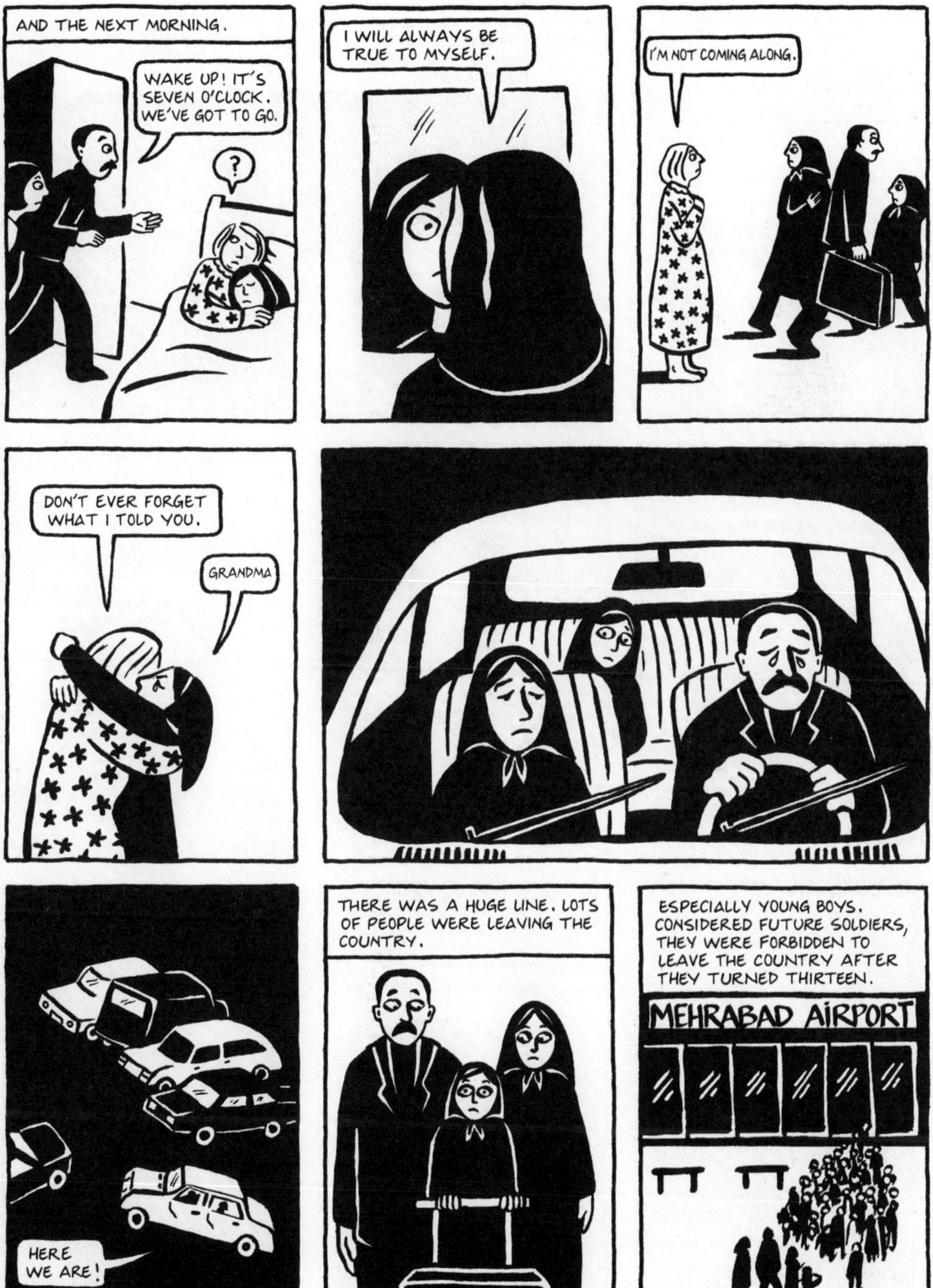
AND THE NEXT MORNING.
WAKE UP! IT'S SEVEN O'CLOCK. WE'VE GOT TO GO.
?
I WILL ALWAYS BE TRUE TO MYSELF.
I'M NOT COMING ALONG.
DON'T EVER FORGET WHAT I TOLD YOU.
GRANDMA
HERE WE ARE!
THERE WAS A HUGE LINE. LOTS OF PEOPLE WERE LEAVING THE COUNTRY.
ESPECIALLY YOUNG BOYS. CONSIDERED FUTURE SOLDIERS, THEY WERE FORBIDDEN TO LEAVE THE COUNTRY AFTER THEY TURNED THIRTEEN.
MEHRABAD AIRPORT

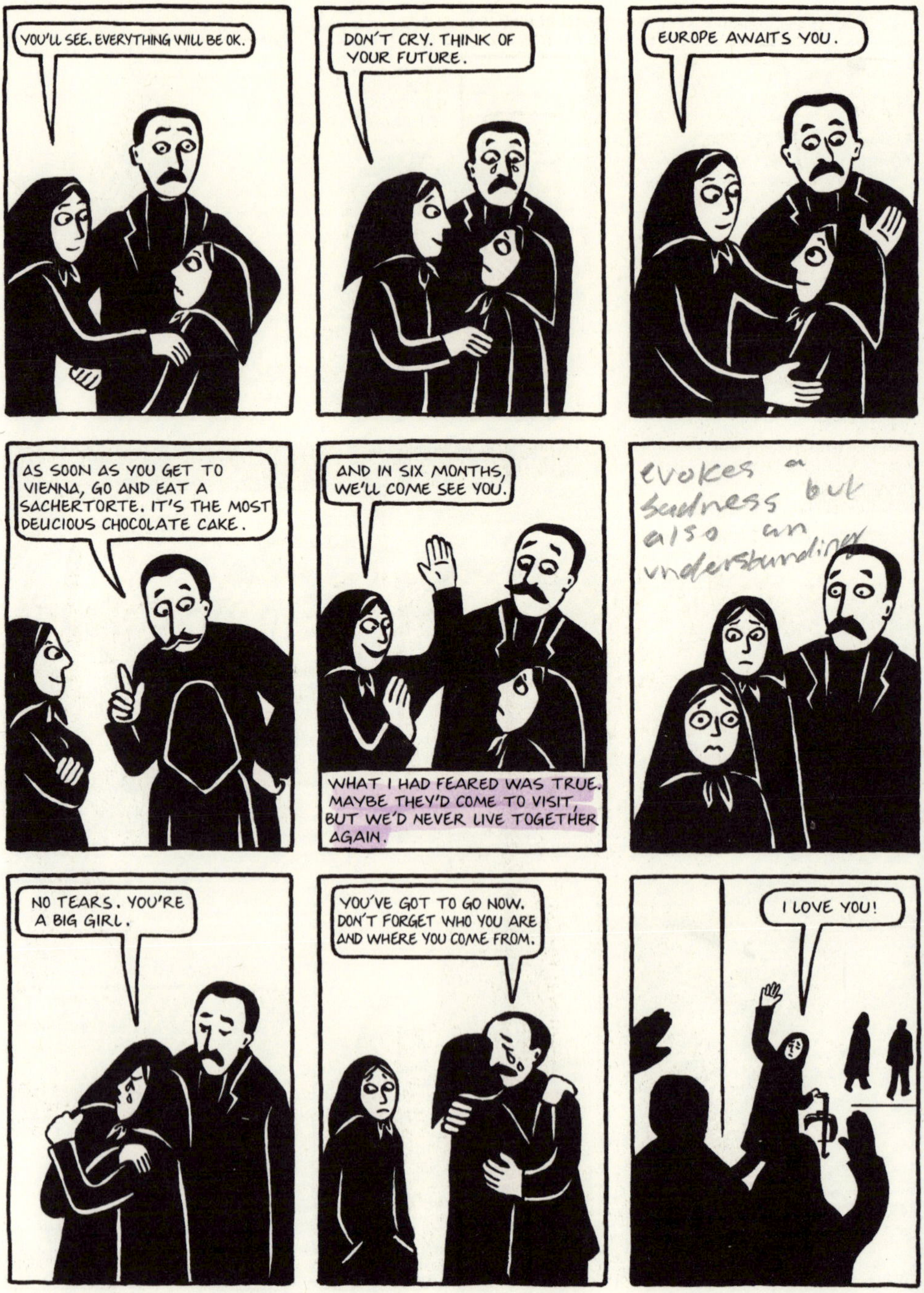
YOU'LL SEE. EVERYTHING WILL BE OK.
DON'T CRY. THINK OF YOUR FUTURE.
EUROPE AWAITS YOU.
AS SOON AS YOU GET TO VIENNA, GO AND EAT A SACHERTORTE. IT'S THE MOST DELICIOUS CHOCOLATE CAKE.
AND IN SIX MONTHS, WE'LL COME SEE YOU.
WHAT I HAD FEARED WAS TRUE. MAYBE THEY'D COME TO VISIT, BUT WE'D NEVER LIVE TOGETHER AGAIN.
evokes a sadness but also an understanding
NO TEARS. YOU'RE A BIG GIRL.
YOU'VE GOT TO GO NOW. DON'T FORGET WHO YOU ARE AND WHERE YOU COME FROM.
I LOVE YOU!

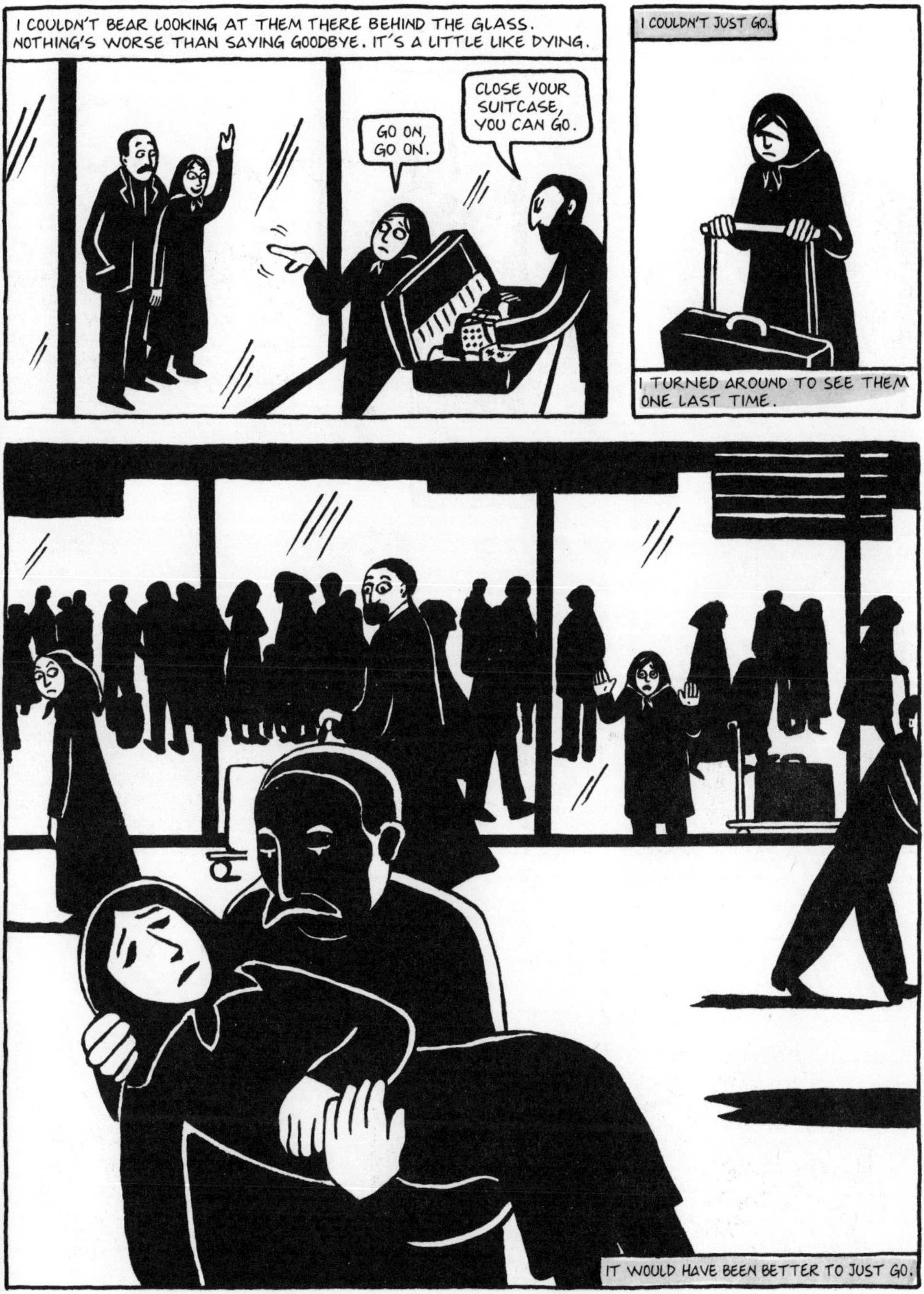

shes alone now

CREDITS

Translation of first part: Mattias Ripa
Translation of second part: Blake Ferris
Supervision of translation: Marjane Satrapi and Carol Bernstein
Lettering: Eve Deluze
Additional hand lettering: Céline Merrien

THANKS TO

Anjali Singh
L'Association
David B.
Jean-Christophe Menu
Emile Bravo
Christophe Blain
Guillaume Dumora
Fanny Dalle-Rive
Nicolas Leroy
Matthieu Wahiche
Charlotte Miquel